Praise for
An Apparently Normal Person

Of the many published personal works on dissociative disorders, there's not a better, more insightful account than this one. Engaging, sincere and sometimes shocking, I was hooked from the start and wanted every detail. The author shares her extraordinary and complex life with clarity, sincerity, dignity and love.

—**Dr. Chris Downs,** psychologist and author

In *An Apparently Normal Person*, Bonnie Armstrong lives a full life, devoted to a career in child advocacy. But when she's plagued by a series of physical ailments unresponsive to treatment, she begins a journey of uncovering and unraveling unspeakable childhood trauma.

Armstrong provides readers with an in-depth look at a world unknown to most. Through the sharing of her story, Bonnie leaves us with an important legacy of breaking down the stigma of a mental health diagnosis. While it's difficult to read some of the painful details, Bonnie Armstrong's vulnerable and honest writing makes it an easy read. This fascinating, enlightening and profound memoir has moved me to my core. Above all, she has shown me the resilience and power of the human spirit.

—**Merle R. Saferstein,** author of
Living and Leaving My Legacy, Vols. 1 and 11

An Apparently Normal Person is a searching memoir of medical mystery, self-discovery, and harrowing honesty as Bonnie Armstrong works to uncover the source of her physical and mental afflictions. As her life is upended, it becomes clear that overwhelming trauma has reshaped both her body and her brain.

The author's searing story invites the reader into a struggle to learn the terrain of complex trauma and recovery. We share her disbelief and her determination as her story unfolds in a page-turning series of advances and setbacks.

Armstrong's writing is personal and steeped in deep feelings as she comes to understand her dissociative disorder has saved her life. The stigma of speaking out about one's lived experience with a mental health diagnosis is transformed into her superpower in her triumphant memoir, *An Apparently Normal Person*.

—**Catherine Klatzker, RN,** author of *You Will Never Be Normal*

Bonnie Armstrong's book, *An Apparently Normal Person,* is a tour de force of courageous storytelling and information, a memoir that offers a path to hope and healing for those who suffer from buried traumatic experiences. Bonnie reveals her personal story, her quest for healing, and the spiritual and scientific ways that mind, body and soul can be reconnected.

—**Linda Joy Myers,** founder of the National Association of Memoir Writers and author of *Don't Call Me Mother* and *Song of the Plains*

I couldn't put this book down! With each page of *An Apparently Normal Person*, Bonnie's unique story unfolds into a journey of self-discovery that anyone can relate to. Through accounts of trauma and adventure, she balances educating the reader with keeping them inspired and hopeful. I learned so much and would highly recommend Bonnie's story to therapists and anyone who is in therapy as a resource for understanding the role of dissociation as an adaptive response to trauma.

—**Andi Fetzner,** PsyD, partner in Origins Training and Consulting

An Apparently Normal Person is an incredibly powerful book for the field of psychology and all human services fields that serve clients. It not only carefully lays out the less understood symptoms of severe trauma that every professional needs to be able to recognize, it demonstrates the incredible resilience that people can experience, especially when given the appropriate tools to do so. I hope it also serves as a reminder to everyone that we have no idea what others are dealing with and why leading with compassion is so important.

—**Carrie D. Miller, PhD,** Clinical Psychology

Bonnie Armstrong is a well-respected educator and advocate for those living with childhood trauma, dissociation and dissociative identity disorder. She continues her advocacy work with her memoir, *An Apparently Normal Person*. Bonnie takes us on a raw and real journey from the unknown physical manifestations, to the eventual diagnosis, and through her incredible healing journey.

—**Jaime Pollack,** founder and director of An Infinite Mind

An Apparently Normal Person is a courageous and empowering book that takes the reader on a harrowing journey. Bonnie shares her truth and illustrates along the way just how the dissociative mind is not only creative but a powerful tool for trauma survival. A must-read for anyone in need of validation, deeper knowledge, or encouragement to stay the course.

—**Larry Ruhl,** artist and author of *Breaking the Ruhls*

AN APPARENTLY NORMAL PERSON

AN APPARENTLY NORMAL PERSON

by
Bonnie R. Armstrong
Foreword by Wendy Lazarus

EMERALD LAKE
BOOKS
Sherman, Connecticut

Library of Congress Cataloging-in-Publication Data

Names: Armstrong, Bonnie, author.

Title: An apparently normal person / by Bonnie R. Armstrong.

Description: Sherman, Connecticut : Emerald Lake Books, [2023]

Identifiers: LCCN 2023053853 (print) | LCCN 2023053854 (ebook) | ISBN
   9781945847783 (trade paperback) | ISBN 9781945847790 (epub)

Subjects: LCSH: Armstrong, Bonnie--Mental health. | Dissociative
   disorders--Patients--United States--Biography.

Classification: LCC RC553.D5 A76 2023 (print) | LCC RC553.D5 (ebook) |
   DDC 616.85/230092 [B]--dc23/eng/20231227

LC record available at https://lccn.loc.gov/2023053853

LC ebook record available at https://lccn.loc.gov/2023053854

Books published by Emerald Lake Books may be ordered from your favorite booksellers or by visiting emeraldlakebooks.com.

To "Julia," my therapist, guide and dance partner
in this incredible ballet of trust, discovery, healing and reconnection.
Your curiosity, attunement and aversion to assumptions created
life-giving magic. We all are forever grateful MO found you.

Table of Contents

Foreword

*A*n *Apparently Normal Person* tells the riveting and inspiring story of how one woman unraveled the chilling truths of her childhood trauma relatively late in her life. It is not just a memoir of how Bonnie Armstrong survived these horrors at the time, but also how, forty years later, she undertook the long and arduous journey of discovery and healing. This book is a serious read, and sometimes it's hard to bear. But Bonnie's is a hopeful story and so well written I found it hard to put down.

Bonnie and I met about thirty-five years ago, when we were both promoting public policies in Los Angeles and the state of California that help children thrive and reach their full potential. At that time, she and I were advocating for changes in how care is provided for kids who had suffered various kinds of neglect and abuse—many of whom ended up in foster care and eventually in the justice system. Ironically, long before Bonnie discovered she, herself, was a survivor of childhood trauma, she became a highly respected and influential leader on these issues at the federal, state and local levels.

I remember clearly the day in 2007 when Bonnie asked me to meet her for lunch. As we sat at a small table outside a stand at the oldest farmers market in Los Angeles, she shared with me her recent discoveries about her childhood abuse and the characters inside herself—her alters—who helped her cope with and survive violent and repeated emotional, mental and physical trauma. She had been diagnosed with a dissociative disorder, formerly known as "multiple personality disorder."

I had seen the movie *The Three Faces of Eve* long ago. But hearing from one of my closest friends about the alters inside her whom she was finally getting to know and who were teaching her about her early traumas was jarring to say the least. I did my best to listen, to support Bonnie, and to do so without judgment. But how could she function so exceptionally well in a high-powered career, be an outstanding mother and wife, and live the life of an apparently normal person? And how could I have shared so many family picnics, phone calls, and committee meetings with her and not had a clue?

That's one of the most important takeaways of Bonnie's story. Her so-called disorder served as her protective armor to survive ten years of unpredictable abuse and to function well despite what she had experienced. Her mind and body's ability to dissociate was the superpower that enabled her to have an incredibly normal-looking life.

Another important takeaway from *An Apparently Normal Person* is that superpowers resulting from trauma don't always last forever, and eventually Bonnie's stopped working. When it did, I watched my friend suffer through a long series of scary and debilitating physical symptoms. Everything that had been locked up inside her ultimately landed her in a wheelchair, in the hospital for weeks, and on medical leave multiple times.

Dissociative disorders like Bonnie's are much more common than many people realize. In fact, millions of US children and adults live with them. Dissociative disorders affect an estimated three percent of the population, making them as widespread as well-known conditions like bipolar disorder and schizophrenia. But unlike those, dissociative disorders are rarely taught in social work, medical or nursing schools. As a result, like Bonnie, most of these people go through years being misdiagnosed, mistreated, overmedicated or dismissed by health providers as exaggerating or imagining their condition.

An Apparently Normal Person shows us how determined Bonnie was to get better. What a difference finding the right response to her childhood trauma made. I had the joy of watching the gradual improvement in her health, well-being and ability to enjoy life. Maybe even more uplifting is that Bonnie's path to healing began when she was in her fifties—demonstrating that it's never too late.

In addition to being an inspiring story, *An Apparently Normal Person* provides a unique perspective for policymakers and practitioners in the fields of trauma and mental health. It is very rare that someone with the impressive track record Bonnie has had improving public policies in these arenas also has lived experience with trauma and healing. Because of this unusual blend, she has uncommon credibility in suggesting how educators, mental health practitioners, and advocates can use her experiences to assist people who face similar challenges.

Hopefully, Bonnie's courage to tell this story and her skill in communicating it in such an accessible way will help normalize healing from childhood trauma at any stage of life. One thing is clear. By sharing her journey, Bonnie has done her part to make it more likely that other children and adults who grow up with unresolved traumas can get the support they need to heal. We all have a role to play in making that happen.

Wendy Lazarus, MSPH
Founder and director, Kids Impact Initiative
Senior fellow, UCLA Center for Healthier
Children Families and Communities

January 2024

Dear Reader,

Thanks for joining me on this journey. Before we get started, I'd like to give you a heads-up or two. A fun fact about the story you are about to read is that a group of us worked together to write it. You see, I live with several dissociated identities inside and parts of this memoir were written by them or by us jointly. Most of the time, I, the apparently normal person of the title, will be your guide. But other times, you'll find more of a collective voice telling the story. You'll also get to hear individually from several of the internal people too. And we'll let you know when that happens and help you keep it all straight.

As you can imagine, pronouns can be tricky in a story like this. I move from being sure I'm a singular "I" to embracing a bright and supportive internal family of other "I's" until all of us embrace our healing journey together as a unified "we." We hope you enjoy reading about how this puzzling world unfolded.

To protect the privacy of people I love, I have changed the names of my family members and everyone else in the story except those who are also in the resource list at the back.

This is one person's story of how dissociation hid childhood trauma and helped me heal. Other people may experience their dissociative disorder or other trauma responses differently. But it's important to remember that virtually every family is touched by trauma in some way, and everyone has a story. Every day, you encounter people who are dealing with difficult issues behind their facade of normalcy. May we all treat each other with kindness and compassion.

And please be sure to take care of yourself. Some of my story may be difficult to read. Remember to breathe and take a break if any passages are triggering to you. But mostly, this is a story about the resilience and strength of the human spirit. It's never too late to begin your healing quest. And I'd love to hear from you after you've read about mine.

Fearlessly, I speak my truth with love.

Part 1
The Body Speaks

Chapter 1
The First Ripple

A wave of brain fog and nausea enveloped me with dizzying ferocity as I sped down the freeway, on the way to a meeting I had to chair. My eyes and head suddenly clouded over, and my body ached everywhere. The meatloaf dinner I had gulped down moments before leaving the house threatened to revolt. The early evening traffic became curiously quiet, with danger lurking as each car whizzed by. My heart pounded so loudly I could hardly breathe.

My first thought was automatic. I have to push through and keep my commitments. This group is counting on me. I can't let them down. But wait! I can hardly see, and I'm so disoriented I'm not safe on the freeway.

My internal dialogue raced. Can I make it back home? Yes, but it'll be safer on side streets. I can stop and rest if it gets too bad. What's happening? Legs feel detached—hard to move them to work the pedals. Everything looks all grey and overcast. What's going on? I've got to get home. I've got to pull myself together! Focus… Don't feel!

Yes, that's right… I heard the old refrain from deep inside. You can do this if you just stay focused.

Luckily, I hadn't driven very far, so the routes back home were familiar, although I don't know which one I took. I turned into our driveway, dragged myself out of the car and, almost on all fours, scaled the four steps to our big, broad porch. The old wooden front door welcomed me home, and I collapsed onto the first piece of furniture I saw—the couch. My husband and fifteen-year-old daughter jumped up as soon as they saw me.

"Bonnie! What happened?"

"Mom, you look awful."

But I couldn't tell them. Words wouldn't come. Wayne took care of calling my colleagues to explain I wouldn't make it to the meeting, while Beth took off my shoes and tried to make me comfortable.

I shook my head, trying to say "No, I don't need anything. Don't touch, just let me rest," and melted into the cushions.

Sometime later, they woke me to insist I go up to bed, although I saw no reason to move. When I tried to stand, I found my leg muscles had turned into something akin to waterlogged sponges with no strength. I looked up at the beautiful, wide, oak staircase that was one of my favorite features of our comfortable, century-old craftsman home and wished we had a single story. Between them, Wayne and Beth got me upstairs, a feat I could barely participate in or remember.

By the next morning, my capacity for speech had returned, but the rubbery weakness in my legs had overtaken my whole body. We decided to go to the emergency room to search for some answers. But how do you safely get downstairs when your legs won't carry you?

Beth offered a solution she and her older brother, Will, had loved when they were little. I sat on a pillow, held her hand, and bumped down the stairs on my bottom, chuckling through the fog at the silliness of it all.

Wayne and I headed off to the hospital where I was born and where my paternal grandfather had served as chief of staff. I focused on holding my body as upright and normal as possible and keeping outwardly calm. I felt myself separate slightly from my body so I could observe the scene as if watching a movie. Wayne seemed upset and worried, but he drove safely. I appeared tired, but normal.

The bright and efficient emergency room felt neither frantic nor welcoming. But as they wheeled me in, I felt a spasm of panic tear into my gut.

Kind attendants listened patiently as I struggled to describe the sensations I felt: a watery weakness in my legs, especially the calves; a general body malaise; trouble finding my balance. No, not vertigo exactly... Not dizziness—but rather, imbalance. And a fog had settled over my brain, fuzzing my thinking and dulling all my senses. Yes, there had been nausea, but that had subsided with no vomiting. Now, it felt like someone had sucked all the vitality right out of me.

The screening tests registered as normal, although my blood pressure was a little low. An earnest young social worker asked about my life and health in general. All appeared normal, with no red flags.

He referred me to a neurologist and an internist for follow-up, but we returned home with no real answers. Even without a diagnosis, I felt reassured that I wasn't facing anything observably or immediately life-threatening. Okay, good. Like my mother always said... This too shall pass.

A FEW DAYS LATER, I walked slowly and unsteadily on Wayne's arm into the neurologist's office. My body and legs had regained some strength, and my brain was coming out of the fog so I could speak more clearly. My description of my symptoms led to more questions and a variety of tests over the next two weeks.

I eagerly anticipated some answers about this weird malady that had so dramatically interrupted my productive life. But the doctor announced all the tests appeared normal. The issue was "probably just stress." Although he knew very little about me, my life or what kinds of stressors I might or might not have, he proffered a prescription for Prozac and told me to follow up with him in six months.

"Wait a minute, mister," I thought, but didn't say. "I'm no silly, hysterical woman. I'm an accomplished professional with many honors to my name. My life and work have been upended suddenly by a mix of baffling symptoms, and all you can say is 'I can't figure out what's wrong with you, so it can't be anything important. Go take a pill, chill out, and don't bother me'?"

Incensed and insulted by his impersonal approach and lack of curiosity, I never filled the prescription or went back to him.

WAYNE AND I KNEW THE PATH back to good health required more exploration, but neither he nor I had any reason to suspect the flood of changes that would soon overtake us and the seemingly solid foundation of our lives.

We had been each other's best friends for nearly three decades, bound together by our love of family, baseball (LA Dodgers for me; Cleveland Indians for him), and politics (we met while taking voters to the polls). As very early baby boomers, we had pushed the envelope of societal convention, but we loved tradition too. (Professionally, I broke the glass ceiling in a governor's office. But I have used the same copper-bottomed saucepan to make the same Christmas fudge for more than forty years.)

We both had lived outside the US, learned other languages, and intentionally pursued early careers far away from our original homes. But after our son and daughter were born in Washington, DC, we moved back to my hometown of Pasadena, California, to raise them close to my six siblings and our large and boisterously growing extended family. Even though my relationship with my father was often strained by what we used to call the "generation gap," I remembered a happy childhood full of family activities and wanted the same for my children.

"Life always has more to teach us than we think we have to learn," read a card from a dear friend on our wedding day in 1972. We had no idea how true this would prove to be.

OVER THE FOLLOWING WEEKS, the mysterious weakness persisted, affecting both my legs and balance, and its sudden onset still puzzled us. Hoping alternatives to Western medicine might be more beneficial, I found a homeopath. She discovered elevated indicators of the Epstein-Barr virus in my blood tests, which is associated with chronic fatigue syndrome, among other things.

Finally, we had a potential culprit for the drastic changes and something constructive for me to do. I worked with her to build up my immune system, shifted to a diet with more fresh vegetables and no red meat, watched for food allergies, took vitamin supplements, and generally became more cognizant of my nutrition and schedule.

She saw my confusion and determination as I worked to figure out what was happening and how to cope with it. Her suggestion that maybe I needed to adjust my lifestyle and expectations for myself as I turned fifty didn't ring true, though. I knew it couldn't be age. Only a week before this thing hit, we'd returned from a three-week birthday trip to show my husband and teenagers where I had lived in Sweden and Germany more than thirty years earlier, during the 1960s. To Beth and Will's amazement, I had planned, guided and interpreted in three languages during the trip. Proud of my capacities, I didn't want anyone to tell me I needed to slow down. I wanted them to help me get back into full gear. Nonetheless, I accepted my homeopath's referral to an intuitive, down-to-earth psychologist.

AFTER ABOUT TEN WEEKS, my strength and energy returned, and I reclaimed my usual vigor, not sure exactly which intervention had helped most or what the actual root cause had been. With the strange interlude over, I moved on with my optimistic life and announced I would run for the local school board after a friend retired from it. I had spent decades working on children's issues in a wide variety of roles and places, and this seemed like a logical step. Serving on the school board would be a new way of making a difference in my community and might lead to other opportunities to learn and contribute—maybe even to serve in a higher office. Wayne and our kids loved the idea and enthusiastically helped me campaign.

I won the election in 1996, continued my service on several local boards and commissions, and resumed my travels around the country, consulting with city councils and school boards about building youth master plans for their communities.

Safe in the knowledge their mother's robust health had been restored, Will graduated from high school and went off to college, while Beth became an exchange student to Costa Rica. In other words, our lives moved forward on their healthy, privileged path.

I congratulated myself for overcoming an odd health hiccup, the importance of which I quickly minimized. And for a year and a half, life sailed along productively and smoothly… until the next surprise wave hit.

Chapter 2
Another Wave

On a cold May morning (for Southern California) in 1998, in a drafty old school building, I sat with a gaggle of school district personnel around a big, square table, reviewing their budget. I had started the morning with a bit of a sore throat and stomachache, and wore a winter coat against the chill. Given my belief that an organization's budget is its most important policy document, I took seriously my assignment as the board's representative on the budget committee. But midway through the meeting, I felt myself grow less connected to the discussions, as if some invisible force was drawing my consciousness away from the work at hand. A grey cloud settled over the proceedings, muting sight and sound. I stood up from the table, confused about where to go, but knowing I had to leave.

As I walked out the door, my legs grew so weak beneath me, I needed to lie down—immediately. A little way up the hallway, I saw a metal table that might serve as a bed, but I couldn't make it that far. Desperate for a place to stretch out, I noticed a nice, soft curve right there in the hallway where the floor met the wall. This lovely space welcomed me as I pulled my long black coat close and melted into the concrete, thankful for a cozy spot to rest.

The next thing I knew, a young man stood over me, asking if I was all right. I couldn't tell how long I had been resting snug in my little corner.

"Oh yes," I responded through a thick fog, tongue barely able to move. "I'm just resting." I pulled myself up to sit against the wall and tried to orient myself.

The school district's excellent health clinic was in this building, and soon, a nurse I knew came by to see how I was doing. She took my blood pressure and pulse and chatted with me as I assured her I had just needed to lie down. Finally, it occurred to me, perhaps it was a bit odd that I was taking a nap on the floor in the hallway during a budget meeting, and we shared a little laugh.

I admitted I didn't feel very good and let the nurse help me into a wheelchair, then down to the clinic to rest. I talked her into letting me see my doctor instead of calling the paramedics. There was no need to draw unnecessary attention to this strange incident.

Wayne picked me up, and my internist, Dr. Miller, saw me immediately. She took an EKG and checked me out, but didn't find anything that explained my odd behavior or sudden symptoms. I felt weak and woozy on my feet, with a sore throat and a head full of cotton candy, but at least my tongue was working again. My doctor sent me home with medicine for the dizziness and antibiotics for a possible strep infection and gave Wayne orders to watch me closely and call if the symptoms worsened or new ones appeared.

It didn't get worse and my sore throat went away quickly, but the wooziness, difficulty walking, and general weakness, especially in the legs, persisted. It took a couple of days before we recognized these issues were similar to the attack I'd had a year and a half before.

This time, the symptoms were not as severe, but they also did not dissipate as quickly, thus disrupting my normal activity for longer. The most visible issues were the weakness in my legs (which made it hard to walk) and the disequilibrium (I had a better word for it now) that kept me off balance.

Friends and family expressed concern, and everyone had theories or recommendations. The idea that it could be the onset of multiple sclerosis (MS) scared me the most, so I found a local neurologist to test me for various neurological disorders. But when the tests came back either negative or inconclusive, she opined she found diagnosing MS "like trying to catch a butterfly."

I wanted to yell, "Well, get a bigger net!" Weeks of upset balance, weakened muscles, and no stamina, and all she could talk about was butterflies!

MY FOCUS AND DETERMINATION were sorely challenged, but I continued my work and school board activities as well as I could. Once those were done, I'd fall into bed early each evening, exhausted, glad the children were gone and Wayne could fend for himself. I needed to find out what was wrong with me.

This neurologist also suggested the cause could be stress. Her completely unrealistic and ridiculous suggestion that I should try to rest more irritated me almost as much as the first neurologist's attempt to fix everything with a bottle of Prozac. I was the primary wage earner in a family with one child in college and one working to graduate from high school early. I had a busy, independent consulting practice that required a lot of travel, my husband was trying to get a small business off the ground, and I served as an elected school board member. When exactly was I supposed to fit in more rest?

Besides, wasn't it obvious? What was happening to my body was clearly too physical to be caused by stress or cured by rest.

Only in hindsight could I realize my peevishness masked (at least to me) the fact that I found it far easier to push myself to meet my external commitments than to listen to my body or focus internally. I didn't even know how to do those things.

Growing up in my family, any illness that didn't come with a broken bone or clear diagnosis—like chicken pox or the plague—was a sign of weakness. My father strongly believed in, and insisted upon, "mind over matter." Anything less was considered malingering. And Mother taught us to "rise above it," whatever "it" might be. I never knew exactly what either meant, but internalized the overall lesson "to pay no attention to what you are feeling and keep moving."

My learned response gave me a clear path forward, even if I couldn't articulate it: push my body to overcome whatever these strange symptoms were, unless or until I received a bona fide, scientific diagnosis that could be dealt with in some other way. As a bonus, I could perceive myself as mildly heroic in the process—not that I was conscious of any of this at the time.

I HAD DEVELOPED QUITE AN ECLECTIC TEAM of healthcare professionals to help me cope: a holistic chiropractor who worked to soothe and strengthen my leg and back muscles; a homeopath to deal with the Epstein-Barr virus and build up my immune system; a Chinese acupuncturist who didn't speak much English but seemed to read my energy flow better than I could explain it (he focused on my head a lot, which he said was too full, even though my complaints were mostly about my legs); a traditional neurologist who didn't provide much help except to order tests to rule out awful sounding diseases; and a trusted primary care physician who monitored symptoms and provided new referrals as needed.

I also liked the psychologist and continued to see her once a month to talk about everything—my health, my marriage (which was showing the strain), my work, and my childhood. With all the upheaval, it was nice to have a smart, curious sounding board.

Since nobody could find a clear explanation for what was happening, I focused on rising above it and waited for it to go away again. And slowly, like before, it did.

I didn't tell anyone about one thing I found really confusing. Even when the leg symptoms were at their worst, somewhere deep inside, I had the strange feeling that if I really wanted to, I could have just gotten up and walked confidently across the room like normal—there wasn't actually anything wrong with my legs or balance. Why did I have these thoughts when the reality was clearly so different? Just wishful thinking, I guess.

This time, it took four months for my body to regain its strength and equilibrium. Again, I felt relief at the victory and returned gratefully to my regular patterns of life and work, with a few changes. First, I decided to get a job with benefits. For more than ten years, I had enjoyed the flexibility, autonomy and diversity of my consulting practice that helped local communities, city councils and school districts across the country on matters related to children, youth and families. More of a calling than a job, it also proved a good source of income for the family. However, these brushes with ill health made me realize I had given up a lot too, like paid sick days, vacations and group health insurance—benefits I'd had when I worked full-time before Will was born.

Years before, Wayne and I had agreed to trade roles when the children started into their teens so he could work part-time, pursue some dreams, and take care of the kids and household as I had done when they were younger. Even though we had been talking about flouting convention in this way since we had become parents, we hadn't considered all the ramifications of such a change.

How hard could it be? First, Wayne would work full-time; then, I would. I had made that commitment to him and had no intention of reneging on the deal.

By now, though, the kids were both gone, pursuing their own lives of learning and adventure as we had hoped they would. They each were blessed with good minds, engaging personalities, and many friends, and both stayed in touch with us while relishing their independence.

When we had agreed on this arrangement, we hadn't considered how long it should last or under which circumstances we should change it, and I still felt I had a duty to keep my end of the bargain until he was ready to adjust it. But my bouts with infirmity had taken a toll, and although I didn't want to admit it, I could feel our emotional partnership fraying.

With some irony, I noted that the heavy responsibility I felt as the primary wage earner had been carried by generations of men before me. Feeling overwhelmed, I knew I needed to take action before some stupid, stereotypical midlife crisis hit.

Wayne laughed gently at my pronouncement about getting a job, wondering how I'd ever find anything that would give me both the satisfaction and freedom I enjoyed in my independent consulting. My response flowed out of my mouth effortlessly, as if I had given it much more thought than I had. I laid out a hypothetical job description, with some specificity as to the type of organization and the role they might want me to play. That conversation took place on a Monday. On Friday, a former colleague from whom I hadn't heard in a couple of years called with just such an offer—a position with almost exactly the job description and organization I had described.

Serendipities like this arose often enough in my life for me not to consider them simple coincidences—more like small miracles or answers to prayers, although I didn't pray to any particular deity. It was enough for me that the Universe (or the Great Spirit, or God, or the Force) would show me I was on the right path as it smoothed the way forward. In this case, it gave me chills of excitement and wonder to see how closely the job that had showed up mirrored my request. I intended to work hard to show my gratitude for this synchronicity, this gift from the Universe.

My new job with a national foundation narrowed my work from the broader world of children's policy and youth development to the improvement of child welfare and foster care services for abused and neglected children. I still had a heavy travel schedule since my new regional office supported eight districts across three states. Locally, in Los Angeles County, we highlighted the needs of teenagers with histories of abuse and no families to care for them or help them heal and make it out in the world.

I felt healthy again and relished the opportunity to make life better for children who bore the scars of physical and emotional abuse. For reasons I did not understand, I felt a special connection to this group of young people, even though the happy middle-class childhood I remembered bore no resemblance to theirs, which were littered with violence, substance abuse and abandonment.

Meanwhile, on the school board, I worked to establish a collaborative venture that ensured access to mental health counseling services for every student who needed them. Our model was later expanded to dozens of school districts, helping many more children and families deal early with mental health issues.

Between work and public service, my long-standing advocacy on behalf of vulnerable children gave me a feeling of deep fulfillment, and I sailed deceptively smooth seas for another year. But then, in 1999, as if the first two waves had been early warning signals, the third hit like a tsunami as a sudden, devastating and yet somehow familiar flood of sensations washed over me.

Chapter 3
The Tsunami

Wayne and I sat chatting contentedly over wine and candlelight in our favorite little French bistro after an intimate dinner celebrating my fifty-third birthday. Then, midsentence, my brain shut down.

It went totally blank.

Fade to black.

Bonnie had left the building.

Mouth open, I lost the ability to form words. The room went quiet. My muscles slackened, and I slumped to the side, almost falling out of my chair. The restaurant became hazy, like in the old days when everyone smoked and such an intimate space would be cloaked in a heavy cloud.

Then, just as mysteriously, my brain rebooted. Like a computer, I came back online. But every sensory circuit in my body had been seized and compromised by some unknown malware.

From far across the small table, Wayne asked, "What's happening?"

In the blink of an eye, I had gone from animated and celebratory to mute and slumped.

"Are you having a stroke?" he wanted to know. "Shall I call 911?"

Before he could decide, I began to return. Slowly, my system geared back up, albeit weakly, hearing coming before speech, sight before movement. Without words, we communicated what we both recognized. We had been down this road before, but this time was different and more frightening—certainly the scariest thing I remembered ever happening to me. I wasn't sure why, but I knew I didn't want doctors or paramedics with a gurney. I wanted my home and my bed. I could make it the short distance to the car if I focused hard enough and got a lot of support from Wayne and perhaps our waiter. Mind over matter; rise above it; focus, don't feel. We left the restaurant shaken, but without any need for outside intervention.

The next morning, I woke up scared, weak and unable to walk without something to lean on. I needed help to fight harder for answers. When I could talk again, I called a wealthy, well-connected friend of Wayne's who'd been living with MS and had voiced concern that I wasn't getting appropriate medical care. I told him what had happened and accepted his long-standing offer to assist me in finding someone who could figure out what was wrong. After many years of experience, he had concluded that the best neurological clinic in the area was at the University of Southern California's University Hospital. His doctor, the director, was about to leave on sabbatical but responded to our mutual friend's request to "take care of her like you would your own daughter" by referring me to a prestigious colleague.

WITHIN DAYS, I had an appointment with a world-class neurologist it would normally take months to see. Dr. Hite was younger than I expected for a person with such a reputation and was very personable. Wayne and I chatted with her about her young daughters and our two children, getting to know each other before an hour-long discussion about my situation. For the first time, I felt heard in a way that gave me confidence she had both the skill and interest to solve the riddle of what was happening in my body. Finding the cause rather than just masking the symptoms was as important to her as it was to me.

I now had excellent group health insurance, and every time I left Dr. Hite's clinic, I saw the big LA County General hospital complex across the street, where people without insurance or connections couldn't hope to get the personalized care I was receiving. I knew it wasn't fair, but I felt immensely grateful I didn't have to worry about the cost of the myriad tests she ordered for all the conditions and diseases that might conceivably have created my symptoms.

As if to give her an opportunity for better observation, I did not show steady improvement this time. Instead, whenever I began to regain my strength and balance, another wave would hit. The cycle became alarmingly degenerative. When each of these smaller attacks pulsed through my body, I felt like I was falling deeper into an unstable hole that I was less and less able to climb out of. One step forward, three steps back.

It all seemed random, but I tried to look for patterns. Unexpected bright lights or loud sounds that were low and rhythmic could cause my head to scramble or my legs to become so spongy they wouldn't hold me up.

One day, Wayne and I walked into our favorite Mexican restaurant and the pattern of black-and-white tiles on the floor caught my eye, grew smaller and then larger, and created a surge of energy through my body that I could neither contain nor explain. A nearby chair gave me respite while Wayne got our food and my leg muscles reasserted themselves.

Other times, sounds from a loud public address system or a siren would swoosh through my head, leaving my brain jumbled and muscles weakened. Any overstimulation could bring on these attacks or "events," as Dr. Hite called them. I don't think I ever lost consciousness, but I often felt like I might faint and had to sit or lie down immediately. Sometimes, I could not speak for a little while. Other times, the mind fog would linger for hours or days, and it could create temporary dyslexia so I couldn't spell or type. And always, my legs and balance would be weaker as a result.

As tests again came back either negative or inconclusive, Dr. Hite admitted she was puzzled. Nonetheless, her promise remained. "We're going to figure this out, and I'm going to give you your life back. I'm used to dealing with serious situations others haven't solved, and I intend to find a solution."

I believed her. Clearly, I had graduated to a clinic with capacities well beyond those of a community physician. I loved my new doctor's confidence and determination and followed every directive she gave.

Between attacks, I had relatively good periods of a few days or weeks. My work colleagues—especially my boss and assistant—were kind, worried and accommodating. Marisol (or "Mari"), one of the women on our team who lived in another city, was also experiencing health issues—in her case, a flare-up of hepatitis C accompanied by disabling reactions to the medications that were supposed to help. Mari and I became good friends, bonding over our lack of stamina and hopes for better health, as well as our passion for our jobs and eagerness to overcome the frailty of our bodies.

And so, I drove myself to do my best to meet my commitments. As soon as I got home, I'd collapse into bed, hardly able to speak, think or move. Wayne would come up to bed hours later, often with the scent of a nightcap of bourbon and ginger ale on his breath.

On more than one occasion, I was vaguely aware of Wayne getting into bed and could feel him reach over to touch me. I knew that meant he was hoping I might wake up enough for a hug or perhaps felt like making love. Still mostly asleep, I remember thinking, "Yes, that would be nice; that would feel good." But as I rolled over to face him, what came out of my mouth was altogether different. I squirmed as if I had suddenly turned into a small child and squealed, "No! No, don't touch me! Go away!"

I heard it but wasn't sure where the voice came from. Then I fell back asleep and was unaware of anything else until morning, when I tried to figure out what the heck was going on.

MY DISEQUILIBRIUM MADE OPEN SPACES increasingly difficult to maneuver. Whether in a large room or outdoors, any open expanse of twenty feet or more loomed like a vast and overwhelming desert.

From Mother's collection of old family canes, she gave me one made of wormwood with a lovely inlaid green handle. Once I gave in and began using it to improve both my balance and stamina, I found I could walk across any room without difficulty and even up a few stairs if needed. The cane had belonged to my father's father. Beyond that, its story was lost with the generations, but it brought me a little comfort to think I wasn't the first person to be so weak and unsteady.

To be able to travel for work, I also decided to conquer my vanity and use a wheelchair in airports and other places where I needed to traverse long distances. My willingness to use the cane and wheelchair allowed me to continue functioning in the world and provided a visual cue that often prompted strangers to offer thoughtfulness and support.

People who knew me interpreted it as a sign of continued, unexplained deterioration. Some, I learned much later, even worried I might be dying. I saw the concern in their eyes even as I convinced myself I was rising above it all with grace, denial and good humor.

During this period of confusion, degeneration and frustration, I continually experienced immense kindness from friends, colleagues, strangers and the wheelchair escorts at airports. For example, my boss pushed our large bureaucratic system to move me to a first-floor office in our refurbished historic building. I know it struck fear in her when she saw me have an event near the top of the stairs at work, but she never made me feel anything but respected and supported.

Both she and Mari have remained dear friends through all the intervening years, encouraging me along my surprising healing journey.

The team who televised school board meetings to our local community offered another example of unexpected helpfulness. Our board meetings notoriously lasted long into the night, and sometimes I didn't have the stamina to sit upright all that time. The production team made it possible for me to leave the boardroom, as if I were going to the restroom, and watch the proceedings on the monitor in their studio next door. They even supplied a comfortably cushioned sofa with a cuddly, grey teddy bear. When a vote appeared imminent, I pulled myself together, focused and went back to continue my participation in the meeting, more rested and alert. With kindness and compassion, they assured me the camera would not capture me leaving or returning. I served out my full term as a productive board member, even with a disability none of us understood. But I had to accept the first major casualty of the illness and didn't run for a second term.

I was pretty good at hiding it, but the uncertainty was almost unbearable. I've always been a person who likes to *know*, and I found not knowing extremely distressing. What was causing this strange erosion of my life and health? Did I have a chronic illness I'd need to accept gracefully and learn to live with? Or was this something I could fight and get over? I'd do whatever I had to, as graciously as I could, to live out my life productively if I could just learn what was wrong.

What more would I have to give up? I cried as I flew over my beloved Sierra Nevada Mountains on a routine flight to Sacramento, worried I would never again be able to feed my soul hiking in their rugged beauty. Would the mind fog take over? Would my intellect— my major asset—abandon me? I endured tests for dozens of illnesses and conditions and looked up each one on the internet. But the frustrating search and unexplained events continued.

During the second half of 2001, events began coming with greater frequency. They were less likely to happen at work, which was a blessing, but they otherwise didn't seem to fit any predictable pattern. I tried to avoid crowds and places with lots of lights or other strong stimuli, but airports didn't seem to trigger them. That meant travel was okay if I paced myself and used wheelchairs.

Dr. Hite suggested I might have an unusual seizure disorder, even though she had tested for that twice without confirmation.

An unusual seizure disorder. Epilepsy. How scary! Deep disappointment in myself welled up when I realized my main fear was the huge stigma I saw in a potential epilepsy diagnosis. Where did that come from?

Back in the 1970s, when I served as the lead health and human services staffer to Florida's Governor Reubin Askew, I worked closely with both advocates for and people with many different conditions, including the Florida Epilepsy Foundation, which even gave me an award. Wayne had also worked with people with disabilities in his professional life. We had friends who lived with various challenges. We were enlightened people who respected all of an individual's differences and abilities! Where did this deep-seated stigma come from? Why was I unwilling to talk about it as a possible diagnosis? Was I saying, "It's okay if you have it, but I can't accept it happening to me?" What a hypocrite!

WHILE ALL OF THIS WAS GOING ON, Will graduated, married his college sweetheart, and moved to Merida, Venezuela, where he and his wife had spent their semesters abroad two years before. Beth had returned from a semester in South Africa just in time to be maid of honor at their wedding and go back to college in Oregon. They all seemed to be thriving.

Not knowing what my future might bring, Wayne and I decided to take the opportunity while I was relatively stable to celebrate a family Christmas together high in the Andes. I wanted to prove to myself—and to my children—that I could still travel and have fun, even if I needed a wheelchair most of the time.

At a long lunch early in our visit, in a little restaurant with picture windows and spectacular views of the mountains, the conversation turned to my health. Wayne and I shared with the children that the working "rule out" diagnosis was a seizure disorder. We didn't yet know what that might mean going forward, but it was my doctor's best guess at the moment.

"Actually," I assured everyone, "it's not nearly as scary as some of the other things I've been tested for."

Will, whose intuitive nature we had always encouraged, leaned across the table and smiled at me. "You know, Mom, I've been think-ing a lot about you, and I kinda think your doctors aren't on the right track. Somehow, I have the feeling it's not seizures or some awful disease. I just really feel like I don't need to be worried about your physical health long term."

I smiled back at him, wishing I could embrace what he was saying without so much skepticism. "Thanks for telling me. That's a hopeful thought. But I wish you also had an idea of what it *is* and what I need to do to get well."

We didn't explore Will's alternative thoughts then, partly because he couldn't be very specific about what they meant beyond saying "don't worry." But his suggestion seemed to lighten the mood.

I only had one major event while we were there, and my stamina held up well enough with naps and a not-too-vigorous schedule. We enjoyed ten days of family time celebrating the holidays and the tra-ditions of another culture.

When I got back home, Dr. Hite continued her detective work. If they were seizures, they were not responding to the medications that should have given me relief. She tried various options, and in the process, to add to my frustrations, I gained more than thirty pounds. The frequency of events increased to more than one a week, and she suggested I talk to my supervisor about the possibility of taking a medical leave if it got any worse. Thank goodness I could do that without naming a medical condition!

ONE AFTERNOON IN SEATTLE, a couple of months later, a hundred or more of us were packed around tables in a dark meeting room watching a PowerPoint presentation on some new child abuse research. Like the ZAP!! or KAPOW!! in a comic book, some sound or frequency from the public address system swooshed through my brain, causing a major break in all my circuits.

I couldn't navigate my way out of the room or lie down, so I grabbed the hand of the colleague sitting next to me. She understood even in the dim light. She held my hand and kept me upright, while I closed my eyes and felt the waves of energy pass through my body from brain to extremities and back again, draining my life force and weakening my muscles.

It was not unlike other major attacks, but I knew something had to change. I sat quietly until the meeting was over and most people had left the room. My friend stayed with me until I could maneuver with my trusty cane to an area with sofas and low lights where I could lie down.

As soon as I could talk clearly, I called Dr. Hite to report what had happened, and she urged—no, ordered—me to get home immediately, stop traveling, and take a leave of absence so we could figure this thing out. My supervisor and I had already discussed backup plans, so she facilitated both my trip home and the paperwork for the leave with dispatch and concern.

"Your condition is not responding to what usually works, so we may need to take more drastic measures," my kind and trustworthy doctor explained in her office the next day. "If this is in fact a seizure disorder, as I suspect, I can implant a device, something like a pace-maker, to help regulate the electrical activity in your vagus nerve to the brain. Intractable seizure disorders can sometimes be controlled this way without increasing medications and other side effects. But, in order to decide whether that makes sense in your case, I need a picture of one of your events."

Without leaving time for my system to recover from the latest attack, she put me in the hospital for a round of telemetry. I knew the drill from twice before.

A jovial technician whose name I can't remember had the bizarre job of gluing forty electrodes onto my head. He prided himself on ceremoniously covering up his deed with an exotic white turban. Laughing and joking all the way, he took me to a special hospital room where the staff hooked me up to an EEG machine and began monitoring my brain waves, 24/7. A video camera kept a visual record of my body's responses to their stimulations—strobe lights, sleep deprivation, etc.

Dr. Hite and I were both determined to get to the bottom of this, but neither of us realized how long that would take.

Chapter 4
A Preposterous Diagnosis

After six days and several events, my body and brain felt like mush. Finally, Dr. Hite came into my hospital room, turned off all the machines, and settled on the side of my bed to talk. I struggled to pull myself up to meet her gaze. Despite my wilted body and fuzzy mind, she had my full attention. I knew she would have my diagnosis figured out and a plan to get my life back on track.

"Are you okay with your husband staying for this?"

That was an odd question... She knew he'd come to most of my appointments.

I nodded. "Sure."

"You've had some events here, haven't you?"

Another strange question... She knew perfectly well I had. All she had to do was look at me.

"Yes, I'm a real mess from them, as you can see." I looked at her expectantly.

"I've reviewed all the tapes and EEGs," she said, "and I can tell you that whatever is happening to you, there is no abnormal electrical activity in your brain. In other words, these tests show you do not have a seizure disorder."

What? Was she trying to give me good news or bad?

"But…" I tried not to show my confusion. "If it's not seizures, then what is it? After all we've been through, I'm really hoping for a diagnosis."

Dr. Hite spoke gently, and I could tell she was choosing her words carefully. "In situations like this, where we have intractable symptoms we can't account for, we have to look somewhere else for the cause. I know I've asked you before, but I want you to think very carefully. Did you have any traumatic events in your childhood?"

Oh, good grief. When she asked me before, I'd told her "No. No falls, no head injuries. I even asked my mother, but she couldn't think of anything."

"No," I said. I couldn't completely rein in my frustration at this point. "Same answer as before."

But she probed deeper, "It doesn't have to have been a fall or injury. How about any emotional shock that might have been traumatic? In my experience, if we don't find abnormal brain activity, we have to look for psychological causes."

Psychological causes?! What was she saying? Does she think this is all in my head? Oh please… just look at my body. I started to say "No" again. But then, from somewhere deep inside, a thought nudged its way to the surface. The psychologist I'd been seeing for help to adjust to all this had been surprisingly interested when I mentioned a silly adolescent prank that clearly didn't deserve the attention she wanted to give it. Trying to be cooperative, I ventured an answer I was sure had no relevance.

"Well, I did try to kill myself once. I took a bunch of aspirin when I was twelve. But kids do silly things like that."

The neurologist looked straight at me with kind eyes and said firmly, "No. Kids do *not* just do things like that. I think if you can go back and figure out what was bothering that twelve-year-old, you'll find what's causing your mystery illness."

That made no sense. Obviously, nothing as silly as that could have caused this disabling condition more than forty years later. I laughed weakly, trying desperately to understand, and blurted out my objection.

"Wait a minute! You can't be saying this is all in my head? Remember, I've been screened and tested, and you even sent me to a neuropsychologist. These issues are real! You've seen me. You're not saying this is just all in my head, are you?"

"No," she responded calmly. "I am saying that what is happening to you is not something we can measure yet. It is clear your symptoms are real, but it is not seizures that are causing them."

"Well, what is it then?" I needed an answer.

As usual, Wayne was taking detailed notes so we could refer to them later. Dr. Hite knew every time she had come up with something new to be tested or ruled out, we had looked it up.

She nodded to him and said, "You would need to look up conversion disorder."

Conversion disorder. Never heard of it. I had heard of things like "hysterical blindness." But I wasn't hysterical, and there was no way I was creating these issues!

"In my reading about epilepsy, I read something about pseudoseizures. Is that what this is?" I ventured, trying to sound reasonable.

"Well, the actual term is 'psychogenic nonepileptic seizures,' but yes, some people call what is happening to you pseudoseizures. You'll find them listed among the indicators of conversion disorder.

"Now, tell me about your relationship with the psychologist you have been seeing."

"I like her, and I trust her," I said, knowing they had probably already talked about me since I had given them permission. (I found out later they had talked at length about the diagnosis and had developed a lot of confidence in each other.)

"Okay, I am taking you off all medications and transferring primary responsibility for your care to your psychologist."

My mind was racing as fast as it could. The fog, like me, had been partially blown away by this discussion. So, I'm supposed to accept a *mental health diagnosis*? What happened to epilepsy? That was bad, but at least I had heard of it! Is she saying I'm crazy? Or that I'm somehow creating all this without there being any real illness?! I longed to go back to the simpler diagnosis of a physical problem—any physical problem.

As she left the room that day in March 2002, her expression told me I had no recourse. No appeal process existed. Somehow, I needed to accept this diagnosis. I glanced over at poor Wayne, who was still writing, and wondered if he was making any sense of it all. Did he think I was crazy?

What did she mean the key to this illness somehow lay with what had happened to me as a twelve-year-old who took some pills? How preposterous!

Part 2
The Mind Opens

Chapter 5
The Green Room

A week after I got out of the hospital, I awoke in the dark with a vivid image disturbing my mind—a scene from something far away and long ago. I saw a baby, wrapped snugly in her blankets, surreptitiously passed through an opening in a ragged fence and into the arms of strangers by her distraught young mother. It was late twilight, and the faces of the townspeople were not clearly visible, but she hoped they would be kind. She prayed they'd offer her baby a more secure future than awaited her family as they were herded onto cattle cars to be ferried to a bleak and deserted prison island in the North Sea. The child didn't realize she was being abandoned, didn't know enough to cry out as she passed through the fence into her uncertain future.

Later that morning, I remembered Julia, my psychologist, had asked me to consider what I had been doing six years earlier, in 1996, on the day before the first wave of symptoms engulfed my body. Wayne, Will, Beth and I had just returned from a trip to Europe that included a visit to the German family I had worked for as a nineteen-year-old au pair.

During our reunion, the family had given me an essay written by their matriarch, the Baroness von Kap-Herr. It detailed her experiences as Russia took over eastern Germany at the end of World

War II, including the demeaning, cruel treatment her landowning, aristocratic family received at the hands of the new conquerors. Not until the 1970s had she felt able to put to paper the details of that terrible period, and I was honored her daughters had shared it with me. When I had lived with them in Hildesheim in 1966, the family's hometown of Dresden was in East Germany and off-limits to Western visitors. But on this trip, thirty years later, we had been able to explore the once beautiful center of art and culture, which was finally being rebuilt from the destruction of the Allied firebombing during the war.

The baroness wrote in vivid High German with all the idiomatic flair of a well-educated person. Back home, I read late into the evening at my dining room table, flipping back and forth between the text and a dictionary to be sure I didn't miss any nuances because of my relatively plebeian German. I had just visited many of the places she referenced, so I had some context, and I particularly appreciated her reflections on what her family had lived through.

My reading had started as an intellectual exercise. I intended to take the essay to one of the local universities to augment their study of the war's aftermath. I was not prepared for the heartbreaking emotional resonance of the reality my friends had survived. The scene from my dream drowned out many others as I remembered what I had read.

But why did this one scene reverberate in me so strongly? I didn't know the family member depicted in it. A baby being passed through a fence into unknown darkness, abandoned for good cause by her frightened mother. It would be years before I understood why this triggered me so deeply.

At the time, I wondered if perhaps the baby connected metaphorically to how I felt as I was passed by my medical doctors to the mental health world to treat decidedly physical impairments. My path forward felt almost as uncertain, unstructured and dangerous as that child's, and it was equally clear I couldn't go back.

Blessedly, the fact I was home on medical leave meant I didn't have to deal with work colleagues or outside commitments. My upstairs home office and bed offered safe spaces where I could hide and read about conversion disorders and pseudoseizures, while I tried to understand how they related to me. I learned that more than two-thirds of people with these conditions had a history of childhood sexual abuse. What? Well, that certainly didn't include me. I had to be part of the other third.

Telling Mother or the rest of the family about the new diagnosis would have been way too uncomfortable. How could I tell them I wasn't sick, that it was all in my head, when I couldn't believe it myself? I simply said we had begun a whole new treatment plan based on what they found while I was in the hospital, and I was optimistic I would fully recover. This seemed to satisfy everyone. Maybe it was even true.

My research showed some of my prayers had been answered. This diagnosis wasn't degenerative or life-threatening like so many of the diseases I had been tested for. It sounded like, with some work, I could recover from this thing. So, with zero understanding of what would be required, I set about to do just that—to recover.

I figured two or three months would be plenty of time to get my head straight and my body back in shape. Denial and optimism, ignorance and overconfidence, all worked in my favor.

I STRUGGLED UP THE STAIRS to Julia's office a few days after leaving the hospital, feeling disoriented, weak and a little scared. Determined to get the process moving and find some answers, I began with something positive. "I'm really glad you and Dr. Hite didn't feel the need to bring in anyone new to work with me. But I don't understand how in the world a psychologist—even a really smart one with a PhD— can help me overcome the very physical issues I'm dealing with."

She responded quietly and with confidence. "I know you've been reading about conversion disorders and you have tons of questions. To get us started, let me just say I have a lot of experience with situations like this, where the connections between body and mind create complex symptoms. I want you to know this diagnosis doesn't mean anyone thinks you are crazy. It just means your body is creating symptoms that don't match your neurology, and we have to find some new ways to help you get your strength back. I believe strongly your body and your mind want to heal and can help you find wholeness."

That seemed only mildly responsive to my concern, but we both knew I'd try anything to get back to normal.

"I want you to get a large three-ring binder, lots of paper, and colored pens," she continued. "Keep a journal each day with your thoughts and questions, capture the dreams you have, and draw any pictures that come to mind. We can meet four times a week to start, and we'll decide later how long your medical leave will need to last."

I had taken a two-month leave and was eligible for up to three months if needed. Neither of us mentioned the lurking truth that we had no sense of when, if ever, I would be able to return to work and to my normal life.

We discussed getting physical therapy to help my body recover now that we knew there wasn't anything medically wrong with it, and I agreed to call Dr. Hite to get a referral. I felt a little more hopeful as I left the office with some concrete steps to take—start a journal, begin physical therapy. Neither sounded like I was crazy.

OVER THE NEXT WEEKS, my world grew to revolve around Julia's office on the second floor of a repurposed Victorian house a few minutes from my home. It had floral wallpaper appropriate to its heritage and a dark green carpet boldly accented by a flowered area rug. I sat on the soft green couch across from her big mission-style chair.

She always wore a matching sweater set with a single diamond on a chain around her neck. With short dark hair and gentle brown eyes, she seemed relaxed, kind and curious. This place gradually became known as the "Green Room"—a haven of safety, open to all thoughts, voices and secrets.

Julia considers herself a "learning theorist," informed by the study of how people learn across the lifespan, especially in early childhood and old age. Her curiosity led to questions like: "How or where did you learn this behavior?" "What is the story your body is trying to tell?" "How did you learn to cope and what were you coping with?"

In addition to asking what I had been doing and thinking at the time of the first attack, Julia expressed continued interest in what happened when I was twelve. But no matter how hard I tried to remember more about that time, my answers were always the same. "I was mad at my parents because they wouldn't let me go to a dance with a special boy. That's all it was—a stupid adolescent prank that didn't deserve any attention." My understanding of it had not magically changed just because my doctors placed such importance on it.

Meanwhile, my body found a scary new trick to play. In the first month after being told my problems were all in my head, I lost more than forty percent of my hair, leaving big empty patches of scalp where thick wavy hair had once grown. "Alopecia areata," my doctor called it. It's often caused by the stress of major emotional shocks. It served as a surprising reality check for just how profound a mental health diagnosis had been to my system as a whole, not just to my ego.

On the other hand, the pseudoseizures stopped. They had been happening with varying severity multiple times a week. Now suddenly, without any medication, they had stopped, like a child's secret game that had lost its allure when discovered. Could my body tell that, for the first time in my life, I was ready to listen to it? But what did that even mean?

I began to see in my mind's eye and feel in my body, brief flashes of horrible images: being beaten with a bamboo switch by my grandmother; her periodic frenzied fits and chaotic energy; strange and scary encounters with my drunk father smelling of bourbon; or my weird uncle with his cackling laugh, heavy on me, my body hurting all over. Flashbacks. The pseudoseizures had been followed by debilitating physical effects and fear of the unknown. In contrast, the flashbacks were followed by physical improvements but left behind emotional devastation wrought by the new knowledge.

Sometimes, the visions came in vivid nightmares, which I dutifully documented in my new journal as soon as I could breathe again. But mostly, they came in snippets in Julia's office. I would describe a physical sensation I felt in my body as I sat on her couch. My chest would tighten until I could barely breathe. I'd close my eyes so I could see better, then witness and feel things whose implications I couldn't believe. But they didn't come with any context or story, just a sensation or picture.

Stranger still, each time something awful was even partially revealed, even if I couldn't tell exactly what had happened, my body responded by walking better the next day or by being able to do more in physical therapy. I saw a clear correlation. The body was getting better each time the mind glimpsed some new detail of a dreadful and forgotten experience of childhood. Although I couldn't directly relate the gains I was making to processing any specific memory, I remember the joy I felt the first time I could do a whole five minutes on the elliptical machine in physical therapy. My strength was returning.

THE IMPORTANCE OF THIS AFFIRMATIVE LOOP cannot be overstated. I experienced real physical improvement, even as the process raised potential memories contrary to everything I thought I knew about myself, my childhood and my family. The concreteness and immediacy of the natural biofeedback told me I had to follow where it led, even if I didn't want to. The alternative was going back to a wheelchair, and I wanted to avoid that if I could. I had to open myself up to the possibility that what I was remembering was real and the path my doctors had led me on was actually helping me get better.

Thus, the journey to find what caused my mystery symptoms, what they were trying to tell me, and how to get on with my life began in earnest. To ensure my story could emerge in its own way, as untainted as possible, I agreed to stop researching symptoms or reading about other people's experiences. The only people with whom I shared small pieces of what I was learning were Wayne and my closest sister, Mary. She was amazingly supportive of me, even though she too had trouble believing what I was telling her. With my children so far away, it sufficed to tell them I was regaining my strength and we still didn't know exactly what had caused the whole thing.

I had read that once the door to hidden memories is open, some people become flooded with flashbacks of such intensity they can't function. My wake-up call had come through debilitating physical symptoms that threatened every aspect of my life but gave me almost no information. As frightening as that had been, these strange and confounding flashbacks terrified me even more. What if I lost my mind? My work? My identity? What if this meant the end of the life I knew? No. I couldn't allow that to happen. I responded as I always had… Focus! You can do anything if you stay focused and work hard.

With Julia's help, I settled in and began listening to the messages coming through my body and mind. She urged me to engage every day in some creative and grounding activity that connected me to nature or to the here and now—things like baking cookies or gardening. (How did the Universe conspire to find me such a highly skilled therapist with the perfect expertise?) Instead of an onslaught, I received only as much new information as I could handle while still being able to function in the outer world.

I am deeply grateful for the measured pace of discovery, even though it meant years of work and came with its share of confusion, exhaustion, overwhelm and impatience. Rather than breaking the eggshell off the memories in one big crack, I was more like a baby chick pecking slowly away from inside, resting a bit, pecking again, and resting some more until I was finally freed.

IT WAS JUST WAYNE, me and our two dogs at home now, and I knew our economic well-being depended on my regaining the capacity to function normally and get back to my job.

But money wasn't the only factor in my need to work again. I didn't understand yet that work focused on making life better for others was not only an important part of my identity, but a key survival and coping strategy. It is not much of an exaggeration to say work had always been my drug of choice. ("Hello, I'm Bonnie, and I'm a workaholic.") I had only an inkling of what this addiction had helped me to cope with, but Julia saw it could be an important ally in the healing process. So, we focused on getting my body well enough within three months to return to my work on behalf of children and families in the child welfare system.

Getting back out in the world also offered another opportunity for positive feedback to push me forward. I had not realized how very sick I had appeared until people told me how good I looked now and how worried they had been. After only three months of treatment, I was back at work, standing straight, and seldom needed my cane. The improvements in my appearance warded off any probing questions I didn't want to answer about my inner health.

Chapter 6
Family Secrets

During my leave, most of my weeks included four hour-long sessions with Julia, two or more sessions of physical therapy, lots of rest, and time to explore my family history. By talking to relatives and reviewing historical records, I hoped to fill in any details of my childhood before I was twelve that I might not already know. Fortunately, my mother enjoyed telling stories about the past, and I didn't need to explain how it might help me regain my health.

Now in her eighties, Mother's beauty, style and active mind kept her looking a decade younger. As a child, dyslexia had masked her intelligence, but she'd learned to trust her intuition and grew into a woman of strength and grace. Her blonde-bombshell, movie-star good looks and vibrant personality had required her to become adept at deflecting unwanted advances without damaging frail male egos.

As adults, my three sisters and I sometimes talked about how we had watched our beautiful mother and learned the moves, while never questioning the dance.

"Boys will be boys. You just have to rise above it," she advised.

Dad had died in 1986, and Mom now lived with my older brother, Peter, about forty-five minutes from me. I visited with her at least once a week during my leave. When she moved in with him, they remodeled to create two master suites at either end of the small, airy, ranch-style house. That gave each of them a private bedroom and bathroom with a shared living room, kitchen and family room between them and a beautifully landscaped backyard complete with hammock, hot tub and sunny patio. They could usually be found in their "his and hers" recliners in the living room, where they read, listened to music, or watched television.

At home, Mother mostly wore long loose dresses, the kind we used to call "muumuus." But somehow, hers always looked elegant—either tie-dye from West Africa, where Peter had lived and worked with the Peace Corps and USAID, or hand-painted pieces she ordered through one of her myriad catalogues.

Peter would visit with me for a while, then go run errands or find some gracious way to give Mom and me time alone. In our conversations, I poked around for new details that might help me understand what had happened when I was young, keeping my questions as innocuous as possible.

"My neurologist was asking again about whether I had any trauma when I was a kid," I began on my first visit, just a week after I got out of the hospital. "I know we've talked about it before, but can you think of anything traumatic that happened back then—either physically or emotionally?"

"Well, I was thinking about your grandfather's funeral, just a month after Claire was born, when I was still so sick." She had hemorrhaged badly and almost died when her seventh child had been born two months premature, even as her father-in-law was dying. I'd been eight and a half years old.

"Your grandmother insisted on having you with her through the whole thing and for the open-casket viewing the day before."

"Yes, I remember sitting on a bench next to her for hours as visitors came and went. What I remember most is how hard it was to sit still and how she slapped my knees if I swung my feet."

Mom continued, more musing to herself than talking to me. "You were with her so much. She wanted you at her house all the time, and I always told you to be good and do whatever your grandmother wanted. That certainly could have been traumatic."

We shared a wry chuckle. Over the years, Mother and I had often tried to understand my father's mother. As a young adult, I had known my grandmother to be manipulative, untruthful and either flat out crazy or just plain evil. But Mother's suggestion that being with her as a child might have been traumatic came as a surprise.

A COUPLE OF WEEKS LATER, Mother revisited the topic. She had obviously been reflecting on it more. "I think I depended on you and used you more than you were aware. I told you, you must go even if you didn't want to because she was your grandmother. Honestly, I needed you to do whatever she said, so she would like me. But I remember sometimes you cried."

"Really?" This was new information. I recalled feeling special because my grandparents (we children called them "Munner" and "Bompa") invited me alone to visit them so often. "Why didn't I want to go?"

"Oh, I don't know," she sighed. "I never asked you why. I just told you, you had to go."

Changing the subject abruptly, she asked, "You remember your grandfather's first wife, Mona, died and they had a son, Edmund, who grew up with his mother's family, right?"

"Yes, I remember hearing about him when Dad died, but I never knew anything about him." I wondered why Mother was raising a secret we had never discussed and an uncle I had never known.

"Well, you may as well know the story since you're so interested in family history, and I only know because Uncle Joe and Aunt Dee stayed in touch with him," Mother began with another heavy sigh. "When Munner and Bompa got married, Munner agreed to raise Ed as her own, which she did until her sons came along."

Mona had died after childbirth in 1911. Dad was born on January 10, 1915, eight and a half months after his parents married. Uncle Joe followed less than eighteen months later.

Mother continued, "Your Aunt Dee told me the police came and removed Ed from Munner and Bompa's home because of the way he was being treated. That's why he was raised by his maternal grandparents. They even had a restraining order, to be sure he couldn't visit his father's home. Apparently, the servants told someone about the things Munner did, and so his grandparents took action to protect him."

"Wow, that's awful." I needed more details. "What happened to him? Child welfare laws weren't very strict or well-enforced in those days. What horrible treatment was he being rescued from?"

"I don't really know the specifics," she admitted. "Mona's father was an important person in town and had the power to make things happen."

"Bad enough he was taken away... But a restraining order? Why didn't Bompa do something?"

"If you want more details, maybe you should talk to Aunt Dee. I'm tired now and want to go lie down." Mother had shared all she was willing to about this little bombshell.

I HAD BECOME THE PROTECTOR of old family papers after our father died suddenly at seventy. It had been my job to clean out his office desk, where I found several file folders full of old personal letters, which I saved from the dumpster my brothers were filling. Unfortunately, I wasn't quick enough to save all the contents of an old chest his father had left, but I did rescue some of Bompa's travel journals and letters. My time off work offered the perfect opportunity to read and organize them to see what light they could shine on our family history.

That day, when I got home from Mother's, I looked up the records and found Bompa served as a physician at Camp A. A. Humphries in Virginia during 1917 and 1918. He must have been away doing his patriotic duty in WWI, leaving Munner with three little boys, when terrible things happened to his first son. That made the entire story more plausible. I couldn't imagine Bompa allowing his child to be abused if he was around. He was such a gentle soul.

However, thinking about my flashbacks of Munner's fits of rage, I wondered what the other children—my father and his four younger brothers—might have been subjected to over the years, with no one from the outside to intervene.

Between the continuing conversations with Mother, Dad's papers, and the timelines I made of family births, deaths, marriages and living arrangements, I compiled the most detailed understanding I'd ever had of our family. I still did not tell Mother my deeper purpose in asking all these questions, but she seemed ready to share her recollections with a forthrightness I hadn't known from her before. Dad had now been dead for sixteen years, and she apparently no longer felt the need to protect the family image.

The first thing that jumped out at me from my new timeline was that, in eight and a half years, Mother had six children and three miscarriages. She and Dad had both been married before. He'd had no children, while she'd brought my older brother into the family. I was born exactly nine months after they married in 1946. Less than nine years later, we were a family of nine.

No single detail of this provided new information for me. However, looking at it on paper filled me with wonder. How in the world did she do all that and still always look so glamorous? It also confirmed my vague sense that during my early childhood, Mother had always been busy with "the baby," and therefore unavailable to me. In fact, being older, I had felt a responsibility to protect Mother from unwanted intrusions.

The timeline also clarified that in less than a decade during his thirties, my father had gone from the peripatetic life of a bachelor traveling salesman, living out of hotels and suitcases, to the owner of both a mortgage and a business, and the head of a family of nine. It gave me a new perspective on what came to be known as the post-war "baby boom."

Both Mother and Dad had always told us they wanted lots of children. In fact, they maintained they were still hoping for twins when my youngest sister, Claire, was born.

But I also remembered a rather strange conversation with Dad on the night before my wedding—strange because he seemed to be seeking an intimacy we had never shared, now that I was all grown up and ready to get married.

As I said goodnight to him, I mentioned off-handedly, "Oh, I've got to remember to take my birth control pill."

"Birth control pill?" He seemed mildly surprised, then mused, "Well, all I can say is if they had existed back then, you wouldn't."

This is the only part of the conversation I remember distinctly, and I didn't think much of it at the time. But it had stuck with me. They may have wanted a big family eventually, but they didn't want me so soon.

Back in the present, almost forty years later, Mother decided my interest in family stories created an opportune time to reveal some of her own secret history. She orchestrated events so her most important story-sharing would take place either in crowded or time-limited settings, allowing her to maintain control. Clearly, she didn't want any probing questions and counted on me not to overreact in public about a private secret.

Mother chose to share her first story in a bustling restaurant, where our extended family had gathered to welcome out-of-town visitors. There must have been more than twenty of us around the table. Having come the farthest, I arrived late, but Mother had saved me a seat next to her, where I settled in and said hello to everyone.

Somewhere between ordering lunch and our salads arriving, as boisterous family conversation swirled around us, Mother leaned over and quietly told me she had saved my place because she needed to tell me she had been raped on a date with a local boy when she was eighteen. She couldn't ever tell anyone about it because her family all knew the boy, but now she felt she should tell me.

I made some attempt at compassion without being too obvious and suggested this was a hard place to have such a conversation. But having said what she wanted to say, she returned to the banter at the table with whoever was on her other side, leaving me shocked, saddened and feeling manipulated.

I don't remember the setting in which she later told me that in her early twenties, after her first husband had left her, she endured another date rape. This time, her sleeping child was in the next room, ensuring she would not scream. At eighty-six years old, she was still questioning herself about what she might have done to avoid, stop or even attract the rapes.

She expressed more emotion when she told the third secret story from the safety of her home. In the small farmhouse where she and her four siblings grew up, they all shared one bathroom with a big clawfoot bathtub. While she was in early puberty, her father was in the bathroom as she got out of the tub. He reached out his big hand and cupped it around her budding breast. This apparently happened only once, but she returned many times to her sense of confusion and indignity, and to her questions. "Why would he do that? His hand was so big and rough. Why did he do that to me? I never could understand." Without giving me time to do more than empathize quickly, she ended the conversation and headed in for a nap.

Another time she mentioned this same incident, she expressed a different sense of confusion. "Dad knew somehow I wouldn't tell anyone. Did he think I was too stupid to tell? He knew he didn't need to worry about me saying anything. He was right, but why?"

Mother had carried the anger, guilt and shame of these experiences (and possibly more?) for a lifetime with her characteristic rise-above-it attitude and highly honed skill for denial. "If I don't think about it, maybe it won't really be true." And finally, she unburdened herself to her eldest daughter.

At first, she confided she didn't feel any better after having told someone. There had been no great, freeing sigh of relief. Later, however, she confessed how good it felt to have someone who knew those secrets—someone who "knows all of me," as she put it.

I understood this desire to be seen, but my need wasn't yet strong enough to dare to open up to her. Instead, I just tried to provide space for her to process her long-held pain whenever she brought it up.

Over time, I began to wonder if her disclosures meant she already knew some of what had happened to me. Was she trying to align herself with me as a sexual assault victim? I couldn't tell.

Either way, I found little comfort in her revelations, just more surprises and horror. Rather than mutual compassion, I felt admonished, as though she was telling me, "We all have our crosses to bear."

I wish she had lived to see the #MeToo movement break the cycle of "boys will be boys" male privilege and entitlement and give women a sense of "we're in this together," instead of the vast loneliness and shame she carried because of these violations.

Chapter 7
The First Granddaughter

The letters Dad had saved from the period of his courtship of Mother and their early marriage included one he had written to his mother after a particularly difficult evening with her. In it, he called her "mentally unstable." I also found several Munner wrote to Mother and apparently gave to Dad, but that he had never delivered. In these rambling religious rants, she quoted the Bible chapter and verse as she railed about why an unclean and wicked woman such as Mother (divorced and with a child) could never be accepted into the family. But the final letter, written while Mother was in the hospital delivering me, spoke of "burying the hatchet" and invited her to bring me to the house when she left the hospital. So, my first stop as a brand-new baby was at the home of my paternal grandparents.

The oft-told family story recounted how, when they put me into the waiting, ample lap of my stern and pious grandmother, "she melted." Oh, the magic power of a baby to unleash emotions you'd forgotten—things like love, compassion and hope.

Sitting in her living room recliner almost sixty years later, Mother added new details to the old story. "As we left their big house, we were both relieved at how she had responded. Then your father told me we were going to have to share you with them. They had never had a girl, and you were the first granddaughter. You looked very much like your father did as a baby, which was also a plus. At the time, I wasn't sure what he meant about sharing you. It turned out later, after we settled down in Pasadena when you were almost two, I had to let you go over to their house anytime they asked. Sometimes, they would just send Uncle Dick or Uncle Ted over to get you, and you had to go."

"I remember spending lots of time there, but this is a new slant on it. Why did they want me so often?" I needed her to continue with these new details.

"Well, you were a darling little girl, and very smart. I knew you had gotten their smart genes—that you would be blessed with your father's good mind and be able to handle yourself. And of course, we had you all to ourselves until then. After that, whenever they asked, I sent you."

I could hear the resignation in her voice.

"So, you had to send me even when it wasn't convenient for you and even if I didn't want to go? This is what Dad meant when he said you'd have to share me with them?"

"That's right. Now, I'm tired, and I'm going to lie down."

IN ADDITION TO THESE PERIODIC COMMAND VISITS, I soon learned, each time a new baby was born, I stayed with my dad's parents for two weeks or more.

Bompa was still a practicing physician, and I didn't remember too many interactions with him, except at mealtimes. Their bedrooms were in different parts of the house, which somehow didn't seem strange to me. My memories were mostly of Munner in her large, airy two-rooms-and-a-bath suite with the sunny patio, down a couple of stairs off the living room. With babies consuming all the adult energy at home, it was nice to feel special at Munner's.

We played endless games of canasta and enjoyed our special books about faraway places. Our favorite was a large, heavily bound orange volume with detailed photographs called *The Cathedrals of Italy.* We never tired of poring over the architectural and artistic details of these magnificent structures, and always agreed the one in Milan was best. Munner was still alive the first time I visited Italy, and I sent her pictures of me at our special cathedral, which felt like an old friend.

As a child, the rules at Munner's house were clear.

- Children did what they were told, without question.
- In the huge, high-ceilinged living room, children walked on the two-foot-wide hardwood path around its perimeter— never on the glorious, dark blue Persian rug that covered the rest of the floor.
- The beds were made with clean sheets and tight hospital corners every morning.
- Children ate whatever food they were served—all of it.
- Good behavior was required (although not always clearly defined).

But for the first almost two years of my life, Mother, Dad and I traveled together. When I was born, my father had famously asserted, "It'll be easier for her to adjust to my way of life than for me to adjust to hers."

He had bachelor's degrees in mining engineering and mineralogy and a master's from the Colorado School of Mines. He worked for a large international engineering company as a salesman and trouble-shooter for mining and railroad operations across the entire western United States and into Canada and Mexico.

Having grown up on a dairy farm in Idaho, Mother was eager to travel with him and see more of the world. When I came along, they decided not to change their plans but to take me along on their travels. Mother happily nursed me and learned to adapt hotel dresser drawers into cribs and bathtubs into playpens. I was healthy, cute and precocious, and, as Mother used to say, I "never met a stranger." She was attentive to my needs, flexible and eager to show me off to hotel maids and local dignitaries alike. I repaid her by seldom fussing and bringing lots of positive attention to my beautiful mother.

My older brother Peter, who had been living on the farm with Mother's parents, needed to start school just before the next baby was due to arrive. We came back to Pasadena, bought a house less than a mile from Dad's parents, and settled down. Peter enrolled in the local elementary school, and Mary was born twelve days before I turned two. And that's the time my earliest flashbacks take me to.

THE SPLINTERED MEMORIES of traumatic experiences did not bring with them the complete story of when it was, where it took place, who was present, or how often it happened. Instead, I'd get fragments of memories—pictures, sensations, emotions—that I had to fit together before I could understand what had occurred, and those always from the viewpoint of a traumatized child.

As the flashbacks started, the first images I saw involved Munner with a bamboo switch, frenetically beating a little girl with long curly hair wriggling on a bed. I realized the girl I saw in my mind was me. But I was also the observer who stood off to the side, wishing the girl wouldn't make the beating worse by squirming so much. I saw the red welts on her legs but didn't feel the pain associated with them.

Then came the ominous visions of Dad or his youngest brother hovering over me, doing something very scary, heavy and dark. Many months later, the sensory clues finally made clear what I hadn't wanted to believe. These images gave way to the feeling of something much too big being painfully forced inside my body and moved around until I felt all wet.

In the Green Room, I recoiled when Julia used the word *rape*. "That's not what happened to me. That happens to adults, and this happened to that little girl." Somehow, I could more easily wrap my head around the less explicit idea of sexual abuse, a term used in the child abuse reports I read at work. It allowed me to remain distant from the case of this girl I was learning about.

Early one morning, after a night of particularly graphic and physical flashbacks and dreams, I retreated to my son's old bedroom. Trying to find comfort and get my bearings, I sat on the bed in tears with my arms clenched around my bent knees and rocked. But all I found was a head full of questions.

"Could any of this be true? Why would they do that? Why would they hurt me like that? Had Daddy really shared me with his brother?! Why didn't anyone stop them?

"And now, so many years later, how is it that those old experiences created all these health issues?

"This is all so surreal, like I'm learning about something that happened to someone else, about things done to other people as children by their relatives. It couldn't have been *me*.

"I can't let these revelations redefine my life. And yet, they do.

"Has anything I've ever thought or done been real?

"Is *anything* real? Yes, I love intellectualizing about abstract ideas. Let's do that. What is the nature of truth?

"But this isn't abstract. This cuts at the core of my life as I have lived and understood it. I thought I knew some truths about myself— but that has all been taken away. How does a person just forget big chunks of her life? And what else have I lost or forgotten? Or am I just making it all up?

"Best to stay removed from the case of this child—empathic, but separate, as with the cases we deal with at work. It doesn't fit at all with what I know about my family or my childhood.

"Yes. If you are going to make it through the day, you must focus on what you need to accomplish today. Put this out of your mind."

I obediently took a couple of deep breaths, wiped my eyes, got up off the bed, and went downstairs to make breakfast.

Chapter 8
A Suicide Attempt

Even as flashbacks from deep within my subconscious revealed unspeakable things, I continued to visit with Mother to probe for what else she might be able to tell me about our family. I couldn't confront her about Dad. I couldn't bear the pain if she had known and done nothing. On the other hand, if she hadn't known, I couldn't bear to hurt her. Besides, she was my best source of the historical information I desperately needed. I didn't want to risk that drying up. I needed, yet also hated, her unwitting corroboration of the plausibility of my new memories.

As we sat chatting one morning, I casually ventured into a topic we seldom mentioned. "You know, I have been thinking about when I was twelve and took all those pills. I've been wondering about how awful that must have been for you—to have your eldest daughter try to do that. What was that like?"

"Oh dear, it was horrible... Just awful. I didn't know what to do," Mother lamented. "But on the way home from the hospital after we had your stomach pumped, your father said he thought the best way to handle it was never to talk about it again. I didn't know what else to do, so I agreed, and we never did."

"Wow, so that's why you never asked me about it. Why do you figure he didn't want to talk about it?"

"Well, I'm not really sure, but what else was I supposed to do?" And she quickly changed the subject.

In a later conversation, she had tears in her eyes when she said, "I should have let you talk about it, shouldn't I? I should have listened to what you had to say."

"Yes, Mother, that would have been a good thing to do," I agreed. "I'm not sure what I would have been able to tell you, but it would have been wonderful to think someone was interested in my thoughts and feelings. Any time an adolescent acts out like that, it's always a message."

With some frustration, I recognized these conversations with Mother about my suicide attempt centered mostly on her and told me nothing new about what had been happening to me at the time. In fact, she still showed a spectacular lack of curiosity about why her daughter had taken those pills. She said something about being concerned my grandmother and one of my uncles were trying to take me away from her and Dad, but never elaborated.

I knew after Bompa died and Dad's middle brother, Uncle Dick, moved up to Palmdale, I used to travel often with my grandmother to visit my aunt and uncle. I liked them and loved the drive through the mountains to the high desert. But the big draw for me was the group of teenage boys who lived with them. I later learned they were probation foster youth, that is, kids who had been in some sort of trouble and couldn't live with their families. To my early adolescent eyes, they were dreamy high school men, and I developed my first serious crush…

Eddie had given me a pearl necklace, which I cherished, and my first real kiss, which had reverberated through me like a gong. (I was a precocious and well-developed twelve-year-old. He was at least sixteen.)

I remembered one afternoon, while we sat around the cozy living room chatting and playing cards, Uncle Dick commented that "Bonnie is Eddie's girl now." Although this startled me, the words settled around my shoulders like a warm cloak of belonging. Eddie's girl. Someone actually wanted me as his girlfriend. And then he invited me to the Valentine's Day dance at his high school. It was so romantic—my first date.

But with no explanation, my rotten parents had said no; not only could I not go to the dance, but I was also not allowed to go back and visit anymore. Why were they treating me like a child, taking away the chance for a real boyfriend? Clearly, they didn't truly love me.

I went to bed mad and in tears, then vaguely remember getting up and taking a handful of pills. Mother said I swallowed a whole bottle, but that was the only new detail she provided.

Mother and Dad took me to the emergency room, but from the way they reacted, I could tell it had been a stupid and shameful thing to do, one that should never be talked about. I don't remember ever trying to understand it beyond that.

Instead, Mother helped me focus my attention outwardly—on doing my best at school, joining service clubs, singing with the Boy's Club dance band, performing in every play I could, and enjoying lots of friends and social activities. That busyness soon pushed any lingering anger at my parents, or questions about the episode, out of my mind.

I never made another serious attempt to take my life, but I often thought about ways to kill myself, which I've since learned are called "suicidal ideations" and are something to be taken seriously. But for more than forty years, I convinced myself these thoughts were just part of life and never told anyone about them, not even Wayne. As an adult, my suicidal thoughts and plans had been consistent companions, their intensity ebbing and flowing with the tides of my stress or sense of overwhelm.

A quote from my journal from near the end of my first year of treatment shows how thoroughly I had normalized the situation I had lived with all my life.

I wonder what life would be like if you never had to spend energy fighting off suicidal thoughts and images and plans. I guess some people may go through life without them. That just occurred to me. Wow! Is that possible? Is that one of the things I'm reaching for in this healing process? That would be a lot of psychic energy available for other things! What an awesome thought... Is it possible?

WITH CONSISTENT THERAPY for the first time in my life, the generalized suicidal ideations—daydreaming virtually every day about my escape—diminished markedly. Later in the healing process, suicidal thoughts arose again several times as I got too close to specific parts of the secrets, triggering the complex protective tools in my mind. Luckily, Julia was always on the lookout for such possibilities and helped me stay safe. But I am getting ahead of myself and the story.

As Julia and I worked to understand my suicidal ideations, we unmasked my longtime fear of driving over large bridges or winding mountain roads (where I would envision myself driving off the edge into oblivion) as a fear of the internal urge to kill myself.

In September 2004 (after two and a half years of therapy), I had to drive through the Bay Area on a work trip with no easy way to avoid several bridges. I called Wayne excitedly from the car. "For the first time ever, I drove across four big bridges without any white knuckles. I didn't get scared of falling from the bridge or anything. I'm getting better in ways we never even imagined!"

He cheered me on, remembering the many times I had needed him to do the driving. This was a truly helpful change in my life. It used to take all my focus and power to hold the car on a bridge or keep from flying off a cliff. But I had never imagined the fear was actually of *myself* and of the possibility I might *intentionally* drive over the edge.

Once I faced it, the fear lost its power. Well, it didn't work quite that magically... but almost.

Chapter 9
Bompa's Science

As I learned to work with the flashbacks, I realized most of them included at least one of three people: Munner, Dad and his youngest brother, Uncle Ted, all of whom were now dead. My adult relationships with them had been complicated, thanks to my perception of their erratic behavior.

Uncle Ted, with his cackling laugh, wandering hands and constant beer drinking, had always made me feel creepy when he got too close. Meanwhile, as Munner aged, she became an unhappy, guilt-tripping victim, always with a new grievance, the veracity of which was never clear. And my father, whose approval was so important to me as a young adult, enjoyed belittling anything I did or believed that diverged from his path or viewpoint. And, of course, there was his binge drinking, which made him unpredictable.

I knew them all to be flawed human beings, but that couldn't have prepared me for the fearful truths the flashbacks revealed about their actions.

Just as I started getting my bearings with these revelations, an even bigger surprise arose... Bompa, my sweet, kind grandfather, began to show up in dreams and flashbacks as a menacing mad scientist.

I was eight and a half when he died, and my conscious memories of him were all positive. I saw him as a gentle giant. Could it be that he had also hurt and used me?

No! Impossible! Totally out of sync with everything I knew about him! If it was true, this betrayal would cut deeper than the others.

BOMPA WAS EVEN BIGGER AND TALLER than his sons. He had a large, round face, light blue eyes that smiled easily, and not much hair. He was a well-known eye doctor, with an office downtown in a lovely old building we visited often. I knew Bompa as deeply religious, a Mason, and someone with a compassionate demeanor and a curious mind. But my flashbacks revealed he also had a scientific interest in unconventional means of probing and improving human potential.

Disjointed memories appeared over several months. First, his twinkly blue eyes, and then the rhythmic sound of a metronome. Slowly, I pieced together the following description of how he began grooming me early to take part in his research and experiments.

One time when I was visiting my grandparents—I think I was two—Munner went into one of her scary, mad yelling fits and threw a heavy, decorative perfume bottle across her bedroom. Glass flew everywhere as it shattered against the wall, and a shard caught my hand, cutting it bad enough to bleed quite a lot. I cried out, as much in fear of Munner's reaction if I bled on the furniture or the rug as in pain from the cut.

Bompa must have heard the commotion, because he came down into Munner's room with his doctor's bag. He gave her a shot that quickly settled her down and then bandaged my hand. Gently, he took me out onto the porch and, blue eyes smiling, told me he could teach me how to keep things like this from hurting. I loved my Bompa and wanted to please him, and I also wanted my hand not to hurt. So I did what he told me to. With his calm voice and twinkling eyes, he hypnotized me right there on the porch and took the pain away. It seemed like magic, and I became a very willing and capable student.

Over time, he taught me to focus on his eyes while listening to a metronome and to go away to a place where there was no pain. Later, I learned I could do it without looking into his eyes—just listen to the ticking or watch the metronome's swinging arm, and allow myself to settle, relax and go away.

As I mastered these early mind control techniques, he taught me more, like counting backward until I could close the door on the outer Bonnie, who would not remember anything. Sometimes, Bonnie would go into a beautiful white light where it was peaceful and nothing bad happened. After I learned to "close the door" and "go away," as we called it, Bompa began to do his "special science" with me.

For that, I lay on a pad on the big mahogany dining room table, surrounded by two other doctors wearing white coats, along with two nurses in white uniforms and crisp white hats.

I especially liked the dark-haired doctor named Ravi. His smile and dark eyes always made me feel calm and important. Ravi gave me shots when Bompa said it was time for me to have medicine. When everyone was ready, Bompa gave the signal, and the nurses used little pokey things to hook my legs up to wires that made them feel really strange.

As electricity ran through my legs until they jumped on the table, Bompa sat in a chair next to my right shoulder and told me, "Stay focused and you won't feel it." Sometimes, Bompa put big black headphones on me with sounds in them or other machines with other kinds of energy that pulsed through my body.

With Bompa's gentle guidance and encouragement, I focused on "layering off" the pain or other sensations when they got too strong for my body to handle. Bompa told me this science and what I was learning were very special. They could help other children—including my little brothers and sisters—and keep them from getting sick. I loved being so special and always did my best to please Bompa and to not feel anything.

A group of important science people worked with Bompa, and I saw them write in little black notebooks. I wasn't sure exactly what they were testing or what they were learning, but the experiments grew longer and harder.

My job was to make Bompa happy by practicing how to make any pain or bad feelings go away so my body wouldn't feel it. I remember he sat by my right shoulder and helped all the time during the science. Nobody else did. He was special, and I was special.

He wanted it not to hurt. That's why he helped. He needed to do this because he could learn more than he could from doing other things, and that would help him with his important work. He was always right there helping and making it okay. "Shall we try one more? Can you do it this way? Can you do just a little more?" Sometimes, he got so excited! "Oh, this is so good! You can do it. Oh, you are so focused! Just stay focused and you can do it!"

So, I didn't feel what was happening because I was making it be somewhere else.

JULIA TOLD ME DURING PARTS OF THESE FLASHBACKS, I moved to the floor in front of the couch in her office, twisting and jerking with the remembered sensations.

As an adult, I was dumbfounded. I could scarcely believe what I was seeing, feeling and hearing. The little girl felt so special and was so patient and tolerant even while she was being used in these science experiments. She clearly was not me, but strangely, my mind could show me detailed pictures of what she remembered.

With Julia's guidance, I had already begun to accept that awful things that happen during childhood can separate from normal memory and be held in other parts of the psyche. Sometimes, a set of traumatic memories can coalesce into a distinct identity, which is often called an "alter." I had heard of multiple personality disorder. In fact, I was deeply moved by both Joanne Woodward's performance in *The Three Faces of Eve* and Sally Field's in *Sybil*. But I never dreamed those stories might have anything to do with me.

And yet, here she was in the Green Room. A young girl, about six years old, whom we called "Bompa's Girl" because she knew herself to be so special to him. She was still inside me, able to explain in detail how special she was and the importance of what she and Bompa had done together.

She had been asleep ever since Bompa died and now, somehow, she had awakened, as the flashbacks showed me on the outside what she had been holding on the inside—the things she had done with him all those years before. Bompa's Girl was a completely separate person from me, describing and showing me images of experiences I knew nothing about but that had happened in a dining room I knew well.

I tried desperately to understand what all this meant. Could it be real? Or true? The sights, sensations and feelings that flooded my mind and body could not be denied, even if their origins weren't clear. I wasn't just imagining things. My whole body was speaking.

Could this mean Bompa used his skills as a physician and scientist, exploring the potential of the human mind, to create a separate part of my psyche, who essentially became a human lab specimen he could experiment with at will? How could he? I thought he loved me!

Beyond anger at his hubris and duplicity, a deep, deep sadness at his betrayal overwhelmed me. I had always known I was special to

Bompa, but I hated to learn it was because I made a good lab rat. I really didn't want this to be true.

But, now that Bompa's Girl had joined us in the Green Room as a real entity, I had to admit to Julia there were also identifiable and quite distinct voices—or people?—connected with my flashbacks involving Munner, Daddy and Uncle Ted.

Whoever or whatever they were, these little people had dealt with rape, beatings and science experiments and kept me from knowing anything about them, even as a child. As a little girl, I—Bonnie—went home, went to school, and carried on an apparently normal childhood, not consciously aware of anything about these experiments or any other abuse. How did I do that? How could it have happened? What would my life have been like if I had known? How could I not have known? Was Bompa's mind control and self-hypnosis training that good?

Julia suggested I must also have had an aptitude for dissociation (going away) and amnesia (forgetting), which are natural survival tools, she told me.

Natural survival tools? So Bompa was teaching me something that also came naturally? I had a lot to learn…

Chapter 10
Four Sisters and a Marriage

The more I learned, the more I felt the need to share what I was learning with my sisters. While Mary lived nearby and was a huge support to me, Christine and Claire, the two youngest, lived in other states and were curious about my recovery. What miracle had brought me back to my "normal" self? I had given them very little detail over the phone, thinking I needed to do this in person. But I didn't know exactly what I was going to tell them or how, nor how they would react to learning secrets no one wanted to know. They were both nurses, so maybe they had heard of stories like mine? Would they believe me or dismiss me as a drama queen?

Mary, just two years younger than me, had been a rock of support through my years of illness and discovery. She had been the first person other than Wayne with whom I shared any details about what I was learning. Somehow, she knew intuitively how to support me—to hold space for my pain—without needing to agree with the things I said. She also didn't treat me as if I was crazy, even when I wasn't so sure. But I hadn't shared the little people inside me with her yet.

We four girls grabbed an opportunity for one of our infrequent "sisters' getaways" when Christine and Claire came to town for a big reunion of Mother's extended family in 2004. We asked our older children to take the younger ones somewhere they could stay all day, so we could have a girls' day at my house.

Earlier sisters' getaways had exposed the fact that we two older girls had different childhood memories than Christine and Claire. For one thing, Dad's drinking had been out in the open for them. Mother's denial and skill at hiding it were no longer successful, as they had been with us. In fact, Christine and Claire told us about nights during which they tried to sleep with the sound of loud arguments and crying coming through the thin bedroom walls, something Mary and I had never heard. Maybe they, like Mary, would be able to accept my new memories as my experiences, if not theirs. Or would they hate me for raising such impossible ideas about our family? I just wasn't sure.

The four of us settled onto my big front porch; waved goodbye to two cars full of happy, beach-bound cousins; and watched the last of the morning haze retreat from the warm blue Pasadena sky. We munched on avocado toast, courtesy of my home's hundred-year-old avocado tree, and fresh-picked Valencia oranges from the remnants of groves that had once covered our neighborhood. With only minor disruptions to forage for more snacks or use the bathroom, we stayed on the porch all day, talking, laughing, crying, sharing.

We started off reliving some of the fun from the reunion, marveling at how cute our kids were as they left, and catching up on the state of everyone's health. They knew I had some weird stuff to share, and I waited my turn.

"You know those awful attacks I was having—the ones that made me so sick and unable to walk? Well, it turns out they were what's called 'pseudoseizures,' and they opened the door to a bunch of things from my childhood that I hadn't remembered at all. Secrets I can hardly believe. But the thing is, as soon as these secrets started coming out, the pseudoseizures stopped and I could walk again. That's why I look so healthy to you. It's a psychological problem that caused all the physical issues."

So far, so good. Christine and Claire both talked about their experience with the body/mind connection. But my situation seemed more extreme than anything else we knew of.

"Well, I've learned one of the reasons I was so good at not remembering is that Bompa started teaching me mind control techniques when I was really little. He taught me how to 'go away' in my mind and not remember the awful, painful things that happened. He was kind of like a mad scientist and did experiments on me and taught me how to hide the memories in another part of my brain so I wouldn't feel the pain and wouldn't remember anything when it was over."

They were both too young to remember him, so it seemed safest to let him be the bad guy first. And then, cautiously, I told them I also remembered Uncle Ted had sexually molested me... and Dad, too, though only a few times and only when he was drunk.

These revelations may have surprised my younger sisters, but they didn't seem to shock them like they had Mary and me. Christine and Claire didn't need a lot of detail about my memories. Instead, they opened up a lively conversation and some rich sharing about all our childhoods.

None of my sisters thought they had been sexually abused, but found it scary and unsettling to realize I hadn't known I had either. At the same time, we shared many stories of the unwanted touching and icky, inappropriate behavior we'd lived with as kids, especially from a very close family friend who was often at the house.

As far as we could tell, I was the only one singled out by Bompa for his experiments, and they accepted I could have repressed memories. They had all heard of that.

"It was like he created other compartments in my mind—almost like other people—to hold the bad stuff, so I could totally forget it and live a normal life. And now, as that amazing survival tool stopped working, it created all these powerful physical symptoms until the horrific memories finally came out into the open."

As we explored deeper, each of them described the protective coping mechanisms they'd developed to manage the denial, lies and behavior in what I now had to acknowledge had been an alcoholic family with its own hidden trauma.

Mary easily adopted Mother's prodigious denial skills and used them well all her life. She said she felt like she kind of floated through her childhood and lamented she didn't have clear memories of lots of things we and her friends remembered—even the good stuff.

Christine said she'd created a bubble around herself and decided what happened "out there" in the family didn't affect her. As a teenager, she was the most openly rebellious of us, distancing herself quite creatively—only to be admonished by Dad, "Why can't you be more like Bonnie?"

Claire had been two months premature and kept in a hospital incubator with little human contact for the first six weeks of her life, disrupting her bonding with and attachment to Mother. She described how, at the age of four, she'd learned the "uncle" she had been named after was not a blood relation at all, merely a very close friend and business associate. Confronted with what felt to her like the crumbling of a major family falsehood, she decided she couldn't trust anyone in the family and withdrew into her own world.

The conversation turned to our relationships and the strange coincidence that we had all divorced our first husbands. I was the luckiest, in that I realized my mistake after only three years and hadn't had any children with him. Wayne and I married a couple of years later and had just celebrated thirty years of a mostly solid, loving partnership. My sisters had all stuck it out longer in their first marriages and became single mothers with complicated arrangements with their exes. Each had also remarried. As different as the details of our stories seemed, sharing them and pondering their meaning connected us.

It was the most open and honest we'd ever been with each other, and it felt totally comfortable, if sadly illuminating. The picture-perfect 1950s family life Mary and I remembered had never existed for Christine and Claire, so they found it easier than we did to accept awful secrets hid behind the facade. Interspersed throughout the conversation, as always, were laughter and happy memories of adventurous family trips and excursions. But even here, the "little girls," as they had always been called, had fewer of these to serve as antidotes and restorative salves than we "big girls." And they were much more clear-eyed about the realities of those trips, which, for all the fun and adventure we'd had, they thought we had romanticized.

All four of us had become useful members of our communities, professionals working to make life better for others, and mothers nurturing fifteen children among us. Each of us developed incredibly adaptive coping strategies to help make that possible. I found it strangely comforting—even liberating—that what I was learning didn't shock the little girls or upend their picture of the family, as it had us big girls.

That afternoon, I learned we could share difficult memories and hard truths with each other without negating the positives that came with our complicated family. I hadn't really tried to explain things in any depth to my brothers, beyond the idea that some very bad stuff involving our grandparents had happened when I was a kid. But this afternoon with my sisters gave me courage to dig in and get on with the work of discovering the truth of my past and continuing to heal.

AT SOME POINT DURING THE DAY, I admitted to my sisters that Wayne and I were struggling, but I was sure everything would work out. Actually, I was desperate to regain the mutually supportive partnership we had enjoyed for so many years, but which I could feel seeping away under the weight of all the changes and uncertainties in our lives. When we tried to talk about it, the conversations devolved into arguments about money. But I knew our financial issues were just a flash point, a symptom of something deeper and harder to identify. After all, we had been through much worse.

Frustrated and urgently clinging to hope, I convinced Wayne we needed couples counseling if we were to get through this, and we began weekly visits with a wonderful psychologist, Cristina, whom we both trusted immediately.

After several sessions, she helped us realize that Wayne was experiencing depression. In fact, once we began talking about it, we identified other times over the years when he had cycled through similar bouts. But this was worse, and our old ways of handling it wouldn't work anymore. He needed me to be who I always had been, to support him as I always had. But I was changing, discovering and coming to terms with my disremembered past. I needed support too. My journal at the time summed up my feelings.

> As I write this, I don't know whether our marriage will survive all the pain and turmoil of the last eight years. We will likely live apart for a while to give ourselves the space to heal and figure out who we want to be now that we have met our childhoods. It has been a good thirty-four years, and I hope to get my best friend back.

Wayne got treatment—both therapy and medication—for his depression, and I continued to work with Julia. Then, we came together in Cristina's cozy office to address our partnership in sessions that were sometimes very painful. Through life's shifts and turns, we had always changed and grown together in the past. This time, we couldn't find that flow.

We decided to sell the wonderful old house we had raised our family in for almost a quarter-century. We didn't need all that space anymore, and we wanted to get out of debt. But I sobbed as I left the neighborhood that had been so much a part of our lives, knowing this truly was the end of an era. That house had supported and enabled my life of motherhood, neighborhood swim parties, school and political gatherings, family Christmases and birthday parties, and so much more.

While it felt good to get out of debt and escape the pressure of deferred maintenance on an old house, it didn't magically revive our partnership. A few months later, we did decide to give each other space for individual healing by living apart for a while. We had bought a retirement home in the city where both our children lived, and Wayne moved there while I found a cozy condo just a mile from our old neighborhood. We agreed to meet in six months to reassess, using the wedding vows we had written and recommitted to each year as the standard for the partnership we wanted.

For the first time in my life, I lived alone. I found it strangely exhilarating to face questions like: What food would you buy if you were the only person who is going to eat here? What music would you play if you were the only one to listen to it? What artwork would you put on the walls if you were decorating for yourself?

Tucked among lots of pine trees, with a stream running through the small complex and floor-to-ceiling windows on one side, my condo felt immediately like a home I could safely heal in, even if I had to do it alone.

Part 3
Surviving the Healing

Chapter 11
Old Skills and New Tools

As I struggled with the changes in my life, my chest tightened so painfully, even sitting safely in the Green Room, that breath could neither enter nor leave. Experience had taught me this meant something deep inside was ready to be released. I relaxed, getting out of the way so others could more easily express themselves. Julia would later help them share anything I didn't see or hear.

First, a little one came, scared and sobbing, trying to get away. She curled up and pushed herself into the corner of the Green Room's soft couch, wondering why her body was so big and hard to move. Her strongest instinct was to make herself either invisible or gone—anything to get away.

Don't let them take me to the table.

She hid in the corner of the couch until her breathing settled.

As soon as it did, another little one came forward. Her body leaped off the couch and over to the wall, where it stood until it melted to the floor.

I saw myself lying on the big table in Bompa's dining room. Something I couldn't feel or define was happening to me. I could see a smoky, ghost-like version of my body get up and move away from the table, yet the other body was still lying there.

Then my muscles went totally rigid: legs out front, hard and immovable; head and back against the wall, stiff and inflexible; tongue very large, round and dry, sticking far out of the mouth, making it impossible to swallow or talk.

Julia asked gently, "What comes next?"

The mind caught on the question and a very clear, strong voice said, "No! We're not going there!"

With that, the muscles softened, the tongue regained its shape and flexibility, and I, the adult, returned to the body, wondering why I was sitting on the floor against a wall.

TRAPPED IN A UNIQUELY AMERICAN CATCH-22, I needed at least two hours of therapy each week. But even my excellent group health insurance covered very little outpatient mental healthcare. So I needed to make enough money to cover my therapy (at a generous discount, thanks to Julia). I had to work to pay for the therapy that made it possible for me to work. That meant I needed full-time employment in my well-paying and moderately stressful job. But the healing process itself, with its wrenching physical and emotional flashbacks, drained what little reserves I had left.

How could I strengthen my ability to cope with all the overwhelming, swirling revelations and reactions in the here and now? Julia wondered whether I might use the skills I had acquired in childhood to help make my adult life manageable while I discovered and healed from unthinkable physical and emotional pain. She helped me to create an adult version of going away, which we called a "pickup."

Unlike their predecessors, pickups were intended to be temporary. Any painful behavior, emotions, sensations or knowledge that stemmed from a different place and time could be set aside and dealt with when it was safe—not stuffed back into secret places, nor allowed to erupt into my day without warning.

To do a pickup, I settled myself with deep breaths, as for meditation, and visualized a detailed image of my junior high. School had always been my safe place, so it made sense the one I attended when I was twelve would come to my mind. I gathered problematic behavior and placed it into the classroom used for after-school detention (although I'd never actually had detention as a student). Difficult emotions went into the auditorium, where they could float around its spacious high ceilings. I put the physical sensations in the nurse's office, where they could be safe and tended to in the little bed, and what I knew, or was learning, about past events went into my ninth-grade social studies classroom, where, in my mind, my favorite teacher, Mr. Clement, still reigned.

Difficult bits of memory stirring internally could thus be kept safe until I got to the Green Room, where we could explore the contents of each room. By doing this, I could still function as what is sometimes called the "apparently normal personality" (ANP) and focus effectively on the present while respecting the need to process the old.

For several years, I led a kind of double life—sort of like I did in childhood, only this time it was consciously. The apparently normal person, now known as "Big Bonnie" to those on the inside, found herself free to slay the dragons of intransigent bureaucracies on behalf of abused and neglected children, while the internal family worked to uncover and understand our history.

Inside, deeply hidden and devastating memories came forward in dreams, flashbacks and body sensations, sometimes accompanied by the myriad alters and smaller parts who had held them in for so long. I used pickups each day to store historical images, sensations and feelings safely in their rooms until each could be documented in our journal or explored in the Green Room.

As various young alters emerged, they called Julia their "Lady Doctor." Being of a different time, they found it curious that a woman could be our doctor. If extra time and energy were needed, the internal folks could regulate the pace of outside life with cold or flu symptoms or an inexplicable day when all Big Bonnie wanted to do was sit and watch old Cary Grant movies.

Protected by her selective and temporary amnesia, Big Bonnie often showed up in the Green Room as the "curious analyst." I had a master's degree in human development, worked in the field of child and family welfare, and kept up with new research on the causes and impact of childhood trauma, abuse and neglect. My job was to apply research in ways that could prevent or mitigate the results of such experiences. In a very real sense, Big Bonnie viewed this "case" with the curiosity of a detached researcher—as something to be understood intellectually, not personalized or felt.

I'd come in with the news of the day, and Julia would engage me in adult conversation, quietly assessing Big Bonnie's functioning. I'd raise a question about some odd physical ailment or thought, or read from my journal, and Julia would suggest, "Let's ask inside what this means." The stored information came forth—sometimes in the words and tears of one of the dissociated identities who was finding its voice, often in excruciating body sensations.

Most of the time, my adult consciousness stayed vaguely present somewhere just behind my eyes, seeing images in the mind and feeling the body, but not hearing much of what happened. A few times, new internal parts insisted I get "completely out of the room" before they spoke. We did a pickup at the end of every session, and Julia made sure Big Bonnie was back in the driver's seat and sufficiently aware of what had transpired to understand my exhaustion, stiff muscles and some new aspect of my story.

This arrangement served us all very well for several years, except for a couple of incidents when someone in the internal system felt an urgency to be out and in control of the body in order to express themself. The first and worst of these breakouts happened after an overnight visit to Mother and Peter's house. After breakfast, Peter went out to run errands while I stayed to chat with Mom until she laid down for her morning "happy nappy." As soon as she did, I planned to leave and go to my office.

Once Mother was resting, I packed up the car and sat in the living room to do a morning pickup before heading out into my day. Settling into Peter's recliner, I closed my eyes. But instead of envisioning my junior high school, in my mind I saw myself get up, walk into the kitchen, pick out a large knife, and take it into the bedroom. Using big downward slashes, I stabbed my sleeping mother over and over again.

Whoa…

What was that? Was someone deep inside me wanting to do that?

I held myself in the chair and tried again to do a pickup. But I couldn't center myself. Who was putting these images in my mind? Why?

I knew I needed to get out of that house before whoever it was took over my body and did something awful. I wasn't even sure if that was possible, but still, I stood up, clasped both hands firmly around my purse, and walked step by intentional step out the front door.

Once in the car, I drove carefully down the driveway into the tidy suburban neighborhood, still not sure who shared my mind with me or what they were trying to accomplish. The small and diminishing part of consciousness that belonged to me, the adult, struggled to hold on as someone assumed more and more control over my body. My plan to go to work was scuttled when the car instead turned onto the more familiar route toward home, then out onto a very busy big street. Who was in control here?

With a great deal of effort, I pulled into a parking lot and shut off the engine. "Let's use the tool that has worked so well for us—a pickup." I said it aloud, pleading for cooperation from this young girl whose voice I didn't recognize. She didn't identify herself with a name or use words to communicate internally, and she clearly didn't want to do a pickup. Instead, she managed to draw on my knowledge about phones and cars while maintaining control of the body's actions. Together, we called and left a message for the Lady Doctor, then sat in the car waiting and trying to figure out what to do. We were in totally unfamiliar territory.

(Pronouns become tricky in relating this story. It is hard to know who "I" refers to, so it's clearer to say "we," given there were at least two of us present. But then, there's a period when only this young, unnamed alter was around. For those times, I'll use the third person "she" since I didn't know yet who she was.)

She decided we needed to eat some lunch, and she wanted mashed potatoes, which she said was her favorite food and something we didn't eat often enough. She started the car and drove out onto the busy street in search of a coffee shop or little restaurant where she could sit and eat mashed potatoes and be sure nobody would get hurt. With cars speeding by on the left, she drove very slowly and carefully down the far-right side of the street.

When Julia called back, the young alter got very confused, trying to do too many things at once. Julia's voice, magically coming out of the car radio, told her to look for the first small cross street, turn off the busy boulevard we were on, and park the car. Even though she hadn't yet found her mashed potato restaurant, she dutifully followed the Lady Doctor's instructions, turned right at the next street, drove a little distance, and pulled into the driveway of a nice, neat white house.

Julia asked for a description of the setting. A large orange tree to the left of the driveway caught the alter's attention and was easy to focus on. Using it, Julia helped us get grounded in the here and now, and Big Bonnie regained control.

I told Julia, "I don't know what's going on here, but I've got a busy schedule this afternoon and need to get to the office."

"Other parts of you have needs too, and you have to take care of them. Why don't you go home, and I can see you at four o'clock this afternoon so we can all talk about it."

"Why aren't my pickups working?" I demanded, more scared than angry.

"That's what we need to find out," she insisted. "Call me when you get home."

"All right," I grudgingly agreed, frustrated at the disruption of my plans.

We hung up. I started the car and drove back onto the main street. But as soon as I did, this young alter, insisting she still needed her mashed potatoes, popped back out into the body and reasserted control. She drove slowly, looking at all the signs, and in a few blocks, found an open and airy diner that looked like it would offer them.

After parking, she walked in, sat in a small booth, and ordered comfort food—broccoli and cheese soup with a side of mashed potatoes. She sat there, smiling and swinging her legs, amused that all anyone else could see was a big person's body—but actually, it was a little girl sitting there! At one point, she thought the waitress was looking at her funny and wondered, "Does she know?"

The food came quickly, and it was perfect. She savored the taste and the way it felt warm and comforting in her tummy. Then she got up and went to the bathroom.

The reflection of the adult in the mirror reminded her she should somehow connect to Big Bonnie. The Lady Doctor had said it wasn't safe for her to drive home, but now that she was out in the body, making decisions, she didn't want to go back inside where she would have less control. "I can handle this if I just stay focused."

Back in the booth, she proudly counted out the money to pay and left to get back in the car.

She didn't like being at Big Bonnie's work and did not want to go there. But she didn't trust that Big Bonnie would go home, so she sat stubbornly in the parking lot until the Lady Doctor returned yet another call.

Julia heard her complaints and promised to make Big Bonnie go home if she'd leave the driving to the adult. Obediently, I drove home with no further drama. The young alter and I were both exhausted and went straight to bed for a nap.

At Julia's office, later that afternoon, the little one spent a lot of time crying that nobody loved or cared for her. As far as I could tell, it explained nothing.

I focused on the scary loss of control, exclaiming to my journal, "Well, now it's clear I am certifiably crazy!"

Becoming stabilized so as to not disrupt my work life felt much more important than worrying about the hallucinations of stabbing my mother—something that did not, after all, happen—or the feelings of a semi-existent child.

Looking back at this harrowing incident with hindsight and some help from Julia, I realized later that my response to the little girl inside was to do just as the adults in her life had always done—not to listen to her needs, but to make it clear that the most acceptable behavior was to ignore those needs and get back to work. In fact, much later, I learned the alter who had taken over that day, BJ, did so to protect us all from the danger she sensed in scary urges coming from somewhere else inside.

After two hours with Julia, I still had no answers, nor any understanding of why someone inside wanted to use a knife to punish Mother. I could see that some parts of me might be angry with her, though, based on their perception that she didn't love or protect us.

The next day, with my pickups working again, I flew to San Francisco to chair a meeting of foundations that focus on youth in foster care. Two days later, in Sacramento, I led a large conference on reforming the child welfare system to offer abuse prevention support to families.

The obvious connection between my work and my internal life wasn't completely lost on me, but I didn't have time to dwell on it. Big Bonnie needed to stay as apparently normal as possible to meet her external commitments.

Nonetheless, this incident clearly indicated internal doors were opening—new secrets needed release and Big Bonnie's control was tenuous at best. Julia understood and, even with the work and travel schedule I insisted on, she ensured we had four sessions in the Green Room that week in order to facilitate these openings safely.

Chapter 12
The Initiation of a Priestess

Less than a week later, a deeply hidden and highly fragmented story began slowly to unfold, triggered in part by the images of the knife. Little by little, splintered shard of memory by splintered shard, a story about my grandparents' strange religious cult emerged. In all, it took more than a year for the pieces to come together into a cohesive story, and the deeper we got into it, the more parts of the psyche we found. Each appeared as a young, frightened child, and each held only her specific aspect of what had happened, sure it was the worst and last.

Maintaining my professional detachment, I was utterly fascinated—and at times horrified—by the capacity of my system to both split spontaneously and switch using Bompa's techniques. Our journals captured the story unfolding in the Green Room. In the process, I learned some of my alters had also dissociated and had smaller parts.

The first part to make herself known stood in the butler's pantry of my grandparents' home, refusing to go into the kitchen. "I did not go in the kitchen!" she yelled, refusing to say why she didn't want to go through the familiar beige swinging door. Somehow, she knew something awful—something she wanted no part of—was about to happen in there. She knew if she stood still, whatever else happened, she would not have to witness or be a part of it. And there she stayed, frozen in terror in the narrow butler's pantry with its floor-to-ceiling, glass-doored cabinets.

If she had turned the other direction, she might have retreated to the big airy breakfast room or, turning left, into the dark, mahogany-lined formal dining room. But no, she stood frozen in the space outside the swinging door, holding the fear she knew could not go into the kitchen.

Later, another part came forward who had compliantly gone through the door into Munner's black-and-white tiled kitchen. She sat on the couch in the Green Room and cried inconsolably because SueJoe, the Siamese cat, had died in that kitchen. She didn't share how she knew this, instead sobbing, "They lied! My grandparents lied. They said SueJoe had just left and gone away." She cried harder as she remembered her sweet cat with two names and different colored eyes. "I named it SueJoe because Munner didn't know if it was a girl or a boy. But SueJoe died that day. She didn't run away. They lied. It makes me so sad."

She stopped crying briefly to add, "Well, at least SueJoe didn't just run away like they said. I knew she wouldn't do that. She loved me. But why did they lie? Why did SueJoe die? How did SueJoe die? I know it happened in the kitchen that day, but who did it?"

Many weeks later, a third child came forward in the Green Room, crying and sobbing. She remembered much more about what had happened in the kitchen with SueJoe. He had been killed. Munner and Bompa were both there, as was a bucket of blood—SueJoe's blood. And a little round thing that was SueJoe's heart. The warm feel of the sticky liquid on her hands and in her nostrils was very strong as she sat on the green couch and remembered the scene.

She saw Bompa silhouetted against the bright sky outside as he opened the back door and took the bucket outside. The nausea that had been building overtook her, and she ran to the little bathroom on the service porch and threw up.

Munner seemed to want to comfort her and put a cool washcloth on her face. No crying allowed back then, but terrible, racking sobs erupted as she spoke about it now and the nausea was very real.

Then, months after the first child had told how she kept herself from taking part in the kitchen ritual, another chapter unfolded. Each story that a little one shared provided a fragmented vision of the whole experience, and as these shards came together the little ones began to realize their experiences were all part of the same story.

The little girl who stayed in the butler's pantry had sadly come to know she wasn't successful in keeping the body outside the swinging door. Now, another one was remembering more about what had happened in the kitchen. "They said SueJoe was evil because he had different colored eyes. He had to die so I wouldn't be evil. And I had to kill him. But I didn't have the knife. I didn't take the knife or use it. I didn't kill my cat!" she yelled forcefully, with a growing grain of doubt, amid many tears.

The most fully formed personality revealed herself as Priestess, who developed her powers through a series of rituals and played a significant role in Bompa's religious ceremonies until his death several years later.

As Priestess listened to all that the little ones revealed, she came forward and put the whole story together. Until then, she had only known the outcome. She was a powerful and disciplined priestess who worked with the High Priest (Bompa) when he summoned her for ceremonies. As she described how that came to be, she shared with confidence and precise diction. In the process, Priestess also put the confusion to rest among us and clarified SueJoe was, in fact, a male cat.

A special initiation took place when I was perhaps five or six years old. A group of adults gathered in the living room speaking in tongues—Munner, Bompa and two uncles among them. Bompa held his spinning white globe to begin the trance that brought me forward, and I took my place in the midst of the group, wearing my white dress. We walked up the four steps from the living room into the dining room in procession. Someone hit the gong hanging from the carved wooden elephant, which stood on the top step, and we walked through the dining room into the butler's pantry with the sound ringing in our ears.

Bompa had our Siamese cat SueJoe—who seemed to be sleeping—in his hands. Some part of me feared what was about to happen in the kitchen and decided she wouldn't go any farther. I walked through the swinging door into the kitchen with them still jabbering away in tongues. But the fear stayed behind, out in the butler's pantry. We knew we could not show fear—could not even feel fear—and get through what we had to do. So, the fear stayed outside the door in its own ball, with its own keeper. Many years later, as I began to remember this day, it appeared as a ball of hot churning emotion in my solar plexus, making it hard to breathe.

Bompa was in his white robe and hat and had the special, ornate gold cross in his hand. I knew something major was about to happen, and I was prepared. Munner sat on a stool, facing away from the door, with SueJoe lying in her lap on an apron. I was brought into the middle of the kitchen, facing Bompa, with Munner sitting next to me on my right, a bucket next to her and the cat lying still in her lap.

A knife was put in my hand, and Munner guided it to cut the cat open and let his blood flow into the bucket. Then she helped me find his heart. I held his warm heart in my hands and felt its power surge through my body. Bompa had coached me it was important to hold a beating heart and feel the sensation of it pulsing strength up my arm and into my being. It was very powerful. When it had done its work and stopped beating, we cut the heart out of the body. I held it out in front of me, as instructed.

Bompa, standing in front of us, looked very big. He did a short ceremony, blessing me and SueJoe's heart with his cross. Then I could feel myself spinning. My eyes rolled back... I couldn't really see, but my eyes were open—felt like floating—in some new kind of trance.

I felt drugged, but there were no needles. I may have drunk some of the blood. The High Priest anointed me as Priestess as we completed this ceremony. The heart was put into a small wooden box with a hinged lid. This box was never to be opened again but was present in ceremonies in the black room as a reminder of this sacrifice and my power.

Bompa and one of the uncles took the bucket and the dead cat outside through the back door. Alone on the service porch with Munner, I went into the little bathroom and vomited, the sensation of warm blood still strong on my hands and in my nostrils. Munner comforted me with a cool cloth and washed me, saying, "You've got to be clean for Him."

Then we were sitting back in the living room. This was part of my initiation as a priestess in Bompa's world. Years later, as these memories emerged, I was sorry to learn the cat had been special to the outside girl and so many other children had been hurt in the process. I was also concerned. It seemed quite inappropriate for these stories to be remembered. I have since learned that for healing to take place, remembering is required.

Chapter 13

Experiments and a Funeral

While Priestess pieced together her story, more information emerged in the Green Room about Bompa's "science" in the dining room. Intensely real body sensations played out, in which I writhed on the Green Room floor or curled up in a fetal position on the comfy couch.

Bompa apparently tested his mind control techniques and coaching by applying different stimulations to my body. I could identify electrical shocks applied to my legs, as well as other energy waves and sounds that are harder to categorize.

In one of the flashbacks, I lay on the dining room table, surrounded by people studying me, with some strange whooshing waves pulsing through my body. As I tried to describe this in my journal, a little one drew a very crude picture of a baby on a big platter being held by a group of people. A big, boxy machine with dials sat off to the side. Lines went from the machine to the baby's body.

A few weeks later, this odd picture seemed to connect to information I learned when I googled Bompa, as I periodically did, using different permutations of his name. This time, I found a letter that documented his involvement in 1937 in experiments with machines created by an inventor named Royal Rife.

With a bit of digging, I learned Rife had demonstrated his new invention, a high-powered microscope, the first one capable of studying living viruses, in 1931, at the local hospital where Bompa had practiced and served as chief of staff.

A university-based research committee worked with Rife on his later invention, the Rife machine, which was designed to cure cancer, viruses and other maladies, such as cataracts, using sound frequencies. The letter I found, signed by a Pasadena physician who had been on the hospital board when Bompa was chief of staff, states my grandfather was the local oculist who examined each patient in the cataract clinic, both before and after each treatment with the Rife machine. The results showed great success in reducing cataracts.

The American Medical Association and others felt the Rife machines were neither safe nor proven effective, and after protracted court battles, all work with them went underground in the early 1940s. I found a picture of one of the actual machines and immediately saw the similarity to the one a part of me had drawn.

Did Bompa keep one of the Rife machines? Did he use it on me to further the research they had begun in the '30s? And if he did, why? As far as I know, I had neither cancer nor cataracts.

Today, there are websites and books devoted to the controversial Rife machines thanks to renewed interest in the 1990s, but this letter was the only mention of my grandfather's association with Rife I have found. Some people still believe Rife's technology can be amazingly beneficial. I hope that's true. I would love to think the experiments performed on me as a child actually resulted in something that helps others heal from their ailments.

I'll never know for sure what exactly Bompa thought he was accomplishing. But the striking similarity between these newly remembered feelings and some of the symptoms that had attacked my body a few years earlier made one thing quite clear: my body and mind had somehow conspired to use the sensations they had stored and hidden for decades to draw attention to the need for healing. If

I ever wanted to find peace, I had to listen to whatever my internal system brought forward. Back in the Green Room, there emerged the following description of the aftermath of the dining room science.

After the experiments were over, I was taken to an upstairs bedroom (normally off-limits to the grandchildren) to sleep off their impact with the aid of medication. When it was all over and the medicine had done its work, Bompa would help close the door in my mind and Outside Bonnie would wake up in the morning in my normal sofa-bed in Munner's sitting room with no memory of where I had been or what had happened—a testament to how amazingly strong Bompa's techniques and my innate dissociative abilities were.

BOMPA DIED AT HIS HOME when he was seventy-five, on May 15, 1955, one month after my mother had given birth to Claire, a premature delivery with such complications they both nearly died. Bompa had had a stroke in March, and while he had still been ambulatory, he had been cognitively gone since then.

Thinking about this timing as an adult made me wonder how my father had coped with the near death of his wife and child, the need to care for the six children at home, and his father's incapacity and death, all at the same time.

Bompa's funeral took place in the big, formal living room at his house, with the calling hours and open casket there the afternoon before. My grandmother requested I accompany her, which, of course, I was required to do. Mother and the other children did not come to the viewing, but she did come to the funeral, against her doctor's orders, and ended up back in the hospital as a result.

For the calling hours, Munner sat near the casket in a big, overstuffed chair, and I sat right next to her on the piano bench. I remained with her throughout the long afternoon, greeting the steady line of visitors well into the evening, remembering to be polite to everyone and to sit quietly without swinging my legs.

Finally, when all the people had left, Munner and I were alone in the room with the open casket. She stood close to it as an emotional frenzy came over her. Apparently, seeing Munner go into one of her fits triggered the tired little girl, making her go away, and brought Munner's Girl to the surface to handle whatever was coming. Outside Bonnie had conscious memories of being at the viewing, but no memory of the events that followed.

To Munner's Girl, a dissociated eight-year-old, Munner appeared to be whirling around in a crazy fury—all swirly, like she was twirling with a white silk scarf or in a vortex of white energy. Munner demanded I get into the coffin with Bompa and make him better. She insisted I was a priestess and should raise him from the dead or accept responsibility for being bad and making him sick and die. But Munner did not know how to call the real Priestess forward, and the little girl who was there with her had no special powers.

Somehow, Munner got me into the coffin and closed the big, curved lid. Being put in a dark box with the cold, dead body was horrible, but it wasn't really Bompa in there. He was soft, and this thing was hard.

Much scarier than that was the confusion about my role in Bompa's illness and death. What did I do to cause him to die? My Mother was really sick too... Was she going to die? Why hadn't she died, while Bompa did? And how was it all my fault?

Rather than being good and quiet as usual, I screamed and pushed up the lid. When this memory came forward years later, I could still hear in my mind a child's shrieks reverberating through the big, high-ceilinged living room.

Finally, Uncle Dick, rescued me. I remember the wonderful sensation of him picking me up and feeling my arms around his body. He was in a dark blue suit, and he was soft and warm and alive. I held him tight. He and Munner argued loudly, but I didn't get involved; I just hugged my uncle. I heard him call her a "crazy old lady" as I caught sight of my Daddy passed out on the loveseat in the sun porch off the living room, oblivious to all the commotion.

Years later, when Priestess first read about this experience, she felt compelled to add her perspective.

Hello. This is Priestess, and I would like to add something here. I now understand Munner tried to force the girl to revive Bompa after he died. I am certainly disgusted with the clumsy and unfortunate attempts that frightened the little girl. Was Munner too stupid to know she needed me for such a task—to maintain the life of the High Priest? I am now not certain even I could have maintained His life, but she should have known that if she wanted me to come forward, she needed His white globe, which spun on the wooden handle and helped me spin into the body.

I was not like some of the others, in that I was not part of the life after Bompa died. I re-awakened in the Green Room. I must admit I was quite stern with the Lady Doctor at first since I did not know or trust her, nor this time or place. Our work was secret and was to remain known only to those who belonged to our group, which met in the black room upstairs. I did not appreciate all the questions this new person asked until I had observed her curiosity and came to trust her motives.

I had been sequestered ever since Bompa had last called me forward to help with the ceremonies. I see he died many years ago, and no one else knew how to engage me. Even though the ceremonies I was created and trained for do not happen any longer, I have made it my business to find appropriate uses for my skills. I shall work with this Lady Doctor who seems respectful and knowledgeable enough to assist me.

Chapter 14
The Table

My life as an apparently normal person continued outside the Green Room with the normal mix of work commitments and family celebrations, aided by pickups and selective forgetting. On a warm spring weekend in 2005, my siblings and many of our children gathered at my sister Christine's home in Utah for the wedding of her eldest daughter.

When we divided the furnishings from Mother and Dad's house, Christine inherited the big mahogany dining set that had been in our parents dining room for more than thirty-five years—the same set that had earlier served our grandparents' home.

On a joyous Saturday morning, we all gathered around that table for a celebratory pre-wedding family brunch. The happy conversation turned to the table itself, and everyone shared fond memories of the countless beautiful dinner parties and the birthday and holiday meals Mother had served on it.

As I enjoyed these memories, it occurred to me that most of the family were too young to remember the very formal dinners we had on it at Munner and Bompa's house. Suddenly, I became overwhelmed with nausea and ran from the room, hand over my mouth, looking for the nearest bathroom. As soon as I found it and closed the door, a young and frightened child took over.

I didn't throw up but stood in the corner, with my back to the wall, shaking with fear and crying because I was afraid someone was coming for me… coming to take me into the dining room and put me on the table. I remembered what happened when they took me to the table. But then I realized these were different people than were there before.

A lady came in to check on me. I tried to hide from her in the corner with my hands over my eyes and started to cry again.

"I love you, and everyone here loves you," Mary ventured, not sure what to say to this very young, obviously scared version of her sister.

That was different. Maybe these were all new people.

I moved my hands away from my face and turned to look at her. I checked to be sure. "They are gone, and they cannot hurt me. They aren't here anymore."

Realizing I meant our grandparents, Mary confirmed I was right. "Yes. They cannot come back. They are gone for good. And everyone here loves you."

I stared intently right into her eyes and realized this was Mary, the little sister, all grown up into a big lady. I had to ask her a very important question. "Were you on the table?"

She looked really confused, but I didn't know how else to ask, and I really needed to know. I tried again, a little stronger. "Were you ever on the table?"

I could see in her face that she had figured out what I meant. "No. I was never on the table for experiments like you were."

Thank goodness. That was really good news. I suddenly didn't feel so scared anymore. But I needed to know for sure. Looking straight into her eyes, I said, "You were safe."

"Yes, you kept me safe." She figured out what I meant quicker this time and gave me the answer I was hoping for.

"They said you would be safe."

Bompa had said my brothers and sisters would be safe if I did my work on the table well, and he had kept his word.

"Yes," she reassured me, "I was safe and so were all the others."

Satisfied, the little girl in the big body sat on the bathroom floor and said, "I guess you want her back."

She left and Big Bonnie found herself sitting on the bathroom floor with Mary. We hugged for a while, two sisters in our fifties, before heading back to the festivities. I stayed away from the table, but quietly enjoyed my niece's happiness and the rest of the events of the day.

THE NEXT MORNING, my siblings were eager to discuss what they had witnessed. We sisters gathered on Christine's king-sized bed to laugh and hug as we wrapped love and support around each other. They were fascinated with this real-life peek into how a seemingly innocent conversation could trigger a switch. My brothers were curious too, and I was able to offer them some new information and insights. But none of us had the time or desire for deep dives into my new reality at that moment.

Everyone inside me welcomed the confirmation that my sisters and brothers had not been used in Bompa's science experiments. I had kept them safe, like Bompa said I would—and at the same time, I had been the only "special one."

Chapter 15

The Room Behind the Garage

As the experiments became harder, the need to keep them secret grew stronger. At some point, all of Bompa's science work moved out of my grandparents' dining room and into the room behind the garage, where the machines were now kept along with a hard, oblong table. It wasn't nearly as comfortable, and it was smaller. The nurses never came out there—just a couple of the men.

The first time the man in the grey coat visited, he commented with surprise, "She's so young!"

"Yes, young," Bompa responded, "but so smart, and she won't remember any of this in the morning." He also assured the visitor that "there will be no permanent damage" from the experiments. He was so confident about the work we were doing.

I'm the one they call Bompa's Girl, and I liked it better in the dining room. It wasn't as fun out in the other room, behind the garage. There were different kinds of tests, harder ones, and different people and different… Well, it wasn't me. I guess I got a little scared.

We made a new girl on the lawn and then… I stayed back on the lawn as much as I could, most of the time. She doesn't have a name. I can kinda see her, though. We switched right on the lawn. She was taller and bigger and older, so she could do more, you know.

Yeah, it was harder out there. I tried not to go there. See, they didn't do the shocks to the head in the dining room, like they did out there. I can feel it right here, on the sides, by my temples. There were wooden shelves, and it was dark, except for this bright light and all the machines…

I always wondered if Bompa knew it wasn't me. Sometimes, you think big people can't tell the difference, and it's like they couldn't tell she was so much bigger. That's a funny thing, isn't it? He should have been able to tell. I guess we were pretty smart about not making it easy for them to tell. Yeah, only I knew she was so much bigger. Boy, that's funny!

Well… I didn't like it out there. And Bompa wasn't the same when we were out there. He didn't get as excited, and he was much more intense. And the other guy was kind of… I mean, it was just "Do it, because just **do it**" out there. I didn't feel so special out there.

I mean, I was still special, cuz I could only do it if I was special. But everybody was there in the dining room, and it was all so new and exciting. And they treated you so special. But it was just work out there, and it was always locked. And out there they shocked the head. Why would they do that?! I can almost feel it again right now. I wish I knew what that means and why they would do that. We know it's experimenting with the brain, but why?

I think he was making it happen. He made us happen. He made it all. That's what he did. So, he proved it could happen. It's true. We wouldn't exist if he hadn't helped make us! So that's why we're so special. He made it into a body that could do those things—make the pain go away and make new parts. That's a good thing to show that it can happen.

We didn't figure it out by ourself! He did it. I didn't know what I was doing, except for what he told me. See, you're supposed to think and know how smart he was and how good, that he could make all this happen that you now get to figure out. That's pretty big! And it's really exciting that it was possible for that little, little, little girl, because he helped her be special and made me. And I'm special cuz I was first. Yes, I was.

The slowly unfolding story of the room behind Bompa's garage brought with it new symptoms and suicidal urges. In this case, they served as distractions to keep the mind focused on the external world. Outside, I forgot from one day to the next what I had learned in the Green Room or written in the journal.

By both temperament and necessity, I kept up my external work and travel schedule, relying more than I understood on selective amnesia and an incredibly cooperative and well-orchestrated internal community.

Chapter 16
Transitions

The beginning of 2006 can be seen as the end of the four-year, Holy-Shit-Are-You-Kidding-Me-This-Can't-Be-Real-Oh-Yes-It-Is phase of my discovery and recovery. Virtually every aspect of my life—my marriage, my job, my health, my understanding of myself and my family—had changed in the four years since Dr. Hite concluded her search for medical causes and turned me over to the psychologist.

The concepts of "true" and "real" and "normal" had lost their meaning for me. Had any part of my life been authentic or honest? Was I crazy and not to be trusted? Had anything I had ever done been real, or had my whole life been one big fat lie? I despaired of ever again feeling like I knew anything for sure—about myself or, for that matter, anything else. Incest, religious cults, experiments with me as the lab rat... I wanted to shout "Impossible!" But denial had lost its magic.

With a gaping hole where my sense of self used to thrive, there was no going back and no clue what going forward looked like. Would it be full of more betrayal and lies, like my whole life had been? Whenever I lost my focus on external commitments, I spiraled into gloom and a gazillion unanswerable questions.

Even my hated mental health diagnosis had changed. Although neither Julia nor I were inclined to focus on labels, we had progressed to the point where the original conversion disorder diagnosis no longer described my situation. We now knew my system had responded to all the violations and my grandfather's training by creating special places in my mind where the traumatic memories and sensations could be walled off from my consciousness. I found this great mystery baffling. How did it all work? How did the alters, like Bompa's Girl and Priestess, function? Julia assured me a diagnosis of "dissociative disorder not otherwise specified" (DDNOS) captured it more accurately.

The change in diagnosis brought both new understanding and curiosity. My symptoms and I were not unique. Almost everything I went through, however random and strange it seemed, actually had a name, and someone somewhere had researched it and written an article, chapter or book about it.

To keep my process as free as possible of outside influences, Julia asked that I not look up the many things I found curious. But from time to time, I'd sigh in utter confusion. "Does this make any sense at all?"

Knowing my deep intellectual curiosity, Julia would answer with the clinical name of my experience and tell me who had done the research and written the most helpful article. It turned out, for example, my habit of stepping outside myself and seeing my actions as if I were watching a movie or listening to someone else talk were common aspects of dissociation, called "depersonalization." I had lived with them all my adult life—unrecognized and normalized clues, like the suicidal ideations. Sometimes, I felt more like a spectator than a participant in my own life.

So much of this involved really scary new territory, leaving me feeling very alone quite often, especially with Wayne gone. I found it strangely comforting that enough other people had had similar experiences to warrant studying and naming them. But on the other hand, when you have been trained to believe—to know—you are special, and that the things done to you were special, it is a little deflating to realize you're not.

In the end, depravity is just depravity, pedophilia is pedophilia, and there are patterns and similarities in how the human organism responds to sustained trauma and abuse. Welcome to the Trauma Survivors Club.

WITH JULIA'S HELP, my internal community and I had acknowledged that my children shouldn't have to deal with the horrors I was reliving. In an admirable display of self-care, Beth had declared she only needed to know that her mother was getting healthier. She and Will deserved the apparently normal mother they had always known (or as close to it as I could manage).

In response, my internal crew created "Mommy-mode." Only the ANP, as the nurturing mom, could be present when with my kids. This seemed to work well and allowed me to continue relationships with my son and daughter, focused on what was happening in their lives and touching lightly on mine. I answered direct questions when asked about my health and healing, letting them determine how much they wanted to know.

And I had good news to share on the health front. My strength, balance and stamina had fully returned. Even though Beth didn't want to know what I was learning about my past, she did know how to celebrate my healing. She organized a camping and hiking trip to our favorite place, above Onion Valley, on the eastern slope of the Sierra Nevada Mountains.

It's a moderately strenuous hike up to several pristine alpine lakes, our favorite being Flower Lake. Beth is an experienced backpacker, but she set a comfortable pace so we could jointly revel in the glories of nature, the resilience of my body, and the gift of being together.

What a joy to again feed my soul in those magnificent mountains; to smell the heady aroma of the plants that give the valley its name; to hear the stream tumbling and frolicking straight down the mountain, singing over boulders and inviting a weary hiker to sit in its cooling, healing mist. It was the perfect antidote to all the heavy emotions—including a few lingering suicidal thoughts the stream happily washed down the mountain. Thank you, Beth.

Even airports were once again easy to navigate. Now, when I exited a plane and saw the line of wheelchairs waiting for passengers, I felt great compassion for those who needed them and great joy that none waited for me. If new physical symptoms appeared—itchy, draining ears or periodic sharp shoulder or hip pain—Dr. Miller would check them out. But generally, these were messages from the body, connected to the stories in flashbacks that were about to appear.

By the end of 2005, it had become clear Wayne and I could no longer muster the kind of partnership we had committed to in our wedding vows. When we gathered with our children for Christmas, we told them we had decided to divorce. Our separation had not been easy for them. At first, they had reacted with anger and disbelief. Why would a couple our age do such a thing after so many years of a good partnership? Is nothing sacred or secure?

After our eighteen-month separation, they'd become somewhat more resigned to the news. We had made an appointment to have a family portrait taken the day after we told them and insisted on keeping that commitment. The children may have felt strange about it, but Wayne and I wanted one last group picture. We were still family, weren't we?

Throughout this whole period, I had maintained my ability to contribute in demanding jobs, even during a time of intense treatment and other personal changes. But work hadn't been exactly stable, either. Without any warning, I had been laid off at the end of 2002 as part of a major downsizing in my organization. Luckily, I quickly found another position in which I could continue my work to improve conditions for children and families involved with the public child welfare system.

When this new employer closed its doors at the end of 2005, I found myself being laid off again. Once more, I had already secured another position in the field—this time focused on preventing child abuse.

But before starting the new job, I decided to use my severance package to take a self-funded, three-month sabbatical to rest and work on understanding my new life and healing path. These four years of opening up had been emotionally and physically exhausting, and I had only begun to acknowledge the grief, loss and abandonment I felt. Such emotions had always been deeply hidden or denied, so I didn't have much experience dealing with them.

The severance package also offered assistance in finding new employment or professional direction. A colleague suggested a four-day course called "Mastering Life's Energies" offered by a friend of hers, psychologist and master coach Dr. Maria Nemeth, at the Academy for Coaching Excellence. Mastering anything sounded good at this point, so I secured Julia's approval, told Maria about my situation, and relaxed into the class, knowing she had my back in case anything erupted.

Thus, the Universe had conspired again to show how every major challenge brings new opportunities. The uncertainty of being laid off and losing my life partner opened space for new ways of making sense of my world as it evolved, even as everything I once held sure crumbled under my feet.

Required readings for the course included mythologist and historian Joseph Campbell's *The Hero's Journey*, a unifying way of understanding the arc of life and change, and Sogyal Rinpoche's *The Tibetan Book of Living and Dying*, with its grounding in Buddhism. These great gifts offered a deeper exploration of my spirituality and a new construct for understanding my response to life's challenges. We all made vision boards at the end of class, and mine resulted in a complete surprise—the vision of being on a spiritual retreat at Machu Picchu within a year!

The class and Maria's mentorship resonated so powerfully, I signed up for the coach training program. With deepening work over the next two years, I became a life coach, credentialed by the International Coaching Federation. Again, this surprise played its own role in my spiritual, personal and professional development.

In this darkest moment of my life, I drew to myself not what I expected but what I needed, including a new teacher, healer and coach, as well as a new cadre of strong women friends and role models. I was in the right place at the right time—not by accident or coincidence—to begin to accept my new and evolving reality, to hear and listen to the inner voices, and to ask for spiritual guidance with an openness I had never known before.

Strangely, despite all this work, I still had no better understanding of what had prompted me as a twelve-year-old to take a bottle of pills. In fact, a new set of questions arose. Why did I wait so long to do it? I could imagine an adolescent might conclude the only way to stop unbearable abuse was to leave life permanently. But as we now understood things, the abuse surely ended after Bompa died when I was eight and a half. The year before that, Dad had turned his den into a bedroom for my two younger brothers. No memories of his late-night visits had surfaced in any other room, so they must have stopped. By then, Uncle Ted had also lost access to me after moving out of his parents' home and getting married.

So, if I was trying to end the abuse, why did I wait almost four more years to take the pills? I no longer thought of it as a stupid prank. I had learned such behavior is always a message. But what did it mean? It still didn't make sense. I made a timeline of everything I could remember or learn from others about what happened after Bompa died. Nothing I could find explained the timing.

Still, even if the mystery remained unresolved, I had a better grasp of the situation. I understood horrific things had happened to my body as a child, had an embryonic sense of how my mind had responded, and had felt the utter abandonment and emptiness that had almost sapped away my life spirit. I clearly needed healing in all three arenas.

Joseph Campbell's comparisons of human quest mythologies in various religions and wisdom traditions rekindled my long-held interest in cultural anthropology. I saw my sabbatical as a perfect opportunity to focus on healing my mind, body and spirit in a more integrated way, informed by indigenous wisdom.

Although I couldn't have articulated it at the time, I had been so sick and so scared for so many years that I welcomed any opportunity to rebuild a sense of trust or meaning. This longing for a larger context within which to understand my struggles and losses opened me to a new phase of healing and growing.

Part 4
Discovering Courage

Chapter 17
Art Therapy

My stated purpose in taking three months of freedom from my work schedule was to use the much-needed time for intensive physical, emotional and spiritual healing. As it approached, I, the ANP who lived in the outside world and forgot the same lessons over and over again, created a schedule worthy of a frenetic tour guide. That's what I always did with free time, especially if introspection seemed imminent.

I planned a two-week Spanish immersion course in Mexico, a swim with the dolphins in Hawaii, some local seminars, and the trip to Machu Picchu. On top of all that, there was the gut-wrenching work required for the divorce that was proceeding through a mediator on its sad, but outwardly amicable, path to closure.

In the Green Room, my internal voices pushed for more quiet time and the space to allow a new approach to processing old pain. Through a combination of forceful verbal requests and uncomfortable physical symptoms, they advocated for a new way of thinking. "Life is not only about accomplishing your to-do list."

Julia helped me understand they wanted me to slow down and take time to allow thoughts to form from the inside out, insisting this was not lazy or unproductive but quite the opposite—a path toward greater ease and productivity of a new kind. We all recognized their requests meant a major shift in the lifelong patterns they had helped create. But I listened and reluctantly cut back on my plans, holding fast only to the spiritual retreat, which I knew had originally come unbidden from inside.

As soon as the holidays and my employment concluded at the end of 2005 and I was alone in my safe and comfy condo, we—the internal voices, Big Bonnie and Julia—set up the new schedule for our free time. I papered one wall of my guest room with huge Post-it easel paper and bought a bucket of colored markers. Julia instructed me to set aside two hours each day to sit quietly on the floor in front of the papered wall and allow myself to relinquish control to whatever part of my consciousness was ready to express itself.

As I breathed deeply, closed my eyes, and relaxed my external controls, I felt my whole being shift. Big Bonnie's consciousness—my agency, cognition and muscle control—moved to somewhere behind the eyes, with very little (or sometimes no) ability to see, affect or remember what happened next.

Later, I would find myself back in my body, looking at childlike, deeply evocative pictures drawn on the paper in front of me. We spent time in the Green Room at least every other day, and the pictures allowed lots of new details and feelings to be expressed without the usually painful body memories or much discussion.

THE FIRST TIME I TRIED THIS EXERCISE, I suddenly felt very young and afraid and wanted to draw something I couldn't express in words. I felt overcome with sadness and started crying instead of drawing.

The next day, a drawing of a girl appeared whose only facial feature was a big, sad mouth. She was in a room with one green wall and a snake skin on another (like the den in the house we grew up in). There was a big red X where her vagina would be, and her sadness almost made her want to get into the bathtub to cut and bleed and die. This little part had no words and no place where she felt safe. Her sense of betrayal and emptiness was so strong, she saw no reason to go on living. When we took the picture to the Green Room, we met Daddy's Girl. Over time, she would find her words and share the reasons for her sadness.

Another day, there was a drawing of a smiling, peaceful lady in a purple dress, with her purple arms forming a protective circle around several small, faceless girls. In the Green Room, this angel came forward to speak to the Lady Doctor. She had a serene countenance, and when asked about the picture, she gave the year as 1953. (I would have been six.)

"That was the year it was hardest to hold it all together." Defiant and proud, she told the Lady Doctor, "But we didn't break apart."

For a while, we called this lady "Angel," but she soon asked to be called "Purple Lady," in keeping with the way she was drawn by some of the little ones she had protected.

Another day in the Green Room, a ball of red-hot, churning fear overtook my solar plexus, making it almost impossible to breathe. I saw a swirling, smoky, dark-grey body appear in midair, very angry with me, with a big head of flying hair and a knife in his hand slashing downward.

Suddenly, I knew who he was. He didn't speak, but I could hear a big voice say, "The Wrath of God shall smite thee." It was me saying this in his voice, and I knew the Wrath of God had come to smite me because I was telling things I shouldn't.

I was so scared I could barely move. But someone else inside realized that this smoky, dark, swirly body wasn't real, that he was just floating in the air. So, she came out into the body, stuck out her tongue, and blew a raspberry at him.

He didn't do anything.

Emboldened, she blew again, and the wind she made moved the smoke, making him disappear. What power! She was more real than he was, but we had all been so afraid of him. Amazing!

At home, we drew pictures of the Wrath of God and crossed him out with a big red X to show he could never hurt us again. We took the drawings to the Green Room and left them there, so we would have no pictures of him in our home.

THE EXPERIENCE WITH THE WRATH OF GOD allowed me to see what I had internalized about religion as a child. I recognized the slashing motion of his arm with the knife from that day at Mother's house, but I didn't know why he would be mad at her. On the other hand, it wasn't hard to figure out that my grandparents' wrathful God of fire and brimstone, fear and retribution, was not a God of healing for me or for the internal alters and parts who remembered those early teachings.

Most of my adult life, I had stayed away from organized religion, though I had explored various metaphysical and spiritual teachings. Wayne and I had eventually settled into a warm and inviting New Thought church, where our children received their early lessons. But even there, I kept it all at arm's length.

Now that I sought a deeper connection with forces larger than this life, however, my healing drew me away from the Christian traditions I had been raised with. In this context, the surprising goal I put on that vision board made perfect sense. Let me seek my own path, with Machu Picchu as an icon of the nature-based traditions of ancient wisdom and sacred places with great healing energy. My spirit had been assaulted and stripped bare as surely as my body had been, both by the childhood trauma and by the crumbling of the adult life I had known. I needed spiritual renewal and healing as much as I needed therapy.

Finalizing the divorce after thirty-five years together required a great deal of time, energy and tears. Other than the trip to Machu Picchu, it was the only major activity I undertook during those three months of my sabbatical—closing out one era and opening a new one. Without a conscious roadmap, doors opened to new healing experiences and a deepening spiritual connection to myself, the universal Great Spirit, and Pachamama (Mother Earth).

I had loved to travel ever since Munner and I sat on her couch reading and rereading a book called *People of Many Lands*. Travel and study had helped me develop a deep respect for indigenous cultures and spiritual traditions, as well as a fascination with natural rock formations and energetic centers. These sacred explorations could now enrich the therapeutic relationship with our ever-more-trusted Lady Doctor.

Thank heaven for Julia, who viewed the benefits of my quest for a healing spiritual framework as being more important than the therapeutic protocols that urged against travel while I was still actively recovering memories. "It was clear to me you were on a mission to find a new spiritual home and a sense of meaning," she told me much later.

Luckily, even with all the upheaval, I had set aside some "mad money," as my mother used to call the secret stash she urged her daughters to always keep. I had sold a beautiful landscape painting after enjoying it for many years, both at my parents' home and in my own. It originally belonged to Bompa, who had known the artist, according to family lore. But as I moved and downsized, everything that reminded me of Bompa felt dirty, fearful and filled with an energy I did not want in my new living space. The painting brought a surprising price at a local auction house, and I set the money aside for special travel and other healing experiences that neither my budget nor insurance would cover. It felt completely appropriate—if not downright vengeful—to have Bompa provide the means for this part of my healing journey.

I still had lots of disconcerting and unanswered questions about my grandfather. Who was he, really? What connection might there be between his science experiments and his religious ceremonies?

Someone inside had drawn on our papered wall details of the ornate cross he used in the ritual initiation of Priestess. My research had produced pictures of the Knights Templar and the Maltese cross, whose similarity to the cross I had drawn made my insides crawl. But what did that mean? Bompa had been a Mason and some believe the Masons were connected to the Knights Templar. Had he simply been a crazy, old eccentric, full of hubris? Or should I work to understand his place in the historical context of movements trying to grapple with good and evil, religion and human potential?

I wanted to run from anything that connected him to my spiritual journey, but did they intertwine? Yes, obviously. What he did to me was wrong, but understanding his whys was more elusive. Perhaps it was all part of something much bigger than his ego, or maybe not.

However, the real question was: Does any of this really matter? After all, it's just an intellectual question—a distraction—with no real meaning for my life and healing. Isn't it?

Realizing that I would probably never know the answers to these questions with any clarity, I decided to keep my focus on my life and not his.

Chapter 18
With Love, Without Fear

I leapt into my version of Joseph Campbell's "call to adventure," crossing into the unknown by heading to Machu Picchu. Never before had I traveled with a tour group. In fact, I chose a group I knew very little about other than their perfect name: "Body Mind Spirit Journeys." I had found their information (along with a $50 off coupon!) the one time in months when I had gone to my neighborhood New Thought church. I had prayed for guidance on my healing journey during the service, then browsed the literature table. Prayer trumped research. Thank you, Universe.

With no idea how my new internal realities might affect my travel, I simply trusted the forces that had drawn me to the trip. As I left, most of the difficult work we had just done to uncover and face hidden fears was no longer in my conscious memory. That doesn't mean it was forgotten, just that I, on the outside, didn't remember it.

During most of my life, I had needed to be at the heart of the planning for any activity, but now I allowed myself to accept without question the itinerary laid out before me. I even risked letting the tour company pick a roommate for me. As a result, I could focus on everything around and inside of me on all three levels: mind, body and spirit. And as promised, each day held a banquet for all three.

I could die on this trip. That possibility felt very real and immediate. As I prepared, I tried to calm myself (and my internal family) with reassurances about the safety of travel in an organized group. But then I realized what Campbell's hero's journey made clear: in a symbolic way, it was true—some things might die. This trip celebrated both the culmination and the beginning of major changes in my life, especially my internal life. Many old ways of thinking and being were ready to die, and I would have to let go of attachments that no longer worked for me—attachments to people, fears and certainties. This quest held the promise that each time I let go of something old, I would create space to embrace something new.

My first encounter with this newness was as mundane as it was poignant. As I sat in the bright, busy Lima airport, filling out immigration forms, I was confronted with a question. Which box do I check? Married? Single? Other? Married for thirty-four years, and with the divorce not quite final, the shift felt disorienting and profound.

My identity in the world had changed, even though I had tried to minimize the jolt by keeping my married name. At the same time, all the changes also opened up the freedom to travel where, when and how I wanted to, with no external person dependent on me or my decisions—although I did have a growing awareness of interdependence among my internal people. Strangely at peace, I reminded myself that the trip's purpose was as much to feel these new emotions as to see the sights.

In fifteen days of amazing experiences, a few stand out as big boosts to my healing journey. The group was small—fifteen of us on a cozy, little bus. My roommate, Anita, and I bonded quickly and paired up for most activities. She was close to my age, and as a recent widow, was grappling with new realities in her life too. During our travels in Cusco and the Urubamba River Valley, our spiritual guide and cultural teacher was Jorge Luis Delgado. He described himself as a *chacaruna*—a bridge person—rather than a shaman, the term the

Northerners wanted to use. Aymara by birth, he had studied with both Aymara elders and the Q'ero, descendants of the Incas. He led us in rituals in the ancient places where his people have held ceremonies for centuries.

THE FIRST NIGHT IN THE URUBAMBA RIVER VALLEY, also known as the Sacred Valley of the Incas, we stayed in an old Spanish monastery that had found new life as a retreat center. Despite its colonizer origins, a quiet, reverent energy filled the rooms and conjured generations of earlier seekers. Our little group gathered in a stone circle behind the monastery, in a field of lush green grasses and fresh breezes, amid Andean peaks bathed in the pinks and purples of a gathering twilight.

Two Q'ero elders welcomed us with a cleansing ceremony after Jorge Luis began his teachings by allowing us to make a traditional offering to Pachamama and to set our intentions for the week. We placed colorful bits of food, sweets, flower petals, leaves and small wooden icons in a square of brightly colored paper, along with our prayers and desires. We folded them together in bundles and offered them to the fire so Pachamama could use their energy to help us accomplish our goals.

Using condor feathers to focus smoke from a sage smudge stick, the elders helped us individually cleanse our minds, bodies and spirits of what they called "heavy energy," lightening our load for the journey ahead. As they reached me, I felt myself step quietly outside my body and watch from just beyond the circle, enjoying the smell of the sage and the ceremonial murmurs of the elders. Inside, some other part of me made sure we responded appropriately and, as always, stayed alert for any sign of danger. Outside, I took in the whole beautiful, peaceful scene and came away with a mental picture of myself standing in a circle of connection with ancient elders, Pachamama and the mountain spirits (locally referred to as the *apus*).

Jorge Luis introduced us to the words with which he would close out every ceremony. "With love, without fear." He spoke this with his right hand over his heart and his left hand at his solar plexus. This salutation is used a bit like other religious traditions use *amen* at the end of a prayer, except that *amen* feels to me as if you are closing something and moving on, while the Inca sentiment feels more like you are taking an intention with you.

When Jorge Luis described the Inca symbols for the upper world (the condor), this physical world (the puma), and the lower world (the serpent), he did so without hierarchy or judgment. Dualities, like good and evil, are not part of this cosmology. Everything has its role and place—no Wrath of God here. In fact, even the cleansing ceremonies were not about getting rid of anything negative, but rather about transforming the heavy energy I no longer needed into energy Pachamama could use in her regenerative ways.

THE NEXT MORNING, our little group departed on the first real test of my body's strength and capacity: our excursion to Ollantaytambo, a small town with ancient temples built high on the cliffs above it. Just five years earlier, I had used a wheelchair most of the time when Wayne, Beth and I visited Will and his wife in Venezuela. Now, I climbed the terraces all the way to the temple at the top with a great sense of healing and accomplishment.

Though I was fascinated by the vistas, temples, stone construction, history and ceremonies, what I remember most is my sense of joy, gratitude and not a little surprise that I was physically able to climb, hike and explore this magnificent sacred place.

In Ollantaytambo, as in all Inca construction, Pachamama was consulted as humans considered where and what to build, and the natural rocks and features of the mountain were incorporated into many of the rooms and temples. Acting in concert with nature was and is a central tenet of indigenous life in the Peruvian Andes.

Coming from earthquake country, I knew enough to be impressed with the longevity of these stone structures, built without mortar but in harmony with the earth's formations. The nature-based philosophy and partnership undergirding all of Jorge Luis's teachings felt warm, welcoming and safe. My chest began to relax and open up, allowing the warmth inside.

THE NEXT DAY, our explorations took us up the river to Pisac. A higher altitude and steeper trail made this hike much more difficult. Our reward included absolutely stunning views of the valley, the powerful Urubamba River, the surrounding Andean peaks, and the abundant farmland—Pachamama in all her glory.

Ancient man-made terraces with rock walls dotted the hills, creating agricultural spaces in areas so steep I wondered how even the llamas could reach them. In contrast, the patchwork of farm fields, separated by rock walls and rows of trees, appeared like a quilt on the larger, flatter stretches of green. Wide-open expanses of Pachamama's natural, uncultivated meadows sloped down from the mountains connecting the terraces and fields. The narrow trail up to the Temple of the Sun allowed pilgrims a loving connection to all of Mother Earth's bountiful, soft, hospitable green.

This welcoming, peaceful scene filled me with thoughts of how glorious it would feel to leave the trail and float down, so Pachamama could hug me in one of her soft meadows. So much easier and more natural than this steep climb.

Why not? Why not just allow myself to drift down, to be with Mother Earth and let her green fields wrap themselves around me in perfect comfort and love? I didn't hear this as seductive or suicidal, more as a longing for a mother's warm, safe hugs. And the thoughts came very close to dictating the body's actions. Several times I thought, *Yes, here. It would be so easy to slip accidentally and fall off the narrow trail, or maybe even to jump.*

Vanity and other internal forces asserted themselves. Suddenly, I became acutely aware that, on the surface, I was just an out-of-shape, almost sixty-year-old woman having trouble with a steep, high-altitude hike. I needed to stay on the trail. I wouldn't let anyone think I couldn't make it all the way up!

At the top, I sat alone on some ancient stones to collect myself before resuming my exploration. I felt pretty shaken. How close had I come to jumping off the cliff? Sitting away from the others, I took a few deep breaths and did a quick pickup to tuck the suicidal thoughts away until we could address them.

Anita found me sitting by myself and checked whether I was okay. I told her what had happened—or *almost* happened. Before joining the others, we sat together for a few minutes, and she gave me a long, caring, hug. It occurred to me that I had been married to Wayne for thirty-four years and hadn't, until recently, shared my suicidal thoughts with him. I had known Anita for less than a week and already found comfort and humor in sharing with her.

In the ancient Sun Temple buildings, on this gorgeous promontory, Jorge Luis led us in ceremonies focused on opening our hearts to the wisdom around us. I know his lessons went deeper, but what I remember is that I came away feeling much more grounded and quite sure Pachamama did not want me to jump off a cliff to show my appreciation for her.

When it came time to leave, Jorge Luis announced he had asked a few local gentlemen to offer assistance with the hike down. I gladly accepted, hoping I wasn't the only one who'd had trouble on the way up. With dusk settling in over the sacred valley, I accompanied a small, sure-footed Q'ero man down the mountain. He spoke very little Spanish (his native Quechua was the other official language in the area around Cusco), but he communicated such nonjudgmental kindness that I trusted him instinctively and completely.

When space allowed, he walked on the outside of the trail, and when it allowed only one person at a time, he ensured I felt safe by

Discovering Courage   **With Love, Without Fear**

holding my hand. At the bottom of the hill, I found it difficult to express my gratitude in any tangible way. He would not take a monetary tip and instead offered to sell me mementos he and his family had made to sell to tourists. I bought two of his mobiles or wind chimes for gifts, but in the end, I kept them for myself and still think of his gentle, life-giving kindness every time I see them or hear them ring in my home.

Hindsight allows us to connect the dots. It helped me realize what occurred on the mountain at Pisac was simply a new and creative twist on something that had happened many times before, when situations arose that allowed for deep introspection. An internal alarm had gone off, signifying that secrets might not be safe. Suicidal ideas and plans answered the alarm, as they had been trained to do.

At Pisac, I did not yet understand any of this. I had no idea some of my internal parts had been tasked with protecting our secrets—with suicide, if necessary. At the time, I treated it as a distraction to be overcome. The forces within me entrusted with keeping us alive had jumped into action and found a way, as they always did.

In this case, my sense of pride and competitiveness kept us on the trail. My protective alters would maintain a higher level of internal control for the rest of the trip, given the impact of these ceremonies. Not conscious of any of this, I was free to open up and soak everything in.

Chapter 19
The Flight of the Condors

Jorge Luis teased our little group with a promise that on our first afternoon at Machu Picchu, we would be able to fly with the condors. No one among us knew quite what he meant, but we were preparing for something special.

The city of Machu Picchu sits in a saddle between two mountains. The older and larger Machu Picchu is said to exude a masculine energy, while the younger Huayna Picchu radiates a more feminine energy to those who are sensitive to the earth's energetic forces. Buildings cover the open area of the saddle right to the edge of the cliffs, which in some places fall straight down to the Urubamba River as she winds her magic far below.

Jorge Luis led us to an area on the lower east side of the city, where few tourists venture. A little cave-like temple sat back a bit from the edge of a rocky cliff. A couple of yards in front of the cave, a narrow rock thrust its nose out over the edge. This is where he said we could fly with the condors.

I watched fearfully as my classmates, one by one, laid back on this narrow rock jutting out into thin air. Jorge Luis gently asked them to relax, open their eyes, and spread their arms as if they were flying in the open sky. Each one appeared to have a profound experience, and although I was scared (actually, petrified), I didn't want to miss an opportunity that seemed so meaningful to the others.[1]

When my turn came, I went forward but asked Jorge Luis to keep his hand on my knee to help me feel grounded and safe. He did, and as I wrote in my journal that evening, his hand "felt like an ethereal guide letting me know all is well—even on the precipice." Confident that I would not fall as long as his hand touched me, I lay back with my eyes shut tight. As I gave myself to the experience, I opened wide first my arms and then my eyes. As I did, two condors flew across the bright blue sky. That was all I could see—just the vast sky and the two high-flying birds.

Maybe I can let go too, I thought. They seem so free. Can I be that free? I lay there long enough to begin disconnecting from the fear inside. As I stood and stepped away, John, a classmate with whom I had a good connection, greeted me with a hug.

"Maybe I don't have to be afraid anymore," I thought out loud, as tears welled up and my body began to shake. I walked a few steps, then sat cross-legged in the grass, closed my eyes, and quietly allowed the tears to flow.

A voice inside affirmed an amazing truth I didn't know I had been seeking. "Bompa can't hurt me anymore. And he can't make me hurt myself. He is dead."

When the tears and shaking ebbed, I opened my eyes to the *apus*, the sacred peaks of the Andes that form a protective cordon around

---

1   When I went back later and looked at it from a different angle, I could see that the rock was well grounded and secure, and that what Jorge Luis had asked us to do was not very dangerous. However, he didn't show us that angle.

Machu Picchu. An internal voice said, "I have nothing to fear. These mountains love me."

THE CLOSEST MOUNTAIN to the east of Machu Picchu is about the same height—not one of the big, craggy peaks, but gentle, curved and covered in rainforest green. Her name is Putucusi, which I was told means "forever flowering" or "happy mountain." Her curvature forms a forested ridge that comes around in front of her like a mother's arm. I felt myself cuddle into her protective embrace. I didn't need to be afraid anymore.

The next morning, the group returned to the area for a sunrise ceremony in which I reaffirmed I could let go of fear—specifically, my internal fear of Bompa, of which I hadn't been consciously aware. During the ritual, we opened our arms wide and reached up with our right hands to feel the masculine energy of Machu Picchu, while our left hands reached for the feminine Huayna Picchu. Our bodies faced east to greet Father Inti (the sun) as he appeared over the peaks. Jorge Luis asked us to allow the sun's light and warmth to permeate every cell.

I let my mind go and permitted my body simply to feel, with no expectations. Colors took over behind my eyelids. In a bright yellow glow, a puma face appeared and winked at me.

I smiled back at it, understanding. "All is well in the world. I don't have to be afraid anymore. Pachamama, Huayna Picchu, Putucusi and Machu Picchu are protecting, loving and blessing me. I am one with them and at the same time in awe of them. With love, without fear."

This simple sunrise ceremony brought such comfort, I recreate it often wherever the early morning sun and I commune. In my home, a picture of Putucusi reminds me each day that I am safe, loved and protected.

Until the trip to Peru, I had never considered myself a fearful person. But the fear that had surfaced, especially the fear of Bompa, was internal, not part of my outer consciousness. And now, my actions in the outside world could support its release.

My favorite physical memento of this trip is a simple textile woven some decades before and used for ceremonies and to carry children. It is purple, about a meter square, and is made with a wonderful yarn whose color transforms with differing light or moods. I hung it on the wall opposite my bed so I could connect to it first thing every morning. With its rich, shifting hues, it immediately became a symbol that helped me center myself each day. With love, without fear.

As the plane lifted up out of Cusco and I looked down at the glorious landscape with which I had been so intimate, an unfamiliar emotion arose. I felt almost giddy with happiness, but without any specific reason. Jorge Luis's words came back as I realized I must be feeling something he had mentioned as a sign of spiritual growth, unreasonable joy—perhaps my most precious souvenir.

Back home, I knew I had tapped into something deeply significant, something I wanted to continue to explore. It hadn't been some conference I attended to learn intellectually, but a soul-warming, life-changing glimpse into a whole new way of experiencing myself as someone connected to the larger universe, to nature, and to my inner family. As a result, I didn't feel as alone or fearful when I tended to my life's new beginnings and endings: 1) starting a job working to help prevent child abuse in my state, 2) finalizing the divorce and dividing up the spoils of our long marriage partnership, 3) figuring out how to express my new sense of openness and the idea that it would be all right if more people knew what had happened to me, and 4) seeing some alters gain clarity around their own voices, personalities and stories.

My new life had begun. The energetic and physical connection to Mother Nature and to the magnanimous spirituality of the universe had lit up a place inside me connected to the "good person" I had always tried to be. The idea of spiritual retreats in ancient sacred places resonated so powerfully that I made a bucket list of the sites that most called on me to study and heal in their natural energy. My mad money would certainly be put to good use.

Chapter 20

The Adverse Childhood Experiences Study

Within a month of starting my new job in the spring of 2006, it and the Universe brought me into contact with Dr. Vincent Felitti, a physician at Kaiser Permanente in San Diego, so I could learn about his study of adverse childhood experiences, their prevalence and their relationship to adult health. Over lunch, he impressed me as both caring and passionate about the importance of his findings—a passion I quickly came to share.

In 1995, he and a colleague from the Centers for Disease Control and Prevention (CDC) started a comprehensive study comparing more than 17,000 Kaiser members' childhood experiences to their health records as adults. They coined the term "adverse childhood experiences" (ACEs) to describe various chronic, unpredictable, stress-inducing events that some children face. These include growing up with a depressed or alcoholic parent, losing a parent to divorce or other causes, or enduring emotional neglect or sexual or physical abuse. Each participant was given a score based on the number of different types of ACEs they encountered in their childhood. These scores were then matched against their health records.

The results amazed even the researchers. Nearly two-thirds of the participants had encountered one or more ACEs. Furthermore, an individual's ACE score correlated with their likelihood of health issues in adulthood with surprising accuracy. The higher your score, the more likely you were to suffer heart disease, diabetes, suicide attempts, substance abuse, chronic lung disease, cancer, liver disease and many other conditions.[2] I quickly incorporated these findings into my child abuse prevention work and began talking about the study in speeches and training sessions at every opportunity.

Consistent with my new openness—but quite uncharacteristically—I told Dr. Felitti in that first meeting that I was living with the adult health consequences of long-hidden childhood trauma. He didn't seem surprised. After all, his study had revealed not only that ACEs are common but that more than twelve percent of adults have four or more ACEs in their background. With straightforward kindness, he asked if I would be willing to write about my story for a medical journal he worked with.

My heart and stomach both did flips of dread at the idea of writing publicly about what happened to me when I still didn't fully understand it myself. "I don't think I'm ready," was my immediate response. He gently probed and found I had attempted suicide, but that this had never been discussed in my family. Perhaps I could write a story entitled something like "We Will Never Talk About This Again"? That sounded a little safer, and I agreed to consider it. I didn't want him to think me a coward.

Internally, everyone busied themselves assessing this new doctor. I heard the discussion but didn't know specifically who the voices were.

"He has grey hair and sparkly eyes when he laughs—but his face is kind of square, not round like Bompa's. No, he does not look like Bompa."

"But his eyes saw deep inside." Several parts knew he had seen them looking at him. "That's the first time someone outside has seen

2   For more information, visit the ACE study page on the CDC website, emeraldlakebooks.com/acestudy. This site also includes many more research papers outlining the results of the study.

inside like that. Maybe he knows how to do it. Could he get inside and trigger something bad?"

"No, he wants us to *tell* the story, not keep secrets. He said it is a powerful story and could help more people understand."

"He wants us to write our story for his journal—about how the body never forgets, even when nobody wants to talk about it ever again. But he wants us to talk about it."

Consensus accomplished. The inside people decided to trust him. But it still felt dangerous to Big Bonnie, who had to live in an outside world that might not be so welcoming.

The ACE study provided some safety as I contemplated writing. I was not alone. I could present my situation in the context of this much larger phenomenon. Julia encouraged it as a new element of the healing process. I was learning to speak my truth out loud—at least on paper.

With Mother still alive, I wanted to be careful not to mention anything that might hurt her (specifically, anything about my father's late-night visits). But I didn't have to worry about confronting any of the others with my newfound truths because they were all dead.

I focused on the suicide attempt and the way physical symptoms had appeared in my fifties. With support from inside, I worked hard on the writing. Before I submitted it, though, I also needed some external validation. I asked Mother to read the draft, both to ensure the accuracy of my renditions of our conversations and to respect her privacy if she wanted to invoke it.

"I wouldn't change a thing. This may help somebody." Her response surprised me. This openness to airing dirty family laundry was new to both of us. With her blessing, I shared the article with the rest of the family. Perhaps as a testament to how carefully I framed my experience—focusing on the impact but not giving any detail about *what* had happened to me—or perhaps because Mother agreed that everything I wrote was true, none of my siblings reacted negatively.

Peter really wanted to understand how it was possible to forget things and then remember them again years later, so we had several conversations about how trauma can affect memory.

Mary continued her gentle support, but I understood her discomfort about me going public. We lived near each other, and our professional networks overlapped. Given the stigma of a mental health condition, my self-disclosure had more potential impact on her life than anyone else's.

My youngest brother, Jeff, didn't want to know the details and may not even have read the article. He was concerned that I not sully Dad's name and reputation, so Mother's approval was all he needed at that point.

Fred, the middle boy and family namesake, had a master's degree in bioengineering. He had been very interested earlier, when I told him about Bompa's science, even though he hadn't been able to discern what Bompa was doing or trying to learn. Later, he maintained a skeptical interest in what his sister said she was remembering.

Everyone agreed I had somehow recovered from what had appeared to be a very serious illness and celebrated that without needing to fully understand how it had happened.

Both my children lived far away in different states, so they could choose whether and how to share this article in a medical journal most of their friends would never see. They responded in their characteristic ways; Will more esoteric, Beth more pragmatic. But their bottom line was pride in what they saw as their mother's courage and desire to help others, along with gratitude that I was healing so well.

My friend and colleague, Mari, read early drafts and, as always, asked insightful questions, pushing me toward greater depth and clarity. She called me "gutsy" for writing it, and we celebrated with dinner and a bottle of champagne.

As it turned out, *The Permanente Journal* was in the midst of making major changes, and my article, "We Will Never Talk

About This Again: Recovery From a Complex Illness,"[3] wasn't actually published until early 2009, in the first issue of the Permanente Press's online journal, *leaflet*. The day it finally went live, I felt like I was living one of those anxiety dreams where you're running the streets naked.

The delay, while frustrating, gave me time to become a little more open on my own and to share the article with friends and colleagues who wanted a better idea of what I was dealing with. As sanitized as it was, it still made the point that childhood trauma can affect adult health in unrecognizable ways. If we want to protect our children, we must listen and respond to them. On the other hand, as adults, we also must pay attention to our bodies when they present us with symptoms, especially mysterious ones.

The story resonated with people. Many whom I shared it with told me they wanted to give it to someone they knew who was facing intractable symptoms no one could figure out. The feedback I received from my friends, as well as from strangers who read it online, reminded me I was not unique. I had a story that could help others. At the time, I wasn't aware of how much more I had to learn, but the idea of using my story to help others began to take shape.

After obsessing over the article, narrative writing became an important tool in my discovery and healing process. Each alter had a special colored pen for the journal and an individual document on the computer to use as they pieced together the fragments of their experiences, fitting them like a jigsaw puzzle into something whole.

Writing also allowed for clearer communication among us, especially with Priestess and Purple Lady, who had coalesced into recognizable and concrete people with clear voices, roles and personalities. Some internal parts still used seemingly random physical signs, like an itchy ear, weak legs, or cold symptoms, to get attention. But most now expressed their opinions, needs and experiences through con-

---

3   Armstrong, Bonnie. "We Will Never Talk About This Again," *leaflet*. Accessed February 9, 2024. emeraldlakebooks.com/leaflet.

versations in the Green Room or writing in the journal. When we read the draft article in the Green Room, six different internal voices came forward to comment, offering Big Bonnie a fascinating glimpse into their diverse—sometimes surprising—perspectives on a topic about which they generally agreed.

Now that I had gone public, even in this limited way, I found I could more directly answer questions about what had been wrong with me and how I had gotten so much better. Introducing the ACE study provided the perfect intellectual cover. I learned to share a few personal details, slowly and gently, and became adept at sensing signs of acceptance, curiosity and kindness, or their opposites, fear, skepticism and judgment. I moderated accordingly how much of my story I told to anyone.

Between the trip to Peru, the article and the journaling, things inside were really being stirred up, and whole new pockets of feelings and memories became accessible. A voice who woke up for the first time during this period gave some new insight into the still mysterious suicide attempt.

I got the sense we needed to die because of the fear we were going to tell someone something that shouldn't be known. The Wrath of God is connected to why I needed to die that night. But it has more to do with Uncle Dick than Munner.

What did Uncle Dick have to do with it? Another puzzle piece that didn't yet fit…

Chapter 21
A Big Exhale

One of my favorite all-time movie moments is the scene in *Waiting to Exhale* when Angela Bassett makes a bonfire of her unfaithful husband's BMW and thousand-dollar suits. As I redecorated after my divorce, this scene inspired my surreal life.

An antique Native American rug that had been rolled up in the back of a closet since we left our big house fit perfectly on the vacant wall over my sofa. But it had an odd odor and the swastika shapes in the design seemed particularly prominent and negative, even though I knew they predated the German version and had nothing to do with it. I tried to draw on the energy of the people who had made the rug rather than those who had used it, knowing it had long ago been in my grandparents' home. I smudged it with white sage to cleanse its smell and used a new shamanic totem to bless it. Even after that, it still felt uncomfortable, but I didn't have something else to put there and left it up anyway.

The next time we were in the Green Room, we asked inside if there was anything we should talk about and an image of the rug on the wall came forward. An inside voice spoke up.

"I don't like that rug," she said. "It shouldn't be here." Julia helped uncover the memories connected to it that had been locked away in the mind and body for over fifty years.

First came flashes of pictures. I could see I was on the sun porch off Uncle Ted's bedroom, upstairs in my grandparents' house. He was the only other person there. Then came the physical sensations. Uncle Ted pushing something into my body—but not my vagina. Was it a stick, like a broom handle, or was it part of him? I wasn't sure.

The girl, whom we called "Uncle Ted's Girl," reminded us she had once shown this scene in a dream. Pictures appeared in the mind, now very uncomfortable to sit through—awful, pain-filled crying, and Uncle Ted's loud, maniacal laughter, complete with snorting.

Julia asked if Uncle Ted's Girl could tell the story in words rather than sensations. She tried to let the feelings fall away but said she didn't have words for them.

What happened next?

"He laughed, and I fell onto the rug. He was done, and he left me there—on that rug, behind the couch. Yes, he raped me, but this time in the poop place. Not like before. I know you call it *rape*. It's not my word. But that rug should go away. It should not be in our new house." The scene from the Angela Bassett movie came to mind, and Uncle Ted's Girl fantasized about burning the rug in a bonfire.

When I got home that evening, I moved almost robotically, like my actions were already planned. I guess they were. With calm determination, I took the rug off the wall, got down the biggest pot I owned, filled the teakettle and a pan with water, gathered matches and charcoal lighter fluid, and took everything out onto the patio. Guided from somewhere inside, with very little emotion, I stuffed the rug into the pot, placed it in an open space with no trees directly above, then doused and lit it. I sat with a glass of bourbon and watched, smiling with the satisfaction of retaliation.

Big Bonnie apologized to the people who had made the rug at least a hundred years before and explained that bad energy had ruined its beauty. I knew it was only a symbol, but it was as close as I could get to burning away the memories. More importantly, this time, Big Bonnie had listened to what Uncle Ted's Girl needed to feel safe and heard.

JUST A WEEK LATER, this same uncle came up out of nowhere in a conversation with Mother. Without explanation, she asked point blank, "Did your Uncle Ted molest you?"

"Yes." I figured I needed to be equally direct.

"I thought maybe he had," she replied, and that was the end of the conversation.

Several years later, a few months before she died, I got an inkling of why she had asked this question. I was at lunch with Mother and my siblings Peter and Mary, and she told us about how awful Uncle Ted had been—always trying to kiss and touch her until she finally told him he was not welcome in her home. She had protected herself from him, but had done nothing to protect her daughter. I couldn't challenge her about it at the time, but Big Bonnie and several insiders were left wondering why, if she knew what he was like, she didn't make more of an effort to protect us from him.

EVEN WITH ALL THE LOSS AND CHANGE, my new life began to feel comfortable. Surely, the worst was behind me now. I committed to move forward, making the best of what I could learn about healing from a dissociative disorder.

Andean Awakening, a book by my Peruvian teacher, Jorge Luis Delgado, prompted a deeper dive into indigenous healing and wisdom. My new spiritual understanding connected to my coach training, my internal work, and the ACE research I devoured as scholars published new papers.

I meditated every day and settled into an exercise regimen that included a lot of laughter while a girlfriend and I walked the three miles around the Rose Bowl stadium most mornings. And, of course, there was my weekly therapy in the Green Room with Julia. Maybe the secrets had all been told, and I could focus less on discovery and more on healing and living.

MY SIBLINGS AND CHILDREN celebrated me with a delightful sixtieth birthday party in November 2006. We invited only people close enough to know at least some of what I was grappling with, and a wonderful crowd of dear friends showed up. No secrets, no pretenses.

About a dozen women, including my mother, sister, daughter and niece, began the evening with a special crone ceremony to start me off on the third phase of my maiden–mother–crone life cycle.[4] My mother and those friends who were already members welcomed me into the Over Sixty Club by presenting me with a string of purple pop-beads. Beth acted as emcee and Will performed a rap he had written to "My Mom, the Crone." I felt loved, supported, seen, heard, growing, grounded and safe—the best birthday party ever!

BUT THE MUCH-NEEDED PAUSE for celebration and consolidation allowed only a momentary opportunity to regain strength before the next jolt of flashbacks a week later, triggered by a gruesome scene in a movie.

In the Green Room, my arms and jaw jumped and torqued into tight and painful corkscrews. Major pain on the right side of my neck and shoulder, shooting pain near my right temple. I'm in a room that looks a little like the basement in that movie: a bare, smallish room out by the garage at Bompa's—behind the middle garage, I think. There's a table, shelves on the wall, and machines. I can't move or talk, and no one comes to get me— like the girl in the movie. Deeper hypnosis or heavier drugs

---

4   This ceremony was inspired by the book *Goddesses in Older Women* written by Jean Shinoda Bolen, MD (Harper, 2001).

have been used here to mask the greater pain caused by the harsher experiments. The well-trained subject doesn't cry out. Who would answer, anyway? No one—like for the girl in the movie. Yet another torture chamber uncovered...

Images of several experiences from my adult life came back, connected somehow to my childhood horrors, including indelible visions from the former Nazi concentration camps I had visited. My strongest reaction was to the concrete table I saw at Mauthausen, once used for human experimentation, with its trough for the blood to drain away. It felt connected to the newly discovered table in Bompa's garage room, and there were dreams of Nazis chasing me, from which I woke soaked with sweat, breathless and terrified.

It would still be years before I understood these connections. In the meantime, these images dimmed as my healing quest led me to deeper spiritual reconciliation.

Chapter 22
Bridging the Americas

Elders from indigenous cultures in North, Central and South America planned a 2007 "Bridging the Americas" retreat and council[5] at Lake Titicaca to activate ancient prophecies many of their traditions shared. Jorge Luis led the South American contingent. They also opened the invitation to a few laypeople—particularly those from prior retreats with indigenous heritage, like Anita, my roommate from the 2006 trip.

When she called about six weeks before the council to suggest we room together again, I knew nothing about the event. Even so, we moved quickly. She got me invited, and I arranged three weeks off work and doubled down on physical therapy for a painful knee. With great excitement, we headed back to Peru to help fulfill the prophecy that "when the eagle and the condor fly together, there will be peace in the Americas."[6]

---

5   If you're interested in Bridging the Americas, some of it was filmed for a documentary. Learn more in the movie *Time of the Sixth Sun*.

6   Prophecies across the Americas foretell a great spiritual springtime that will come after five hundred years to cleanse the pain of the colonial past and ancestral wounding on these lands. In the prophecy of the eagle and condor, the eagle represents the indigenous people of the north and the condor represents the indigenous cultures of the south. The prophecy signifies not only a reunion of the peoples of the Americas, but of the entire human race.

Jorge Luis had taught us about this prophecy. He and many other wisdom keepers believed we were in the midst of a major shift in cosmic and planetary energies that the wise ones had anticipated many generations ago. As sentient beings graced with the blessing of living on the planet at this time, it was our duty to do all we could to activate this new energy. Eager to do my part, I knew my personal healing would also benefit, as it had on the first trip.

The council took place at sacred Lake Titicaca on the high plateau just north of the Peru–Bolivia border. We stayed in the small lakeside town of Chucuito, in a newish hotel and conference center, where various elders presided over sunrise and sunset observances. Each day, we ventured out to explore and participate in ceremonies of connection held in sacred places throughout the area.

The first was a joyous joining-of-the-waters unity celebration on the sacred lake, performed in reed boats made in the ancient style by the people of the Uros Islands. Our boats, filled with elders dressed in ceremonial finery, gathered in a circle under a cloudless sky that mirrored the deep blue waters. They had come from Alaska, Hawaii, Chile and all points in between with sacred waters to be joined in this ceremony. I sat in awe that my WASPy self could be so intimately in their presence, taking part in rituals of connection that resonated deep in my soul.

The Uros people themselves are a reminder of how flexible and ingenious human beings can be when survival is at stake. The more than forty floating islands on which they live are also made of reeds. Imagine escaping a conqueror by making floating islands to live on!

My childhood survival strategies are simply another example of this ingenuity.

ON ANOTHER BRIGHT SUNNY DAY, our throng of one hundred fifty or so people hiked through a series of sacred rock formations to arrive at the legendary doorway of Aramu Muru. The oldest of the

North American elders began the ceremonies by speaking of a dream in which the ancestors asked each of us, individually and jointly, to seek to heal the pain of our families, going back twelve generations.

"Only when the suffering of the ancestors is alleviated and released will our prophecy of peace be realized," the elder said. I reverently accepted my role in addressing the historical pain of indigenous people in this setting. Regardless of where they lived in the Americas, they had all been subjugated by conquerors over the past three centuries. If we could heal the wounds caused by all that violence and upheaval with our ceremonies and prayers, it would help bring the lasting peace we all wanted.

But on a personal level, it didn't seem quite as clear. I had been so focused on my healing I'd never considered the pain of those who hurt me or those who hurt them. With some humility, I realized how very little I knew about my father's and grandfather's ancestors. I saw them both simply as privileged white men who felt entitled to use, hurt and betray me. The elders asked that I expand my view.

On either side of the Aramu Muru doorway, circular shafts scored out of the red rock rise thirty feet or more to the top of the outcropping, open to the sky. It is said that the one on the right as

you face the doorway carries masculine energy and the one on the left, feminine energy.

The warm air smelled of white sage smudge sticks and wildflowers as several elders led group prayers in English and Spanish. Ceremonial chanting, soft flutes, and the steady beat of a Lakota drummer created a sacred symphony. We took turns, first in the right shaft, then in the door, and finally in the left shaft, each bringing our personal prayers and the larger intention to bridge the Americas and heal centuries of generational pain.

I held back to be respectful of the elders and their ceremonial work. But the people around me made it clear we were holding space for all of us. If I was there, I belonged and had important work to do in bringing forth the new energy, the new era of peace.

I stepped into the first stone shaft and immediately became aware of energetic strings connecting me to my male ancestors—my father, his father, and his father before him, going back twelve generations, as well as all their brothers. The energetic cords attached to my body were drawn taut up through the shaft. I turned slowly with the energy flow, wanting to break the cycles of pain. A huge pair of scissors appeared above my head and cut all the strings in one powerful snip. The release I experienced felt so real I lost my footing.

Regaining my balance, I exited the shaft, walking the few feet down the red rock pathway to the door with gratitude and wonder. As my forehead touched the stone opening, a surge of oneness, of connection, with these rocks and with the universe, filled me, while something unnameable but almost tangible left me.

I turned from the door so dazed I couldn't even make it to the left shaft. Instead, I sat in the wild grass, soaking in the meaning of what I had just experienced. Had the stirrings of compassion let me cut the cords of pain?[7]

---

7   That night, I had a vivid dream about several women being hurt and chased by men. When the women told anyone or sought protection, the men would become enraged and resume the chase, trying to hurt them again. But someone intervened, at their own risk, to protect the women, using a large pair of scissors.

As our individual turns at the doorway finished, the elders gathered in a circle to create a large ceremonial space. Abuelita Marguerite from Nayarit, Mexico, invited all of us who were at least sixty years old to sit with them in this circle, as elders of our own "tribes." She said we had each learned much and had many experiences in our lives, and that we could now use the wisdom we had gathered to help others on their own journeys.

I felt honored by this acknowledgment (and thrilled with the offer to sit for the ceremony). The truth of what she said struck me. How was I going to use my new freedom and whatever wisdom I had gained to help others?

My learning and healing—this long, arduous process I'd been going through—was not just about me. Clearly, it connected to something much bigger. I had to be open to and searching for ways to use myself to break cycles of violence and pain in my family and beyond.

Sitting on Mother Earth, in this circle of wisdom keepers, all of us supported by Pachamama, I felt deeply grounded and connected. Inside the space we protected, a young Hopi man performed the traditional Eagle Dance in full ceremonial dress. All of his ancestors, who had performed this same dance and passed it on to him, blessed the ceremony.

At the end, on behalf of all the northern tribes, he presented Jorge Luis with an eagle feather; Jorge Luis, representing the Southern tribes, presented him with a condor feather. They celebrated growing unity, while I celebrated a kind of severance from my male ancestors.

I didn't realize it yet, but this separation from the fear and control of the past was a major step in developing a unity of spirit within my internal system. Snipping the cords connecting me to the past patriarchy allowed me to free myself from their pain and control, while opening the door for compassion. The Inca salutation "With love, without fear" resonated deeply. Could I live that way?

And so, as we sat in our ceremonial circle, we prayed again for our ancestors going back twelve generations. Mine, all northern Europeans, came to North America in the eighteenth and nineteenth centuries as part of the horde that rained pain and terror on the ancestors of many of the people with whom I sat. Finally, I began to understand what they were saying.

First, the elders were telling me I was there to do my own work, not to help them with theirs. I needed to use my energy to heal my lineage, just as they worked to heal theirs. Second, they talked in terms of wounded souls needing healing, not victims and perpetrators. The anger I felt toward my ancestors for their actions in relation to me and the people who surrounded me may have been understandable, but compassion would be required if our intent was peace and healing.

The inclusive goal of unity and healing for all humanity offered a powerful statement about the new energy we were activating. It took me years to grasp the depth of that day's lessons or to appreciate how Purple Lady internalized them into our system.

The next two days were filled with unity ceremonies and opportunities for learning and sharing at the conference in the hotel. I met Silvia Calisaya, a powerful Aymara healer, who read my coca leaves and confirmed I was on a productive healing path. We connected, both personally and energetically, and agreed to stay in touch.

When the council closed, those of us who had chosen to stay longer and visit Machu Picchu and Cusco boarded buses and drove north through the Altiplano—the high plateau of the Peruvian Andes—to Aguas Calientes, the small town at the base of Machu Picchu. The next morning, while Anita slept, I awoke early to take the first bus up the mountain. After the packed schedule of the council and conference, I wanted quiet time to meditate, talk with the birds, and visit with Putucusi, my special mountain. The group met at the little cave temple we had been to on the first trip for the sunrise ceremony and flying with the condors. I needed no hand-on-the-knee security blanket this time.

After the ceremony, Jorge Luis talked with several of us about where to go and what to explore during our free time in the after-noon. One group hiked all the way up Huayna Picchu, but he sug-gested I go the other direction, up onto the Inca Trail high above the city to a huge boulder that presides over a small cemetery where the Grandmother of Lightning was buried. She had been one of the most important priestesses of Machu Picchu. He suggested I hike up to commune with her and see what would happen. So, I did.

To me, many of the natural features of the rock looked like faces, some of which had tears of moss flowing from the eyes. Was she a priestess of women who had known great sorrow? I settled onto a rock on the east side of the little cemetery, across from a small, makeshift altar where other seekers had left trib-utes to her. The sun's warmth helped me absorb the energy of this sacred place and recover from the steep hike.

I meditated for a while, seeking her presence and whatever guidance she might have for me. Then, I reverently explored the area, noting that my internal priestess was co-present with me and encouraging the investigation. Priestess didn't usually spend much time out in the body, and Big Bonnie welcomed her strength and curiosity. If we intended to learn from an ancient priestess, obviously our internal priestess should be present.

In my pocket, I carried the *khuya* Jorge Luis had given me—a special stone given by a teacher to a student as a reminder of lessons learned. My knee ached, so I sat again and placed the *khuya* on it, perhaps to ease the pain or even to heal it.

Immediately and indignantly, the Inca priestess admonished us. "Get your own rock!" she ordered.

We didn't quite hear her voice in our mind, but her words were clear, powerful and unmistakable. When we opened our eyes, we knew which rock was ours—a flat, dusty, orange one about the size of our palm, sitting on the ground right in front of us. We clasped it to our heart, then held it up for her blessing before sitting back down and placing it on our knee.

The pain subsided as we meditated, now fully in her empowering presence. We didn't hear anything else with that level of clarity, but the message came through loud and clear. *Get in touch with your own power, your own truth. You need not rely on power—or on rocks—given to you by any man.* In our mind's eye, we saw a red rock formation and knew a trip to red rock country would be next on the agenda.

With gratitude for her powerful medicine, we placed the healing rock on her altar as an offering. We knew of the taboo against removing stones from Machu Picchu, and besides, it was too big to fit in my pocket. As we stood giving thanks, a small, triangular, deep orange stone caught our eye. Priestess asked the Grandmother for permission to take this one as a *khuya* to hold her teachings for our altar back home, and it was granted.

Quieter inside, and yet more powerful, we made our way back down the Inca Trail into Machu Picchu with Priestess co-conscious in mind and body, and with a new *khuya* in our pocket. The dusty paving stones conjured the centuries of walkers who had worn them smooth and uneven. The feel of a breeze on the skin, the trees so tall and swaying, and the sight of the ancient city below as we rounded a bend enthralled Priestess. Big Bonnie felt the difference too and wondered if this could be what it felt like to be whole and fully present in the moment, with all my selves in harmony. I burst out with a laugh of discovery, then found myself crying with joy, gratitude and love. And that knee never caused another problem.

While Big Bonnie returned home with a fascinating story, for Priestess, communing with the Ancient One was transformational. When we got home, Priestess insisted on having a blown-up photo of the huge rock at the Grandmother's burial site framed and hung on the wall of our bedroom, next to Purple Lady's textile from the first trip. It became our iconic symbol of the emergence and ownership of our feminine power. Priestess wrote:

> It feels good to look up and feel her power through the rock; to know she is watching over us, and that we are together as we were when we were with her.

It felt good to Big Bonnie, too, to wake back home in my bed and contemplate the sequence of miraculous events. Cutting the strings to my masculine ancestors prepared me to hear the Grandmother's call and allowed my most powerful feminine alter to come forward and be more present in my outside life.

We weren't yet ready to focus on the feminine energy at the door. Instead, we waited through several days of ceremonies and travel until the most influential Inca priestess, the Grandmother of Lightning, pushed us to open up to our own power.

The ceremonies accentuated the imperative to acknowledge and break generational cycles of fear, pain, abuse and violence, both personally and universally—even if that meant growing some compassion for those who had hurt us. And the Grandmother of Lightning helped me see I must go beyond the wounds that brought me here and accept my personal power and my calling to break these cycles.

Her message rings in my ears often when I feel weak, unsure or lonely. "Do not rely on power given to you by others. You have your own power, your own truth. Get your own rock and use it!"

Chapter 23
New Jobs for Old Friends

Aided by Julia's incredible, gentle skill, some of the internal people began to feel safe in this new world. Meetings in the Green Room became opportunities to appreciate the unique contributions of each of us and to transform them creatively to accomplish new tasks and activities. Assured that the skills and jobs we had once performed had been essential to survival, we understood those jobs were no longer needed because those dangers were no longer present. Instead, we could take on new roles to lead and support the important work now at hand: healing from the past and growing into a new future.

Purple Lady motivated Big Bonnie and helped her set up a personal altar on a side table in our home. We populated it with special stones and small carvings from our travels, which we arranged and rearranged according to our evolving needs and intentions.

Our spiritual ceremony emerged as an inclusive moment each morning in which all parts were welcome to engage. Based on the wisdom traditions we had studied and our growing understanding of our internal community's needs, our morning altar ritual reinforced our meditation practice and our connections to nature and the Universe.

Over time, we added new artifacts and stones from each sacred place we visited, and a stone representing every alter who wanted one. Today, the circle of stones symbolizing the internal family offers an opportunity for each to make their needs or concerns known. The Inca salutation "With love, without fear" serves as a helpful prayer and a reminder of how we want to approach the world each day.

Priestess announced that, after giving it some consideration, she had found a good way to assist us in the here and now. "I am large enough to hold the anger for many. Powerful enough that it can do no more damage. Heavy energy released to the Grandmother Rock in ritual does not consume. We have many coca leaves and much to release to the Earth Goddess. Do that ritual each week. I'll assist inside and heavy energy will flow away. It is good."

And that became our method of handling the anger associated with the various experiences we learned about. When we did a pickup, we gave our anger to Priestess to hold so it would not interfere with life or with the revelations and release of new pieces of the story. Each week at the altar, Priestess and Big Bonnie used our version of a ritual Jorge Luis had taught us in Peru. We took three coca leaves from the stash we had brought home and fanned them out in our hands, creating a *kintu* into which we could blow all our pent-up emotion. Then we took the *kintu* outside to the stream that runs past the front door of our home. With reverence and gratitude, we blew the anger-filled leaves into the stream, releasing back to Pachamama all the heavy energy that had served its purpose and we no longer needed.

There is no good/bad or sinful/righteous duality in the ancient cosmology, as there had been with my grandparents. Heavy energy can be useful. Then, when it has served its purpose, it can be given to Pachamama so she can reuse it. Nothing is lost or wicked, and everything can be recycled.

Priestess had internalized the Grandmother of Lightning's message at a much deeper level than Big Bonnie, and she used it to make a transformative shift from Bompa's teachings to her own rock, her own power. Able to think for herself now, she used her considerable intellect, strength and energy on behalf of the entire internal community.

Jane, a cheerful, expressive young girl who was very comfortable in the body, had become a regular in the Green Room. She had even gotten to know a couple of Big Bonnie's outside friends, interacting with them to share her joy at being alive. She took on the new job of helping other little ones find their voices or express themselves with feelings or tears. When flashbacks and body memories continued, not connected to anything that gave them context, she made sure we recorded them in the journal until they were ready for the Green Room.

With leadership from inside, rather than resistance, I developed a more consistent meditation practice than ever before, using Deepak Chopra's guided meditations to get started. His nondogmatic approach and Buddhist-based but eclectic mix of wisdom traditions complemented my growing spiritual cosmology. And his focus on the chakras—the seven energy centers of the body—opened a means of befriending my body and feeling its energy.

I realized rather sheepishly that all my earlier attempts at meditation had been focused on *looking* like I was meditating, without really internalizing anything too dangerously intrusive. In the old days, each time I tried provided nothing beyond a little relaxation and a lot of posing—life as performance art. Now, with no partner or class to pose for, and with the help of Priestess's new openness and Purple Lady's guidance, our practice connected us to energy and messages, both universal and internal.

My coach training provided a new tool that helped me become grounded in the present and reminded me I had choices about how I showed up in my life each day. Before starting work with a client or engaging in any interaction, I settle myself with a couple of deep breaths and ask, essentially, "What qualities of my being do I want to demonstrate in this interaction?" From a list, I choose five attributes that I want to shine through in this setting. Sadness, abandonment and fearfulness are not on the list. The second question asks, "Am I willing to approach this interaction openly, without a bunch of preconceived assumptions?"

For years, we asked these questions at the altar each morning, and they came to augment and even replace the traditional pickups. I didn't realize then that this process resonated internally because of its similarity to the way my internal community had always worked in difficult or threatening situations. They used to ask, "What skills do I need in order to survive, hide and not be damaged by what's likely to happen here? Where within us can we find those skills?"

All these shifts inside were clear signs of healing, and my new understanding of my history gave the apparently normal person on the outside hope that we had reached the end. Again, I became impatient with the therapeutic process. Hadn't I done enough by now? Hadn't I learned everything I needed to live my life without all this drama? I knew I didn't know what I didn't know, but that only made me more impatient. I didn't *want* to know any more. Soon, my annoyance drew an ethereal response in the Green Room in the form of a quieting message.

Julia and I had been talking about my teenage years. I wanted to figure out how and when the alters had structured themselves. They hadn't just popped into place after I was twelve, I now saw. As Julia so often did, she suggested, "Why don't you ask inside?" So, I settled myself, moved Big Bonnie out of the way as much as I could, and waited to see what would come forth.

The images were very real. Something like an umbrella or a mushroom cap of energy, twice the circumference of my head, floated down from the transom above the door and slowly settled over and around me. I imagined it felt similar to being caught in an extraterrestrial energy beam. Warm. Safe. Kind.

There was a strong awareness that I was all of my energy field—seven layers out. This organism saw us as one entity—only partly physical. That's why it was so big around. It encompassed the whole, coming down from the top. It came with no words, so I opened up to it silently, closing my eyes.

When the eyes re-opened, they hadn't been in the Green Room before. They took it in knowingly, with familiarity. They looked gently at Julia for the first time, but again with recognition.

Julia asked, "Do you have words?" and there were none. But the intent, the message to her, was clear.

"You are doing a good job."

And to me, there came a great peaceful centeredness. *All is well and is unfolding as it should. Don't sweat the small stuff.* I knew this, not in words, but by a feeling in my whole energetic body, including the physical. Then the presence rose and left me uplifted, serene, awed. A higher power had made itself known with deep stillness and peacefulness—even deeper than when Purple Lady first visited.

Julia, also moved, said the two of us had been given a gift. I was not sure how to understand, hold and use this gift. But I knew Purple Lady connected deeply to this experience. I could see that the energy field of the Andes was nurturing and re-energizing my system; that was why we were drawn there for learning and ceremonies of connection and unity.

My irritation softened, and the sense of well-being produced by this experience allowed me to return to my healing path with peaceful confidence. But the details were quickly moved to someplace outside of Big Bonnie's conscious memory, where alters like Priestess and Purple Lady could retain and reflect upon what the apparently normal person couldn't hold on to. Thank goodness I wrote about it immediately in the journal!

Chapter 24
An Intentional Grandmother

After my eighteen-month child abuse prevention job ended in the fall of 2007, I went back to my consulting practice, thinking that the flexibility would be helpful and would allow me to reduce my hours. Instead, I learned that the more structured, external schedule and control of a job helped me function in the outer world.

The internal work had deepened and expanded, and my alters pushed for a schedule they could count on, including more balance between the hours available for external and internal work. As if by plan, right on time, the perfect opportunity arrived. The national organization I had worked for earlier approached me to lead their local work, without responsibility for any far-flung offices.

My longtime friend Marisol would now be my supervisor, and her boss was also someone with whom I had worked closely in different settings over the years. Both were mental health professionals, and I was open about my diagnosis and my ability to perform while continuing in treatment. Although we never discussed it as an accommodation under the terms of the Americans with Disabilities Act, I requested a four-day/forty-hour work schedule. They agreed, and we built an atmosphere of trust and respect that was conducive to my growing health and wholeness, while giving me the opportunity to contribute fully to the field and community. With a better understanding of why this work to strengthen families and improve child welfare resonated so passionately with me, I jumped into my new role with vigor, and perhaps a bit more wisdom.

ANOTHER PERIOD OF INTERNAL CONSOLIDATION allowed me to catch my breath and believe, again, that the worst was over. My three-day weekends allowed me to see a few coaching clients, which I found quite rewarding. But I used the time mainly for my regular therapy sessions in the Green Room and whatever follow-up my internal community needed. I could feel the spiritual work aiding the physical and emotional healing inside, as we all came to know each other in new ways. Maybe there was finally light at the end of this long, dark tunnel.

Around the same time, Will and his wife excitedly announced they were having a baby. They had returned to the States after years in South America and had settled in Oregon. About a month before my first grandchild was born, Priestess and Purple Lady raised some concerns about the kind of grandmother we would be. They provided internal leadership, insisting, "This is something we can all come together around. This baby only has one grandma in his or her life. We can all work together to be sure we show up as a consistent, loving, protective, authentic grandma," Purple Lady urged everyone. "We are willing to be that kind of grandma together."

"And also smart, strong and wise," added Priestess. "Yes, we can all bring our strengths and our lessons to help. We know we want the child to see one grandmother with all these qualities. We know it can be confusing and scary to see a grandmother who is wildly unpredictable."

From that time forward, with great consistency no matter what else was happening in our world, when the grandchildren are present (I've since been blessed with five), there is never any question that everyone internally will help Big Bonnie display the qualities they would have liked in their own grandmother. My grandchildren came to call me *Oma*, the German word for "grandma," and we call this being in "Oma-mode"—another great example of the always evolving, protective, creative and collaborative brilliance of our internal community.

With the birth of my first grandson, I felt the universe shift. My world forever changed. I was now an elder in a new way. In the Green Room, as we discussed this transition, I felt the fullness of my energetic and spiritual soul in my consciousness. It reminded me that I was on my path, and it was unfolding as it should. I could be more generous and loving toward the small vexations in life. I had the sensation of being present in my entire energy body—the physical body was more amorphous, still present but more spacious. It reminded me we're all so much more than we appear.

At the time, I did not connect these sensations to the experience three months earlier with the ethereal presence in the Green Room. I thought this was the first time I'd been aware of the comforting sense that my life was part of a much larger universe and that I was playing a part orchestrated by a higher power. As before, I wondered if this perhaps confirmed we were finally finished with the revelations and could focus more on the present and future, and less on the past. *No need to delve deeper. Accept what happened and that we may never know the totality of it or understand the motivations of all those involved—and let that be okay. That's the path to peace, even if you still have physical symptoms you don't understand and can't reconcile. You are so tired of all this painful work focused on the past. Give it a rest. Besides, there's probably not much of anything more to explore.*

Was I seduced by these thoughts or guided? Either way, they let me focus more on being and thriving in the present and taking on my next nature-based adventures in the growth and healing of my body, mind and spirit.

THE FOLLOWING JOURNAL ENTRY from my sixty-second birthday reveals our collective thoughts as we worked to understand what was happening to us.

In the end, we are all parts of a soul whose role is to break cycles going back generations—cycles of deceit, cruelty, denial and hubris. The very way I was trained to absorb whatever anyone could dish out helped me not become one of them.

So now, together, we are seeking and finding peace. Lasting peace for any of us seems to require that each of us finds our own... and that may take many more birthdays or a lifetime. Each little crack and crevice in this psyche—this soul, this being—has its own memories and responses. Most are stuck in a single time and place. Only a few are more fully formed into adaptable, sentient personalities who can help others find their peace.

I remember a couple of times sensing the whole energetic being, and in those moments, knowing that we are one and that our journey is unfolding as it is intended, like it says in the poem "Desiderata."[8] It is easy to lose sight of that truth when caught up in daily struggles.

The hubris and folly of thinking Big Bonnie controls anything becomes clearer. But I still have to make money to pay my way in this world. Yes, we could simplify our existence. But it often feels like just getting through the day—surviving intact—takes all the strength there is. Intact... An interesting choice of words. Often, lately, we feel like we're coming apart, each in our own struggles—not intact, but with separate battles. But I guess it is all the same war.

---

8   This poem, written in 1927 by Max Ehrmann, had been important to Wayne and me. It includes a line that states, "And whether or not it is clear to you, no doubt the universe is unfolding as it should."

Part 5
A New Baseline

Chapter 25
Uluru, Australia

I have been blessed with the opportunity for lots of travel since I was a baby. And I love the mobility of my children's generation. My daughter, Beth, became fast friends with Phoebe, an Australian, when they were both high school exchange students in Costa Rica. Through their college years, they traveled together, and Phoebe visited California often, becoming like a second daughter to me. This awesome young Australian fell in love with an Israeli man whom she met in Laos on vacation and then corresponded with by email and Skype after they returned home. Love without borders.

When they announced they were getting married in 2008, I jumped at the opportunity to visit Australia, celebrate them, and check off another entry on my bucket list by studying indigenous wisdom traditions there.

As with Peru, preparations for the trip facilitated internal shifts. Big Bonnie found herself more willing to accept the new realities of life rather than defaulting to old ways of thinking. I was more than one, and all parties needed to be consulted on things that affected them.

Julia reminded me I had never been alone. I had always had an internal community supporting me, a fact I had only just begun to grasp. We made decisions about the trip jointly—with Julia's help, of course—and planned to learn and travel for at least two weeks before arriving at Phoebe's for the wedding. In the process, a whole range of emotions emerged inside, from fear to curiosity to courage. For this trip, we needed enough structure to feel safe and enough freedom to explore and discover, with allowances for time to ponder and assimilate... to just be.

The image of red rocks I saw while visiting with the Grandmother of Lightning at Machu Picchu looked just like pictures of Uluru, where the creation stories of many local wisdom traditions are centered. So I knew where to go. Uluru is the traditional name of what the colonizers called "Ayers Rock," when they came and renamed things that had had perfectly good names for many thousands of years.

As Phoebe and I discussed over email what and how I might learn, she told me she had a friend in Alice Springs. Like Phoebe, she was a linguist working with indigenous groups to preserve their languages. At the close of all of Phoebe's emails was a quote from an activist, Lila Watson, and her indigenous community, aimed at curious outsiders.

> If you have come here to help me, then you are wasting your
> time. But if you have come because your liberation is bound
> up with mine, then let us work together.

These words reminded me of the lesson the elders in Peru had tried to teach me through their actions. Humbly, I continued my quest to glean guidance and liberating healing wisdom from the ancient cultures.

I DECIDED TO STOP FIRST in Alice Springs for a few days, before heading to Uluru, another hour's flight deeper into the Outback. Phoebe's friend had agreed to meet me and help focus my studies and explorations in the limited time I had. Desert Mob (one of the nation's most significant Aboriginal art events) had been held the week before I got there, so the galleries and museums she guided me to still overflowed with indigenous art.

I immersed myself in the various types of artwork that, until a few decades earlier, had been created mostly in loose red sand. Once people began making pictures that didn't blow away with the next stiff breeze or swipe of the foot, they had to rethink what they put into them. The art carried sacred and cultural lessons, some of which were not meant for the eyes of outsiders. Even while respecting that limitation, though, it still seemed the most accessible window into the culture. The dot art of this region included many symbolic shapes and figures, some with multiple meanings, and I wanted to understand the stories behind the paintings as best I could.

The moment we rose into the air on the short flight to Uluru, I saw that the land below looked like the dot artwork, with a red earth background and green and white shrubbery dotting the landscape. There are no high mountains in this area—no places where you can get the bird's eye view of the land that these artists or their ancestors clearly had. Their cosmology—Tjukurpa—is the basis of their culture, law and moral systems and incorporates past, present and future at the same time. It includes the concept of "Dreamtime" to describe their understanding of their origins and deep interdependent connections with the land and its other inhabitants. I wondered if the ancestral beings who created the features of the land had floated above it and passed down their aerial views through the generations.

On my first full day at Uluru, I joined a group led by a local Aboriginal guide on a walk around the entire circumference of the rock. The caves and crevices, the configuration of the cracks and openings, all have meaning, rendering some of them too sacred for outsiders to see. These stories about Uluru offer another glimpse into the teachings of a culture that has survived and evolved over at least 65,000 years.

Pictures from afar usually show Uluru as a massive outcropping of stone. Even the sight of it from hotel viewing areas at sunrise and sunset does nothing to prepare a newcomer for the size and intricacy of the markings or the complexity and sheer power of the rock when

seen up close. From one angle, it looks to be made up of sedimentary layers stood upright and then rounded by erosion. In other places, it has such supple flowing curves, worn so smooth, that it's like a polished carving. The surface is punctuated by holes and caves of all sizes, the nuances shifting with every step.

During the walk, I found myself thinking about my father; his presence almost palpable. He seemed to want me to remember the wonderful family adventures we had together, even as I was learning about the other, not-so-wonderful things that had happened.

At one point, I separated from the group and heard myself talking to him out loud. "Please leave. I know you would have loved this place. But can't you see it without using me?"

I tried to listen to him, wondering if he had some message, but I didn't hear anything clearly, only the sense that, yes, it was a place he would have loved to visit. I really didn't want his presence around me, though. Maybe he would have liked it, but I was the one here now. This was my time.

As I resumed walking, an internal masculine presence, of whom I had only been vaguely aware, came forward. He called himself "George." It had been his job to protect the little girl from Dad and others, and he made it quite clear (albeit not so much in words) he didn't want Dad's spirit around.

The next day, we felt Dad again when we drove out to Mt. Conner, another huge rock outcropping in the middle of the vast desert. I heard him imploring, "Remember the trips and the good times we had."

"I'll grant you that." I acknowledged. "Family trips were positive times, and you never touched alcohol or hurt me when we traveled together. I gained a lot from those adventures, including my love for the desert and red rocks. It is true you were a complex person. And you're right, the awful things you did do not erase the good things that were also part of my childhood." None of that changed the fact that his presence felt creepy and unwanted.

George asserted himself again and made it clear we did not need Dad to help us enjoy this place or to learn what it had to teach. We worked together to clear Dad out of our mind and presence.

Back at Uluru, in the cultural center that acts as art studio, gallery, educational museum and shop, we continued our pursuit of the perfect painting to bring home. Big Bonnie had led the search so far, but with great indecision. I asked for help inside and called on everyone who had an interest to weigh in.

A French family who had been on the same walk drew our attention to the back wall, where they had become very excited about a painting with squares of dots—which meant it was just of a landscape. The one above it—too big and too expensive for Big Bonnie to consider it seriously—caught our collective attention. It depicted six people around a common meeting place with the red rocks as backdrop. Then we saw a picture of the artist next to it, a matriarch from a nearby community. There were no more questions inside. We needed this one. Almost crying with excitement, we made a joint decision, deeply felt, without further discussion. Breathless, we found it hard to let anyone be alone outside to make the purchase.

We named it "Bonnie's Dreaming" because it helps tell Bonnie's Dreamtime story. It shows the coming together of masculine and feminine aspects around a common purpose and on common ground. In *Bonnie's Dreaming*, six individuals are sitting together, pursuing peace with each other and with their past. The red rocks watch, guide and help the process along.

In the artist's morality tale, as outlined in her description of the painting, there are two scenes separated in time. In the first, a male is pursuing the two females. In the second, after some higher intervention, the man comes back seeking to establish peaceful relations rather than leading with his penis. (Note the connection of the native artist's story to my father's attempted overtures, something I didn't consciously see until years later.)

As I left Uluru, I knew everything had unfolded exactly as I needed it to. That included both my active engagement with the powerful red rocks of Mother Earth and the quiet time to absorb a nascent connection to Aboriginal Dreamtime and Tjukurpa.

At home, a photo of Uluru joined the one of the Grandmother of Lightning's rock on our bedroom wall, denoting the emergence of my internal masculine energy and power. And the painting, *Bonnie's Dreaming*, began its life in my home directly above the bed. Over time, it migrated into the dining room, then to the living room; each step representing the greater openness with which we began to acknowledge and share our story.

ULURU HAD BROUGHT ME a reconnection with my dad. No, not a reconnection; more a recognition that we shared many things—pains and passions, joys and sorrows. And yet, there remained the certain knowledge that I was choosing a different path. I don't think he ever got to a place where he could seek wisdom from the rocks or the pain. He was still seeking peace. But that doesn't come unless you face your demons—another lesson reaffirmed by the Dreamtime stories. I've been willing to face mine, but sometimes I lose my way.

Dad's spirit wants me to be successful but can't help directly. He knows I find solace and power in the red rocks and wants them to bring me courage—something he never found.

Even in the conscious world, my interactions with Dad throughout my life were stormy and often emotionally hurtful. Learning what he had done to me as a dissociated child brought forth more disgust and anger. This reminder of the good times we had shared—and there were many—and how they, too, had shaped my life came as a welcome counterpoint. Coupled with my new understanding of who his parents were, it allowed for compassion—not yet forgiveness, but compassion—for what he must have gone through as a child, and how that might have shaped him. I even came to wonder if he, too, had been dissociative; if the sober father I knew in the daytime didn't remember or know anything about the drunk one who took me into the den at night. After all, they seemed like such different people... But I'll never know.

Chapter 26
Balance and Unity

Australia's red rocks were not alone in calling me to visit. My bucket list and the push for a deeper connection to the land, Mother Nature and the spiritual cosmos opened up several more opportunities. I hadn't visited Sedona, Arizona, for many years when I heard that Jorge Luis would lead a workshop there in 2009. A dear friend from my years in Florida agreed to meet me, and we rekindled deep bonds with each other and with Mother Earth by enjoying a couple of days of hiking and exploring before and after the workshop.

Again, Jorge Luis's nonjudgmental, nondogmatic, I-accept-you-wherever-you-are clarity and his we're-all-on-this-path-together teaching style drew me in to the ancient wisdom he embodied. I learned as much by observing his interactions with others as by listening to his words.

My friend and I also attended a class on Native American totem animals, where I confirmed my longtime sense that my spirit guide was a gentle, male bear. His unobtrusive guidance and protection had been with me at many critical moments over the years, but I had never fully acknowledged him until then. In my mind's eye, he is a large, furry brown bear surrounded by golden light, with a kind face, warm smell, and gentle demeanor. In Navajo culture, the bear represents healing and nurturing care, which fit perfectly. I bought a small stone Navajo fetish for my altar and began thanking and calling on him in my rituals.

Soaking in the lessons and natural energy, I sat in meditation on the rocky bank of Oak Creek beneath Cathedral Rock, my feet dangling in the cool springtime water. The deep orange of the afternoon sun reflected off the high rocks into the river. Balance. Actively peaceful, peacefully powerful energy filled me. The masculine energy and heat of the rock formation balanced the feminine energy of the running water. Now that both these forces had been awakened in me, I could be intentional, with a new sense of equilibrium in my life. A

picture of that setting became the third icon on my bedroom wall.

Since then, the glorious natural rock formations and cosmic energy of Sedona have served both Big Bonnie and many of our alters as a place of deep connection, opening and introspection. It's close enough that we make the drive often, sometimes with Mari or other friends, sometimes alone with my internal selves. We go to attend organized workshops or gatherings. But more often, it's a time for individual exploration, hiking, meditation, writing and gratitude for Pachamama's blessings.

I HAD FINALLY ACCEPTED I had a dissociative disorder and tried to read what I could about healing and what the future might hold for me. For decades, therapists and researchers had thought integration was the most successful outcome for a person who had used dissociation to survive childhood trauma. By their definition, this meant the point of therapy was to become a single personality with no internal voices or alters. More recently, the field has moved toward a focus on healing from the underlying trauma and developing peaceful, consistent functionality in the world, with or without multiple identities. Functional multiplicity has become an accepted goal.

I didn't care much about the labels, but I wanted to be free of the painful and annoying body symptoms still lingering from the awful things that happened when I was young. I wanted to be able to think clearly and contribute to the world around me as a professional. And I wanted to be authentic in my relationships with the people I loved. We discussed all this in the Green Room, and Julia was open to exploring options and letting us consider the goal, timing and approach that felt most healing for us.

However, as I allowed more openness with friends and family, well-meaning people could set off terrible feelings when they blithely (or sometimes impatiently) asked how soon I would be integrated into one person again. From their perspective, this crazy multiple personality stuff was all new, and they wanted the Bonnie they remembered to be "back to normal." (Whatever that is!)

No matter what it looked or felt like on the outside—including to me—"normal" hadn't existed since I was two, and it was impossible to go back to it. To many in the inside community, any discussion of integration felt like they were once again being asked to devalue their experiences and courage—to cease to exist or become invisible again. It was as if they were being asked to go away.

Another trip to a sacred place for a workshop with Jorge Luis offered the opportunity to deal with these questions and decide on unity and community—not integration—as our goal.

MANY PEOPLE CONSIDER MT. SHASTA to be one of the key energy centers on the planet. The rustic village nestled at its base caters to spiritual seekers and hikers in equal measure. When I heard Jorge Luis was to lead a five-day workshop with some locals there in November 2010, I invited my dear friend Mari to join me in experiencing a place neither of us yet knew. I was also eager to share Jorge Luis's teachings with another fellow seeker.

A group of twenty-five gathered in a rustic retreat center, where Jorge Luis explained the three mainstays of Inca teachings about how to live a good life: *munay, llankay* and *yachay* (love, service and wisdom). He talked about unity and the oneness of all things. Priestess became very present early in this retreat and wrote about it later in our journal.

> I like the woman who went with us. We have become good friends. We had already met each other, and she has proved herself trustworthy. Then we got to know each other better on this trip to Mt. Shasta.
>
> There was a large bonfire, and I listened as the leader urged the people to burn away things they no longer needed. I came forward and chose to throw sticks into the bonfire, representing Bompa's hold on me. I was able to say as I threw them in and watched them burn that he could no longer control me or do anything to me.
>
> The leader asked us to release them with love. That seemed harder. What is love? What does it have to do with my relationship with Bompa? Something new to think about.
>
> This was at the beginning of the retreat, and I made myself available for more of the work there, as it was an important step in releasing his hold on me. I had been considering it ever since our visit to the Grandmother's rock. In the end, I have had to admit Bompa was wrong about a great many things.

Priestess and Big Bonnie stood together looking into the fire for a long time—looking into the unknown of a future free from Bompa's strong influence. We don't have to do what he says or try to please him anymore. Or keep his secrets. However, we can enjoy this moment together—the light of the fire against the dark sky, the cold air and burning heat, the stars and trees surrounding us, the sound of the gurgling stream just down the hill.

Sensing my altered state, Mari drove my car back to the retreat center. Quite uncharacteristically, Priestess decided to explain to her new friend what had happened. "Bompa is dead. He's in the fire. I don't have to carry him around anymore. I burned away the heavy energy in the fire. But the love part was confusing and made it hard. Thank you for driving the car."

"Thank you for talking to me," Mari responded. "I think you show a lot of courage."

"Yes, I do. But I don't like being here, and I'm leaving now." Priestess did not spend more time out in the body, but she was very present inside during the rest of the retreat.

As Jorge Luis discussed unity, it made sense to Priestess as a way to co-exist and still respect the roles each alter was playing now and had played over time. She helped other internal skeptics see that unity simply means knowing about each other and working collaboratively with each other, not going away or becoming an invisible part of a "onesie."

The concept of collaboration played a large role in our professional life, but when Julia had suggested similar internal work to the strong-willed Priestess, she had been reluctant to see its value. However, with Jorge Luis's guidance, Priestess felt it grow organically. As within, so without, as we were learning.

ONE HIGHLY ANTICIPATED EVENT of the retreat at Mt. Shasta was a gong concert to demonstrate the healing nature of sound. Or

AN APPARENTLY NORMAL PERSON

rather, I should say it was eagerly anticipated by those who knew of this musician and his healing work. Mari and I, on the other hand, had never heard of him and didn't know what to expect.

After dinner, everyone brought blankets and pillows into the meeting room, which contained dozens of gongs of all sizes. We all settled in comfortably on the floor, the lights dimmed, and he began to play.

Almost immediately, my body felt the sound waves swoosh through it, like during the old experiments. Some made my legs jump right up off the floor, others assaulted my ears and caused them to itch painfully, still others made my eyes water, as if I were terribly allergic to something. My conscious mind tried to remind my body, *These sensations connect to things that happened many years ago, not to what's happening now in this peaceful place. If we let them come, feel the memories, and release them, then we might enjoy the music today.* But the body had been hijacked by the old trauma response. Any possibility of listening to the mind was shut down.

Big Bonnie felt robbed and embarrassed. It was painful to acknowledge the deep vulnerability. I couldn't tolerate these sounds. Something so uplifting to everyone else in the room was torturous to me. Intellectually, I knew I was safe here, but that made no difference to the body. I could hardly call it *my* body, since I was no longer in control. Defeated, I bundled up my belongings and limped back to my room, leaving the concert to those who could enjoy it.

The gong musician stayed with us the next day, joining in our ceremonies. He had a peaceful demeanor and seemed likable and knowledgeable, so I engaged him in conversation to see what I might learn about the healing possibilities of sound. Royal Rife's work was familiar to him, and he expressed compassion about how it had affected me. He urged me to write about it and to continue my healing work, not only for myself, but for my grandfather and my grandchildren's children—echoes of the indigenous teachings.

THE NEXT DAY, at the river, Big Bonnie focused on the cleansing and healing ceremonies, letting the water wash metaphorically through me. The churning of the white water cleansed my energy at the center of my being as it passed through.

Having cleansed ourselves—Priestess with fire and Big Bonnie with water—we went up onto the mountain the next day for a wind ceremony. Here, Purple Lady became fully engaged for the first time. She had previously created an internal "golden circle," where she welcomed each alter as they came to know their story and chose to join with others to find new ways to be together. Purple Lady experienced the wind ceremony as joyous and open and made the following notes as she came away.

> *I need not hold the circle so tightly anymore. It belongs to all of us and to none of us and is part of the great golden light that grows as we open to it. Today and this moment are our gifts. This is why we survived. Now it is time to let go—open to oneness outside and oneness inside. As within, so without. As above, so below. The necessity for separateness is no longer strong. Humor, joy, love—many gifts. Joyous faces show me the gift I can bring as we come together—the light that shines from inside.*

Purple Lady's peaceful, spiritual presence began to shine through the eyes and support the outside life in new ways, always seeking harmony and connection.

During the final ritual of the retreat, Big Bonnie, Priestess and Purple Lady all stood together in the small ceremonial circle at the center of the big ring of celebrants. We repeated the affirmation. "I accept unity with gratitude and love in the center of the circle of circles, open, expansive, luminous."

BACK HOME, we hung a picture of Mt. Shasta, with her three cones and uneven surface, on our wall to symbolize unity. And at our altar, we added to our morning ritual the intention of living in unity with gratitude.

I noted some thoughts about the retreat's impact in my journal:

> I seem to have brought home an open and joyous center that's cleaner, less cluttered. Internal disharmony is greatly diminished, and everything feels less compartmentalized. I hear and sense a difference in the quality of my voice, a groundedness and clarity.
>
> Purple Lady feels freed up to play a different, closer-to-the-surface role, allowing her kind, peaceful nature and great equilibrium to show through.

The deep connection to the mountain, river and trees followed us home. The site on the mountain where we celebrated the wind ceremony became a favorite meditation place whenever we were in Northern California. It's also our go-to spot to visit mentally during guided meditations. Once again, ancient spiritual wisdom, offered in conjunction with Pachamama's powerful natural energy, created a healing environment that allowed me to release old fears and become open to new connections.

I felt like our healing work, both in Sedona and Mt. Shasta, had laid a solid foundation for the next phase of my journey. But releasing the past comes with losses that must be grieved. My path would still prove to be full of twists and turns, rather than a linear one.

Chapter 27
Losses and Grief

On the second morning of 2011, I sat alone with my journal in the king-sized bed Wayne and I had owned since we bought our first home in 1975 in Tallahassee. A friend with far better taste than ours had nudged us to invest in a beautiful, midcentury modern, dark-wood bedroom set. It had served our family well through years of breakfast-in-bed birthdays, Mother's Days, and Father's Days. The expansive wall facing me in my condo held the icons of my healing adventures, while the sliding glass doors on my left opened onto the patio to let in the comfort of Southern California's sunny morning light.

I had been mildly ill and hadn't worked between Christmas and New Year. It's hard to tell how much of that was an internal need to slow down and reflect, and how much was actually a bug. Either way, for the first time in memory, I had not partaken in Pasadena's special form of New Year's celebration, the annual Tournament of Roses parade. However, living near the Rose Bowl, I still maintained one tradition by providing a warming lunch to a family group of six as they transitioned from the parade to the game. Otherwise, I spent the holiday alone.

Looking across the room, I played with the right language to describe the journey chronicled in the photographs on my wall. After a while, I settled on the following:

> This is how we put ourself together for the first time in our life, drawing on the mind, body, spirit and nature connections of indigenous peoples in places of natural wonder and potent energy.

I couldn't make sense of the healing process that engaged so much of my life on a daily or weekly basis, but this statement helped articulate the last five years. Retreats in four special places had empowered the symbolized progression: Peru awakened our feminine energy and ownership of our own power; Uluru enabled us to more comfortably express our masculine energy; Sedona fostered a balance between the two; and at Mt. Shasta, we found unity within and without, with gratitude and love.

I noted these were all places made by the forces that formed the earth, not creations of man. They joined in healing a being splintered by human manipulation, helping to reconnect the natural being—the spirit born into this body—to itself and to wholeness. The essential energy of each of these places bonded directly with my own.

My travels had, of course, been interspersed with countless hours of skillful therapy, lots of hard work, and many days of questioning everything. How could this all be possible? Where is it leading, and why did it have to be so hard? Even as shared experiences and memories grew inside, I felt a sense of loss alongside the new unity—grief for the brave parts who had helped us survive and thrive over the years, who now found their skills no longer needed. Each was so tired that, having mustered the courage to come forward, they weren't sure what to do now that they no longer needed to stand ready to deal with impossible demands.

Julia provoked us by suggesting neither I nor any of my internal family had ever learned to grieve in a healthy manner. She encouraged me to allow a recognition of each loss, each betrayal, each splintered humiliation. I felt permission to grieve. Sitting alone in a bed full of family memories, both the precious moments and the losses flooded in. I could almost smell the warm croissants, fresh coffee, and children's morning breath that had filled this bed for many years and would do so no more.

I knew my kids were supposed to grow and leave the family nest, and as much as I missed them, I cherished a close relationship and frequent visits with each one. But an empty nest is still an empty nest. And I had lost the nest along with the chicks. I missed our wonderful century-old home, built in Pasadena's popular Arts and Crafts style, with fruit trees, a pool and ample room for parties and celebrations, inside or out. I missed our heterogeneous neighborhood, where we all babysat, house-sat and dog-sat for each other and created a communal nest that helped our families flourish.

And my partner? Weren't we supposed to age together into that cute old couple holding hands in the park? Why am I going through all this alone? I still didn't understand what had happened to what had been a mutually supportive life partnership. Having once had it, I felt doubly alone without it.

At the same time, the sense of loss continued in my professional world. A colleague who had become a trusted friend was subjected to a political hatchet job and was hounded out of her position and my daily orbit. I had witnessed such painful unfairness before, but her loss struck a much deeper chord. Back in Washington, DC, while working for the governor of Florida, I had served on a child welfare reform task force that contributed to the landmark legislation that became the Adoption Assistance and Child Welfare Act of 1980 (Public Law 96-272). Jimmy Carter signed it into law just five months before losing his bid for re-election.

His successor, Ronald Reagan, intent on proving his belief that "government is the problem, not the solution," proceeded to implement the letter of the law while stripping out the budget for services to support vulnerable families that the law was predicated upon. Predictably, within a few years, the number of children in foster care skyrocketed, but that basic breach of trust was never remedied. Instead, the government warriors trying to keep children safe and families together were singled out as the problem and scapegoated all over the country. It's always been far easier for short-sighted politicians to blame the people than to fix the system. My friend was just the latest example, and the closest to me. Had nothing I worked for all these years made any difference at all? The resounding answer that morning was, "I guess not."

Who goes through three layoffs during their fifties? I had come to terms with the fact that what matters is the work, not the job, and I had been able to continue what I was doing for children and families. But each change disrupted relationships, and I wasn't very good at maintaining them, especially given the intense time commitment of my healing work. So, my friendship circle shrank, first after the divorce, then after each work disruption.

Let go of the way we were, so we can make room for the changes needed to go forward peacefully, came the internal voice. Was that you, Purple Lady? *So many options, so much potential if we can accept the loss and grieve those people and things that cannot take the journey into the future with us. Then we can move ahead with excitement to see what it will be like when no one internally needs to hold old pain or sadness or anger anymore, when stories are safe enough to share both internally and externally.* A deep, cleansing, peaceful breath went through the whole internal community as we realized we could happily release fear and separateness to come together and celebrate our connections. At last, we were safe enough and strong enough and unified enough that no one needed to be alone or scared anymore.

My little pity party at an end, I reveled in joyful serenity at the achievement of a state where *no one needed to be alone or scared anymore.* It felt like we were finally finished with this long, painful process. Now we could consolidate all we'd learned.

As USUAL, I didn't know what I didn't know. The welcome sense of safety provided just the opening for yet more deeply hidden secrets, body memories, and fear to come forward over the next year.

While the oblivious Big Bonnie maintained a busy external work and travel schedule in 2011, our journal chronicled a new and sporadic constellation of symptoms: burning, watery eyes that sometimes puffed up and became hard to open; draining, itchy ears; and hip and leg pain. Stranger still was a thing we called the "sleepies." I could be in the middle of writing or talking (usually trying to figure out some new aspect of the story or the meaning of a new symptom) and suddenly become so sleepy I couldn't keep my eyes open.

At Julia's suggestion, I checked in with my trusted primary care physician, Dr. Miller, who found no medical cause for these new symptoms and left us to figure them out in therapy. However, that visit to her office added an interesting piece of new information. As I waited in her exam room, lying on the table wearing a simple cotton hospital gown, I felt agitation grow inside—jumpy nerves with butterflies and even a little nausea. I wondered out loud why anyone inside would be nervous waiting for this doctor we knew and loved.

"This looks a lot like the white room," came the response, but I couldn't tell from whom.

With hindsight and the detailed journals, it's easy to see these symptoms escalated during the second half of the year, even as my denial and amnesia carried on strong. Day to day, week to week, I treated the physical symptoms as minor, unconnected irritants to be overcome or endured with grace rather than as pieces of the puzzle of my life.

Chapter 28
A Celebration of Oneness

In November 2011, I fulfilled a wish on my bucket list by float-ing over the Sedona landscape in a hot-air balloon with several friends to celebrate my sixty-fifth birthday. We had a time-share for a week, where six of us played, ate, meditated and held ceremonies to open ourselves to the next phase of life, to celebrate our friendships, and to sit in humble gratitude for all of nature's plenty.

At 11:11 a.m. on 11/11/11, we were not where we had planned to be, but we were where we were. We stopped in the open desert and celebrated an impromptu ceremony on the day of the ones at the time of the ones, honoring the oneness of all people and the universe. As within, so without.

For the first time in my life, I spent an entire week with friends, including my sister Mary, with whom it was safe to be completely open and fluid about all of who I was and what I was experiencing. At my wonderful sixtieth birthday party, only Big Bonnie was allowed to be out. But this time, my friends already knew and loved several alters, especially joyous Jane. They accepted us just as we showed up, whoever showed up. We celebrated not only our birthday but also the ability to be co-conscious without fear.

This trip came directly on the heels of a child welfare leadership symposium I chaired on behalf of the foundation I worked for. We had invited experts and local leaders to explore new neuroscience research related to the impact of trauma on a child's developing brain, the burgeoning field of trauma-informed practice, and needed improvements in child welfare policy. My work put me in a position to help others learn from the latest research and then make connections between what we know and what we need to do to support families and children. Such a blessing!

During a pause in the action, while others were in breakout sessions, I sat quietly with our keynote speaker, the brilliant and personable Harvard researcher Dr. Jack Shonkoff. I asked him the same question I had asked every researcher I came in contact with. "What do we know about how dissociation works? Is it possibly some sort of protective factor for the developing brain?" Maybe he could help in my search for answers about how I could be a smart and productive professional, given the assaults on my developing young body and brain. I had read there are many of us who are highly functional in the world, despite—or maybe because of—a dissociative disorder.

Dr. Shonkoff was brief in his immediate response, saying with a twinkle in his eye, "I love this type of question because I actually have a clear answer. I don't have a clue!"

This was essentially the same response I received from every researcher I had queried. Again, I was left with the dissonance between the *science* that says early trauma impedes full development of the brain and a *life* that had been lived as a high-achieving, multilingual, glass-ceiling-breaking professional with solid relationships, a loving family, and a master's degree.

Chapter 29
The Base

After spending Thanksgiving 2011 with my children and grand-children, I returned home with the usual cold, but this one developed into a rotten flu that kept me down for two weeks. While the flu was very real, I also understood that my internal system was signaling a need for downtime to process new information. What-ever was opening up was somehow connected to these painful eye and ear symptoms, and to some place they called "the base," which they now saw as the location of the mysterious white room.

One day, while surfing the internet for research on dissociation, I happened upon a description of mind control experimentation run by the US government during the Cold War—a secret CIA program called MKULTRA. As I read about what they did to people, my body resonated powerfully, as if to say, "This connects with the symptoms and flashbacks we've been experiencing."

The next day in the Green Room, Julia asked what that had felt like inside. Slowly, and with help from Jane, a shy new girl made her way forward to talk with Julia. We were wearing green sweats and the rug in the Green Room was a similarly deep hunter green. The new girl asked if she could use the green pen as her color in the journal. She wanted to figure out who she was and what her role was, both now and back then.

"I don't even have a name," she complained.

"Would you like to give yourself a name?" Julia offered.

The girl thought for a while. "I'll be Carol. Aunt Carol was always nice to me."

As she talked and remembered, I could feel lots of smaller voices around her, frightened shards filled with horror. The whole body suddenly felt immobilized and heavy, with legs twitching.

"This is what it felt like after the experiments," Carol quietly told Julia.

Experiments? What experiments? Big Bonnie was close enough to the surface to hear and wonder. Had the body again remembered something my conscious mind knew nothing about? This wasn't like at Bompa's, but I recognized the feeling in the legs as very similar to what I felt when I first got sick.

I didn't want to overshadow her, but I did want to talk directly with this new person who sat there with me on the green couch, so I came forward enough to say out loud, "A lot of us are really interested in what happened to you. We want you to feel safe because we have learned that once you share what happened a long time ago, it loses its power to make us feel bad anymore. We all want to help you tell your story so we will know what you and your other parts lived through. And I promise whatever they did to you won't ever happen again." Deep down, I could feel Carol's certainty that no one could make good on such a promise.

A surge of paranoia dominated the next few days. No matter what Julia or Big Bonnie said, the mind was gripped with fear that some ill-defined "they" could, and would, still "get us."

Carol used her green pen to express her fears and questions in the journal.

Someone could come and take me away and put us in a room and do those same kinds of things to us—to this body. That could happen. Now we are scared and can't breathe.

It does happen. People do disappear, even today. Will I disappear if my story is told?

A stranger might come and give me a shot in my arm and then take me away.

Are they still following and watching me? Or is the fear all inside me?

Who were the people and what was "the base"?

The morning paper carried news of a child kidnapping, which made her point. Her fear resonated with me. I'm still not comfortable in dark or crowded places, like movie theaters, where a stranger could sit next to me, inject poison or sedatives into my arm, and drag me away unnoticed.

I realized Carol and I shared several fears. But, of course, that made sense! We were both housed in the same body.

Was there any possibility that whatever had happened to Carol was part of the secret mind control projects in that article that had felt so familiar? I found a website for survivors of the MKULTRA experiments and considered joining it to get more information; perhaps a list of any local projects. But Carol didn't feel safe doing that. Her deep concern filled the body with tension. If someone found out we were on that website, they would come and get us.

In typical ANP fashion, I didn't take any of this too seriously as I attempted to move on with my life. But the scratchy, draining eyes developed into conjunctivitis, canceling an eagerly anticipated trip to spend Christmas with my son and grandchildren. I felt terribly disappointed not to be with the kids for the holiday, but I had to admit I was exhausted and relished the time alone at home. After all, I had just seen them at Thanksgiving. The energy to spend another week in controlled Oma-mode was just more than my system could muster.

When I did try to learn what I could from the internet about these government mind control projects, I found myself falling asleep as I read. I couldn't stay focused. Eventually, I tried reasoning.

"It would be so helpful if we had just a little more of the story from those years after Bompa died and some idea of what happened at the base—wherever that was." But clearly, someone (or several some-ones) was intent on making it very difficult for Big Bonnie to read about the experiments.

I knew, and tried to convince the others inside, that as long as someone thinks something has to remain secret and hidden, we will have body symptoms. But why were the eyes being affected? What was the message? Was there something I wasn't supposed to see? Or didn't want to see? Or, heaven forbid, did they do experiments on my eyes?

The symptoms continued unabated as my frustration grew. Why couldn't I just get well and feel good again permanently? There can't be much more story to reveal.

Part 6
The Door for Dying

Chapter 30
Riptides

The whole world seemed to know 2012 was destined to be a pivotal year. Movies and Western popular culture misrepresented and exploited the ancient prophecies and the shift in the Mayan calendar with scenes of doom and apocalypse. But to Mayans and many others, prophecy foretold major energetic and spiritual changes would usher in a new era of peace, compassion and love.

Before I could immerse myself in that shift at the winter solstice, I first had to face Joseph Campbell's metaphorical "supreme ordeal" in my hero's journey. As Campbell warned, to move forward, I had to let go of even more of what had always seemed so important—my work and professional life, my mother, and any remaining innocence or illusions. Letting go and opening up always come together, and they bring their friends, pain and grief, on the road to growth and healing.

The year started with what seemed, at the time, a capricious but fairly harmless request by my new supervisor. I had been working forty-hour weeks or more on a four-day schedule since 2008, which gave me three days for therapy, a few coaching clients, and a much-needed respite from the internal work of maintaining the outer professional persona (although I wasn't much aware of this third element). But now, without warning or explanation, my boss asserted this was no longer possible. I would need to be in the office five days a week. My original supervisors had moved on to different jobs and, although I had received a promotion in the process, I no longer felt safe being transparent about my ongoing mental health issues. Besides, everything was going so well… Surely this wouldn't upset anything.

I only had a couple of coaching clients at the time, and they were easily moved to evening or weekend appointments. So, with only mild pushback, I accommodated my supervisor's unexplained requirements, moved my therapy appointments to evenings and showed up in the office five days a week. I wish I could say this was accompanied by a decrease in hours worked each day, but old habits die hard.

Soon after I made this accommodation, other rule changes and sudden shifts in expectations followed. Why was so much changing? I loved my work and hoped to continue to contribute for a few more years, which would also help me build my savings before retiring.

So, I set about using my supervisor's unpredictability and negative energy as a test of my growth in the art of controlling my responses without resorting to the old dissociative techniques. I practiced staying calm in the middle of the drama and worked to respond to perceived attacks without fear, but with compassion. She must have been under a lot of pressure.

That worked pretty well on the outside, but inside, a very different response unfolded. Soon, whenever I needed to interact with her, my breathing tightened and my blood ran hot, like boiling oil coursing through my veins.

Thanks to all my reading about the physical impact of trauma, and with Julia's help, I understood this as stress hormones (like cortisol) being unleashed while, deep inside, my nervous system went into its learned trauma response mode. Even though nothing happening in the here and now warranted this panicked response, there it was. Where did it come from, and what was it related to? Why did I feel such strong revulsion every time I saw my supervisor smooth her hair to the side, as she did so often? Why had the body begun again to exhibit barely manageable physical symptoms, including more itchy, painful, draining ears and scratchy, swollen eyes?

I began to see things that were only visible to me: a menacing, large, black bird watching me from a perch on the ficus bush just outside my big office windows; creepy black lizards and desert bugs that scampered across my floor. As I sat at my conference table with a colleague, a black cloak suddenly appeared around her shoulders, taking my breath away and ending the meeting abruptly.

These new symptoms bled into my interactions with others in ways I could no longer conceal. On several occasions, I did not recognize people I knew. I met and talked with one woman three times over a period of a couple of weeks, and each time, until she reminded me, I did not know who she was or that we had ever met before. So embarrassing and unprofessional! This had to stop.

In the Green Room, the radical idea arose that perhaps we no longer needed to use external demands as our motivation to hold ourselves together. Maybe healing and wholeness would be better served if internal needs and commitments became as important as the external ones had always been? A life-altering thought, indeed. But as these weird symptoms encroached more and more on my ability to function at work, I began to get the message. Why were they getting this strong now? Which scary old memories was my supervisor's behavior triggering? What messages hid in these hallucinations?

For the first time in more than ten years, I began a daily log, trying to see patterns in the symptoms and rushes of cortisol. But I couldn't make sense of it. I just wanted it all to go away.

Both Julia and Dr. Miller became concerned as symptoms I kept trying to downplay continued to escalate. They urged me to take short-term leave—a couple of months away from my job—to do the deep work necessary to find some answers. That in itself felt really scary because the only diagnosis I had now was DDNOS. For the first time, they wanted me to admit to the world that I had a mental health condition that interfered with my work.

In response to my concerns, my doctors pointed out the obvious. For some reason, my internal community was not willing to keep Big Bonnie functioning out in the work world as it always had. We needed to find out why. When it seemed there was no other way, I finally agreed and requested medical leave, knowing I had some protections despite not invoking the Americans with Disabilities Act.

Julia urged me to set aside some time of "extraordinary stillness," when I could let go of all other worries. But life had other plans.

How is it that challenges so often come in bunches? As soon as I left work to try to find relief from my internal mysteries, a series of family crises intervened. To be worthy of Campbell's supreme ordeal, I guess mine had to be multifaceted.

First, within a week, my ninety-four-year-old mother began to fail quickly. All our younger siblings were busy working, so I spent as much time as I could with her to help Peter, who had lived with and cared for her for fifteen years. He could not bring himself to face the fact she was dying. So, with his tacit acceptance and that of our other siblings, it fell to me to make the difficult and necessary call that brought in a hospice team to help us all prepare for her transition.

That same afternoon, while we waited for hospice to make a first visit, I got a series of disjointed phone calls from my daughter and learned, while pacing Peter's beautifully manicured back lawn to improve cellular reception, that Beth, who was traveling with friends in Thailand, had been attacked in Bangkok. Some random man passing her on a street corner had thrown acid in her face. A passing cab driver heard her screams and took her to the police and then the hospital for emergency care. Now, she was trying to connect with her mom, who was having immensely frustrating phone issues while tending to her dying mother and waiting for the hospice nurse.

The next morning, we were finally able to arrange a Skype call, and my anxiety was greatly relieved to see that her face had been burned but not disfigured by the acid. She was deeply shaken but felt she had received good care in the Bangkok hospital. At her request, I got compassionate cooperation from the airline so she could fly home the next day.

In the midst of everything, I was thrilled to know that my space and our relationship were where she wanted to be. She didn't need the details to know I had found a healing path that felt safe for her. Everyone internally agreed and felt affirmed in how we had handled the relationship. Her needs would complicate how we used the time off work, but so did Mother's condition, and right now, they came first.

Beth's physical injuries turned out to be superficial enough that they healed well and quickly. My doctors said the Thai emergency care had been excellent. Her ever-present water bottle, with which she immediately began rinsing off her face, combined with the good medical care and the protection her glasses offered, saved her sight and her looks. I arranged for her see a therapist who specialized in the immediate aftermath of trauma to help her cope emotionally with the randomness of this act of violence. In a lovely case of serendipity, Beth's healing coincided with her grandmother's dying and allowed her to be present for the last two weeks of her grandmother's life.

Mother died peacefully at home in her own bed, having said a lucid goodbye to each of her seven children and many of her two dozen grandchildren. She had an amazing ability to see the uniqueness of each person, and every one of us felt special to her. She told me she was glad I "saw all of" her and had forgiven her mistakes. I knew this was hyperbole, but I also understood she had been unusually open with me about her fears, her experiences, and even her faults. I had a nagging sense though that we would never know what stories she had chosen not to reveal.

For my part, of course, I kept busy. She had entrusted to me several pages of last wishes and plans for her service that I needed to implement. I was sad she was gone, but glad the end had come quickly and without great pain. I felt compassion for her, without condoning the acts of omission and commission that had left me so vulnerable and unprotected as a child. And I held space for the traumatic experiences that had warped her life. Still, grieving her death would prove complicated.

Will and his family, who had visited to say goodbye to her a couple of months earlier, came for the funeral. But he had to get back home to Oregon for surgery to correct a very painful, chronic gastrointestinal condition. Because of the grandchildren, I was always in Oma-mode when I was with him and his family, and we had only a limited opportunity to talk about what I was going through. Even so, I always felt his interest and support. His worrisome pain and gut issues had defied diagnosis for almost a decade, and we all hoped this surgery would help.

EVEN WITH ALL THIS GOING ON, I knew I had to maintain my commitment to seeing Julia three times a week during my leave. On the outside, I seemed in control, functioning as the eldest daughter, sister, mom and Oma, helping others through difficult times. I later wrote the following memory of this period.

> My internal system held back the expected onslaught of symptoms, flashbacks and memories, so Big Bonnie, with a new level of internal unity, compassion and spiritual centeredness, could be present with the external family. I was remarkably symptom-free during the first month of my leave, so I could be present for my children and grieve with my family as we watched Mother die and planned her funeral.

Talk about rose-colored glasses! That may be the picture I remembered, and it probably is how most people saw me, but our journal reveals quite a different reality.

In the Green Room, Carol, George and Jane continued to help little shards of memory without name or voice explore painful, scary experiences at this place they remembered as "the base." They didn't put much detail in the journal, except to note the difficulty breathing, or the shooting pain on the right side of the head, or the burning, watery eyes and itchy skin.

They also processed with their Lady Doctor all that was going on around us in the outer family, and on that topic, some chose to express themselves in the journal.

George wrote about Mother's death:

Sadness for her and because of her. Her father was bad to her, and her husband was bad to us. Both not protected, even though I tried. What did I think I could do? Children can't really protect adults, can they?

Another strong part (later identified as BJ) was furious with Mother for not protecting her oldest little girl. BJ wrote a eulogy of sorts for her.

Don't like hearing all the stuff about how loving she was—what a wonderful woman—all that, with no mention that she felt she was "less than" and damaged. Molested or fondled by her father, raped twice as a young woman, never felt pretty or smart enough as a little girl, so had to work hard to be the one her mother could turn to for sewing clothes, cleaning and caring for her sick sister, and trying to protect her father by hiding his drunken messes from her mother. Then marrying a dashing, exciting alcoholic with a totally crazy family. Using her second child the same way she had been used—or so she thought. This precocious little girl can manage okay if I use her to keep the crazy mother-in-law occupied, so she leaves the rest of the family alone—especially if she'll like me better and not be so mean. It worked—so why try to figure out what was going on when they took the child so often?

Why worry about the strange noises late at night or why the husband sometimes passed out on the floor in the den, half undressed?

And the father-in-law! Such a sweet, kind man—brilliant doctor—no worries about letting him take such an interest in the girl, even if she sometimes doesn't want to go.

Someone else picked up the black pen and scrawled in big, thick letters:

I HATE HER! I HATE HER!

If she had done her job of protecting her oldest daughter better, there wouldn't be an us—a we—we wouldn't have needed to figure out ways to protect ourself—even if they didn't really protect—just gave us ways of surviving so it didn't hurt so much.

Not sure how to handle all these emotions, Big Bonnie requested help from Priestess. *You have held a lot of anger—helping us all to process it, being the strong one who would not be consumed by it. How shall we proceed now?*

Priestess responded in her distinctive orange block printing:

Let us ask... Who do you hate? Not the old lady who died. The mother in the picture. The beautiful blonde. Do you hate her? No—You want to be beautiful like her—But you can't, so you must protect her. And you did. So, who should we hate?

Yes, what we hate is when people only talk about one part of her, when there are many things that are true about her. She did not protect her oldest daughter. She married an alcoholic and then worked to cover up the impact of his drinking, like she learned from her father. She was beautiful and smart.

She was strong and did what she needed to do to survive and to build the picture of the life she wanted. And eventually, she got the life she wanted, with many grandchildren and enough money to be generous and buy lots of gifts. And seven children who were good to her.

She got most of what she wanted out of life, it looks like. Hard to know who to be angry with now. Angry about what happened then, and at her back then.

I reflected on the baroness's story I had read the night before my body first began to speak so loudly. These voices inside felt every bit as abandoned by their mother as the baby who was passed through that fence. And now Mother was dead. Dead, without ever acknowledging her culpability for what had happened.

Thanks to Julia's incredible skill and the amazing cooperation from our internal community, we managed to get through that first month of leave from work with minimal disruption to the outer picture of an apparently normal, supportive sister and mother. Yet all the while, we were exploding internally with emotions that, at least for the moment, overshadowed the horrific secrets the body was getting ready to divulge.

As if this weren't enough, a new set of flashbacks showed us what happened in the fearful place we had come to know as the "white room." The sensations of terrible body-torquing electric shocks and of sounds that shook everything and scrambled the head were not accompanied by any context.

Blessedly, these flashbacks erupted in the Green Room, where they could be contained, if not fully understood.

Chapter 31
The White Room

Once things outside quieted down, I sequestered myself for several hours a day with a papered wall for drawing pictures. With Julia's help, we created safe places in our mind where parts could huddle together and feel comfortable. Another long process of piecing things together had begun. We saw Julia every other day so she and Carol could help each small fragment release body sensations, heavy emotions, and visual memories.

Some of the physical sensations were similar to those from Bompa's garage room, but more severe: electric shocks that torqued and twisted the body; something poking the eyes that made them scratchy, watery and painful; and big sounds that rumbled through the body, causing it to shake and shut down. These memories lay hidden behind much stronger barriers of amnesia and mind control than earlier memories had been. But why? Who put them in place? All we knew at this point was that the people wore uniforms.

In the meantime, Carol and George insisted we read back over our binders full of journals from the previous decade. Our task was to identify early memories that didn't make sense at the time but now might fit with what we had learned since.

As we read, we noticed a pattern. Every time the "white room" arose in flashbacks, something seemingly disconnected—often related to suicide—distracted us from attempts to understand what and where it was. Now, Carol connected these old flashbacks to more recent information and produced a narrative that filled the gaps between Bompa's death and the twelve-year-old with her pills.

While Bompa's experiments were still going on in the room behind the garage, a man who wore a grey coat began to visit. Then, one time, two men with thick German accents came, and we helped Bompa show off our skills for them. After that, Bompa took me to some kind of military place to let them test me using his mind control methods. Those three men were all there.

After Bompa died, the man with the grey coat (who, George reminded us, did not always wear his grey coat; that just became a way of identifying him) came to Bompa's house in a big black car and packed up all of Bompa's machines and research notebooks from the room behind the garage. He took them and me and my Uncle Dick to some big place where the air was very bad and hurt my eyes.

As far as I know, I never saw the man in the grey coat again, but I sure wish I could find him and get Bompa's notebooks back!

After that, my Uncle Dick or Aunt Carol began regularly (maybe four times a year or more) taking me to a different place, which was on the other side of the mountains, possibly somewhere near Palmdale, where they lived. I only knew it as "the base," and the ladies who greeted me as I walked alone into the big front room of the low, drab building wore blue uniforms.

I was eight when we started going there, and the ladies looked glamorous and welcoming, like Pan Am stewardesses. The "white room" was sort of like a doctor's examining room. The Blue Ladies helped me change clothes and put my things in a locker in the hallway.

People in white coats took over once I was in the white room. Sometimes, they gave me medicine in apple juice, or pills, or shots, to get ready for the "testing rooms." That's where the awful experiments happened, with teams of doctors and attendants. We recognized how their actions connected directly to the physical symptoms and scary memories that had been coming out in flashbacks for so long. We had to layer off the experiences, creating little pieces of memory that the outside girl would not feel or remember. Maybe this was the skill they (whoever "they" were) wanted to test and understand, or replicate, or deepen, or something...

We would need the full attention of everyone in the internal community to learn enough about the awful events at the base to face, release and heal from them. No matter how unbelievable and surreal it all sounded, to heal, we had to honor both the physical sensations stored in the body and the perspective of each traumatized fragment of the little girl's mind.

In the process, we found explanations for many mysteries. For example, we recognized the weakness in my legs—specifically, the spongy, watery feeling in my calves, so central to the early symptoms that left me barely able to walk—as the body's memory of what those same legs felt like after experiments with electric currents coursing through their muscles. Likewise, the strange and disorienting waves that whooshed through my head were body memories of experiments with sound waves and radio frequencies.

Oddest of all, the way my current work supervisor habitually stroked and smoothed her hair resembled the mannerisms of a woman at the base. Even though that woman looked nothing like my supervisor and I had no conscious memory of her, seeing that behavior day after day over several months helped jar loose the context of this whole set of confusing physical and emotional symptoms. The fact that I suddenly perceived my supervisor as unpredictable, capricious and punitive also proved immensely helpful, for these were also traits of the woman at the base whom we now needed to remember—a woman Carol called "the Brown Lady."

This woman was large and dressed in a dark brown suit. She sat at a wooden desk in her room, which was bigger than the others. After they completed the tests or experiments, I was left alone, strapped to my rolling bed in the hall. Then someone would come with my clothes and take me to the Brown Lady's room, where she asked me questions from the papers on her desk while writing on a clipboard. She wasn't friendly and didn't smile. She wore her dark hair in a pageboy cut and often stroked it on the side and plumped the curl from the bottom.

She might ask, for example, whether I remembered the numbers or figures that were on the ceiling in the room where I was just tested. Or she would ask about things I might have seen in the first big room—like how many desks there were and what was on them, or how many people were wearing this or that uniform. I was anxious about getting the answers to her questions right, to prove both how smart Bompa was and how well I had done. But my training with Bompa had always been about *not* remembering anything that happened, while she wanted me to tell her what I did remember.

This was very confusing and scary, and I never knew what the right answers were supposed to be. Her big, square-shaped body reminded me of Munner, and memories of Munner's periodic rage at wrong answers added to my fear. The Brown Lady made me feel very little, frightened and vulnerable on the inside, but only the stoic, determined and controlled girl showed on the outside.

A big screen hung on one wall in her room, behind a wooden railing. Sometimes, she would come out from behind her desk to sit at a projector and flash slides of numbers, shapes, maps or pictures on the screen. She sat right next to me, and I could hear the fearful *click-click* of the slides being shifted into place in the projector. The maps and pictures may have been places shown to me during the experiments. I was supposed to identify the map that went with the picture of the place.

If I didn't get it right, she would yell at me that I was a stupid child. But I was never sure how she defined right. She would say things like, "You stupid little girl. You can't get this right. You aren't even trying."

But I was trying!

She had a straight, rounded stick that she used to hit me on the back of the head. Munner used to do the same thing during piano lessons, and it brought fear and confusion.

"Don't you cry!" the Brown Lady ordered. "You are useless to us if you can't even do this!" The worst possible insult, based on Bompa's training, was to be called "useless."

Some of the Brown Lady's pictures had large black birds—maybe turkey vultures—flying in the sky. To underscore her points, she yelled that those birds would be watching me and would swoop down and claw my head open, and maybe even peck out my eyes. They would be watching me to make sure I was good and didn't tell anyone about the base and what happened there. They would follow me wherever I was until I came back again—and then forever. I left her room knowing that birds with cameras in their wings would know if I ever told any of the secrets. I was obviously too stupid to be trusted to keep secrets myself without supervision.

The Brown Lady was very good at this part of her job: to make me (a child between eight and twelve years old) feel worthless, stupid, frightened and without power, to demoralize me in preparation for the final chapter in each visit to the base—time with Major Ken in the green trailer. But what happened in the green trailer with Major Ken was hidden in yet another compartment of the mind, where it was even harder for Carol, and those of us supporting her in this excavation, to access. The alters here were suspicious of everything and everyone. They gave only fleeting evidence of their existence, and for a long time, they deflected attempts to connect with them.

Major Ken had the dual job of helping the girl recover from the aftermath of whatever experiments or tests were done that day and of solidifying the mind control messages that would keep the secrets safe. He was a younger man with a nice tan, a muscular body, and a sandy-brown crewcut. When the Brown Lady finished with me, he came into her domain, they exchanged papers, and he led—or sometimes carried—me out the back door and down a short path into the green trailer where he ruled.

He had originally been known as Dr. Ken, but had apparently received a promotion sometime during our four-year relationship to become Major Ken. We remember him as being nice, even solicitous, as he sought to help us recover enough to be released without raising suspicions on the outside about what had happened at the base. His trailer had two twin beds, a messy desk, a little bathroom, a sink with a bunch of cupboards, and a cot that held the overflow of supplies from the cupboards.

He gave me medicine and let me rest until I felt well enough to get up, work with him, and then get picked up to go home. He reinforced how important it was that no one—not even Bonnie—know about the base and the work we did there. Over time, he helped make at least four closely related alters, although he may have thought they were all one.

The first two gave themselves the names "Molly" and "Mallory" when they finally came out, and the other two were "Claudia" and "Gloria," who were a little older. Each held some form of self-destruction as their imperative if they ever thought there was a chance the secrets would be revealed. They were told that if anyone ever found out I had even been to the base, my family, especially my mother and sisters, would be hurt. No other parts of Bonnie could know that anything had happened—or even that there was anything to know. It was that secret, and it had to stay secret.

And we knew the people there would somehow find out if we told anyone—either from the birds with cameras, from the men in dark hats and coats who were watching us, or in other ways.

When Major Ken was finished, there was no question I should die if the secrets might be exposed. As Carol described it, "He opened a new door—the door for dying."

Chapter 32

CanDance

Through all these horrifying revelations, I, the observing adult, marveled at the strength of the pre-adolescent girl Carol represented. How did she (together with her many smaller parts) survive all of it? What gave her the strength, the fortitude, the desire?

Part of the answer surfaced when we came into contact with an intriguing protective presence whose origin remains unclear even now. She is definitely feminine, but not exactly an alter or part, like the others. Maybe she was created in the room behind the garage, as part of a safety net against the generalized sense of danger to our existence. But she became most needed at the base, where the very soul of the place and everyone in it was drained of all kindness and empathy.

Other internal parts, including Jane and George, had to coax her to come forward and help her find her voice. When we asked her name, she called herself CanDance.

I am a good person, and I do not deserve to be hurt. As long as I survived, I knew a good person with strong values would survive to contribute to the world and that no one could destroy her. We had to maintain our core—a part that held tight and stayed no matter what else happened or how many parts had to be created to handle different things. A part that said, "I am a person. I have a soul. You can't destroy me."

Each time we got back into the car to leave the base, I knew we had won again because I was still there. They couldn't reach that part; they couldn't touch the center of our being! And now I can sleep.

She knew she was in a war and that it was up to her to make sure someone capable of being kind, honest, compassionate and loving would come out on top and go on to make a good life in the world. George protected this central core with tenacity and care.

Wow! As exquisitely complex and elegant as my internal system was, with all it had survived, it placed the highest value on maintaining a "good person" to live in the outside world. Deeply humbled, I hoped I had lived up to their standards over the years of my clueless adult life.

Chapter 33
Endings and Beginnings

B ack in the here-and-now world, my four-month leave came to an end, and I returned to work. I lasted less than three months. By November 2012, it was clear to my doctors, if not to me, that forcing myself back into a setting where the external professional demands on the ANP needed to override the internal demands of a community working to heal had become counter-productive. Even my vaunted capacity to rise above it and stay focused wasn't enough to cover the turmoil of alters in life and death struggles over which secrets could be safely told and to whom.

I went to see Dr. Miller on a Wednesday, knowing I wasn't handling things as well as I wanted to, but holding on to my usual optimism and denial. She asked how I felt. Without warning, I burst into tears, knowing I was a failure. We talked as she checked me over, and I admitted to my deep exhaustion and overwhelm. She also talked to several alters.

At the end of the visit, she declared that my health required me to stop working immediately—by Friday, if possible; by next Wednesday, at the latest. She insisted I had to accept I would not work full-time again anytime soon; not because I was a failure, but because I needed to heal. My work in the external world had proven itself no longer conducive to healing. She knew how important my professional life had always been to me, but, uncharacteristically, she left no room for discussion.

Julia helped me hear the internal voices saying, "You need to do something different now." After a lifetime of getting up and going to school or work, pushing through any pain in mind or body, they were saying, "You don't have to do that anymore. You can't." My double life could no longer remain separate. We needed more connectedness.

Leaving my job so abruptly robbed me of the chance to say goodbye to the people and work that had enriched and held together my external life. There would be no retirement celebration with colleagues telling funny stories or applauding my contributions. The organization's policy would not even let me announce I was leaving for medical reasons. They just put out a terse note that I was gone.

The last vestige of my old life was taken from me without ceremony, and I had no idea who I would be without it. I had often passed on to others the wisdom that when the Universe closes one door, it always opens another. I desperately needed that to be more than a stupid, tired cliché.

Without my dear friend Mari's encouragement, I'm pretty sure I would have sulked for a long while, mourning the door that had closed and not even noticing the unexpected opportunity the Universe offered. Both Mari and I had been looking forward to the 2012 solstice, because in the Mayan calendar, it served as a marker for the shift in global energy so many traditions' prophets had foreseen.

When the opportunity arose to join a small international group of celebrants for the solstice in Maya country, in the Yucatan, Mari insisted we grab it. A check with my internal family found some excitement and little resistance. So, in early December, Mari and I set out on a new, life-affirming adventure that allowed me to find my post-professional footing as an adventurous spiritual seeker and a grandmother with her own rock, her own truth, and a newly articulated purpose—the Holy Grail, if you will, of my hero's journey.

Chapter 34
Winter Solstice 2012
in Maya Country

In the pre-dawn glow of the winter solstice of 2012, celebrants filed out of the LOL BE Mayan Cultural Center near Chichén Itzá, Mexico, in orderly rows, to gather at an outdoor altar. The chilly air made me glad we were packed in so close together. Mostly dressed in white, we sat cradled by Pachamama to await the first sun of the new era. I recognized at least six languages being spoken around me, but knew the two to three hundred of us gathered there represented the whole globe.

In the processional, I'd gotten separated from Mari and sat among people I'd never met, feeling immediate kinship. That was the point, wasn't it? That was why we'd all come from the four corners—to celebrate our oneness, our connections, and to welcome, with our Mayan sisters and brothers, the beginning of their new calendar symbolizing unity. Most important to the Maya, it was a time for introspection and recommitment to each other and to Mother Earth.

A reverent hush held the group together. This was *the* solstice I had been looking forward to since my first trip to Peru in 2006—the apex of the period of energetic transition. People all over the world were bringing the prophecies to life in their communities, and here I sat, in the heart of Maya country at this pivotal moment.

I deeply needed my little life and struggles to be connected to something larger than myself. And here I was, celebrating cosmic forces that connected my healing work to the breaking of global cycles of violence, fear and patriarchy. The Mexican government, in its wisdom, had forbidden ceremonies at this auspicious time at any of the ancient Mayan temples or shrines created for these purposes. Therefore, people gathered in other locations, such as this private cultural center on a large plot of land in the countryside a few miles from Chichén Itzá.

Mari and I had traveled with a group of twenty pilgrims from the US and Europe during the week prior to the solstice to celebrate and explore several of the ancient Mayan cities. Our preparation focused on opening our hearts, acting with love, and releasing historical pain, so we could embrace the new consciousness, the new era.

Signs and billboards all over this part of Mexico urged everyone to *prepárate a renovar tu mente*. I mused I had been "renovating my mind" for a long time, and together with my internal community, I felt absolute joy at being there to celebrate with love and without fear.

I also relished the chance to speak three languages each day, given our multilingual traveling companions. We had several German speakers in our English-language tour group, in a Spanish-speaking country. Mari is a native Spanish-speaker, so the languages flowed and brought together parts of my life and mind.

Jane and Priestess, in particular, experienced this trip with deep interest. Since Mari had already met both of them, we felt safe with a

level of co-presence that allowed them to see and enjoy the ceremonies. I had never been in this part of Mexico, so everything was new and exploring the ancient cities stimulated the mind, body and spirit.

All of us (inside and out) were deeply moved by the feminine energy of the temple at Uxmal, with its oval curves and exquisite details—even sculpted birds on the roof!

We celebrated sunrise on the last day of the old era at Mayapan, with deep meditation time to let go of the old and open up to the new, working on both personal and global transitions.

The first rays of solstice sunlight broke through a stand of large trees on the other side of the meadow. We didn't need words to hear the message. Global healing is possible, and we each have a role to play.

The ceremony at the altar unfolded in three languages—four, if you counted Pachamama's poetry of birdsong, breezes and sunrays. Afterward, we each walked through a ceremonial Mayan arch, signifying our acceptance of our responsibilities in the new era. The global message was actually very personal. *Each one is charged in this new era to do all we can, in every interaction, to increase the flow of love and harmony, and to decrease fear and aggression.*

I felt my true purpose in this next phase of life was revealed, filling me with joy and an almost evangelic fervor. Surely, this simple message was beyond any single religion and yet encompassed all

religions. Wasn't it the very essence of how major religions tell us to treat our fellow beings?

Then the party started; a large circle celebration of song and dance. People from several continents and many countries shared special ceremonial presentations of dance, music and commitment. We all sang and danced with joy and optimism, swaying and connecting as one.

FROM THERE, our small group moved on to the ancient city of Chichén Itzá. Our leader ushered us to a small temple she called "the Queen's Temple," where we connected with our feminine energy. To avoid anything that might look to authorities like a ceremony, we sat in the woods and meditated on the prophesied shift and each person's role in bringing forth a more peaceful, balanced world.

After the group meditation, I stood at the side of the old temple and opened up to ask if anyone inside wanted to be in the body. Jane had been present earlier, having joyful fun during the singing and dancing. Now, Priestess came forward. The body stiffened, the eyes saw more precisely, and she felt the energy of the place.

> Yes, this temple is old and may hold feminine energy, but it does not hold a real Priestess like in Machu Picchu. It is good to be here, but it does not connect as the Grandmother of Lightning's rock did. I sense big energy and feel no anger and no fear in it.

Our group moved on to the Temple of Kukulcán (or *El Castillo*), adding our energy to the shift toward a more peaceful and collaborative feminine energy. I walked around the large, iconic, masculine temple for the first time and was struck by how its energy felt wan and used up. What had once been a powerful energy source felt dissipated and withered; its usefulness and power was almost at an end—just like the power of the men who had once dominated my life and would do so no more.

As I heard many times on this trip, "In every interaction, act so you increase love and harmony and decrease fear and aggression." People around the globe were now called to bring this simple essence of the great spiritual awakening to fruition. This charge provided a central theme for my healing and learning, and a focus to keep me going through the hard times—a clarity about the "why" that makes my "how" and "what" feel more manageable, to borrow from Victor Frankl's *Man's Search for Meaning*.

I still had hard times coming, but I now had the freedom and capacity to face them without resorting to dissociation, whether in the old style or using my new, more temporary methods. I worked to wrap my head and arms around the truth of my life. No more hiding in the distractions of work, family and external involvements. I had to feel the discomfort, the loss, the grieving, and to grant each part and alter time to cry as they looked the horrors straight in the eye. Then, maybe, we could accept it all with greater compassion, candor and love.

Again, Joseph Campbell helped me to understand where I had been and to view my quest for health and wholeness in a larger context.

> ...we have not even to risk the adventure alone; for the heroes of all time have gone before us; the labyrinth is thoroughly known; we have only to follow the thread of the hero path. And where we had thought to find an abomination, we shall find a god; where we had thought to slay another, we shall slay ourselves; where we had thought to travel outward, we shall come to the center of our own experience; where we had thought to be alone, we will be with all the world.[9]

Yes, I had traveled far to find my truth, and the healing was infinitely bigger than just being able to walk again. Campbell's metaphors helped me see the truth in something Mari had suggested. Perhaps the healing journey of a person with dissociated identities can be

---

9   Campbell, J. *The Hero with a Thousand Faces* (MJF Books, 1997), pg 18.

seen as a metaphor too. As each part and alter heals, it helps the whole being to heal. Likewise, as each individual heals, it helps the whole of humanity heal.

Chapter 35
The Day Everything Changed

When I got back home, I worked to put this spiritual lesson into action while also continuing the painful excavation of my past. Carol requested help to piece together the rest of the puzzle of the base and its connection to the suicide attempt, using her preferred tool of writing out the story. George coordinated our efforts. BJ realized she had been more present at the base than she had thought and could help fill in some details. Priestess offered her particular skill in figuring out the timing of things. Big Bonnie asked questions, typed and stayed in touch with Julia.

We started again by plastering the wall with easel paper and drawing pictures of whatever came forward. Carol made a diagram of the building at the base, naming each room. We created a page on the computer for every one of them so we could offer each fragment of memory a place to go, either with Post-its on the diagram or with words on the computer. In the mind, we created big, soft green cushions where little ones could snuggle up and feel safe as they shared.

This process honored the fact that these memories, and the work of retrieving them, were anything but linear. We uncovered much more detail about the suicide attempt and the sources of the painful symptoms, both physical and emotional.

After some discussion, we decided to share here a summary of the last day at the base—the day that changed everything.

We will tell the story of what happened when we tried to save our family by taking a bottle of pills. A bunch of us are writing this together—mainly BJ, Carol and George, with help from Big Bonnie. We figure it's important to tell you together because we can now see what happened on that day everyone's been so curious about—the one that ended with us taking the pills. It also turned out to be the last time we were ever at the base.

Like always, Carol was out, with BJ behind her, when we got dropped off alone at the base like we had been several times a year ever since Bompa died.

As usual, the Blue Ladies welcomed me and got me ready. After the experiments and questioning were done, Major Ken came to the Brown Lady's room and took me (now a twelve-year-old young lady) to his green trailer. It's hard to know which experiments they did on which visits, but BJ thinks they must have done eye experiments that day, because she remembers the eyes hurting and recalls feeling pretty sad and unloved.

"This is BJ, and I'll tell this part. See, the doctor who did the eye experiments was really handsome and looked like a movie star, and I dreamed he would realize I was now old enough to be his partner and we could go all over the world, saving people and doing our special science. He always smiled and talked nice to me as he started his work. But when it was all over, he didn't ask me to go away with him. He didn't even say goodbye. They just wheeled me out of the testing room to recuperate, strapped to my gurney, until the Brown Lady was ready to question and berate me. To make me feel even worse, she seemed especially mean that day."

So, I already felt unloved and disappointed when Major Ken took me out the back door of the Brown Lady's room, into bright sunlight that assaulted tender eyes, down the three steps, and up the short path to his green trailer, as usual. I laid down to rest on one of the twin beds in his messy office, and he gave me some medicine to help the body recover from the experiments. This time, that would have included drops that soothed the eyes.

But on this day, before he let us get dressed and ready to leave, he prepared the child to accept one more cruelty. The German guys were coming for a visit. When we heard that, we knew what it meant. All the other people at the base appreciated me for my skills, even as they tortured me. They didn't care enough not to hurt me, but unlike these two, they respected that I was a human who had some special capacities.

We had created a special part to deal with the Germans at the base. She chose the name "Jean" because that could be either a girl's or boy's name.

Major Ken gave us explicit instructions to "be nice" to them, which meant letting them do whatever they wanted, being passive, and not remembering it. At Bompa's, when they visited, these guys with their thick accents had just observed and discussed his techniques and my prowess with him. Whoever they were, now that Bompa wasn't there, they treated my body like an object, made available for their pleasure once Major Ken had left the three of us alone in the trailer. Jean remembers that they laughed with each other while they hurt me.

I was not a human being to them; I was an animal over whom they had complete power. When they were finished, they zipped up their pants and laughed together with no regard for the child, the object they had just used. They left in good spirits, and I went numbly into the little bathroom to wash out my mouth, clean up the body, and erase any remnants of these events, leaving Jean to hold them locked away inside for many decades.

Another part came out to sit dutifully on the bed and get ready to go, buttoning up her blouse and dully brushing her hair. Major Ken re-entered the trailer to do the job he did so well: frighten me into willing submission. He used his own hypnosis and mind control techniques to create and instruct parts of the mind and remove all memory of what had happened so the girl could safely go home.

That day, Major Ken talked more strongly and harshly than usual to the parts he had made, although we don't think he really understood how many of us there were. The younger ones, Molly and Mallory, remember he told them the secrets of the base could not be told to or learned by anyone—even Outside Bonnie. Terrible things would happen to my mother and sisters if anyone ever found out about the base or the experiments that were being done there.

The older ones, including Gloria and Claudia, remember him saying, in his deep, gravelly voice, "Your family lets you come here because they want you to do this. You were chosen to work with us and to protect your family by holding these things only in this part of your mind—secret from all other parts. No one will believe you if you try to expose the secret, and many others will be hurt. You can't tell anyone anything. If you do, you will be bad and deserve to die. You'll get sick in your own head—sick of yourself for being so bad, for being a bad person who should die."

When he was finished, there was no question the girl should die if there was ever any chance of the secrets of the base coming out. In fact, I was so worthless and useless, I should probably just have died anyway.

Then we began the process of shutting the doors in my head so I could leave. But Major Ken was in an unusual hurry and was not very careful to close everything. As always, a different part—strong and mostly male—came out to walk the body out of the trailer and buffer the transition. But nothing was normal about what we saw in the driveway between the two buildings where Uncle Dick usually picked us up.

Uncle Dick was there, but hung back while Daddy got out of the driver's seat of his blue Cadillac to greet us. No, he didn't greet us. He stuck out his hand to Major Ken and greeted him. He didn't pay any attention to me. It seemed like the two of them must have met before because they greeted each other like old friends, shaking hands, and laughing that man laugh that says, "I'm important and you will look important, too, if you laugh with me."

Major Ken handed Daddy an envelope, cut open at the top with a lot of folded papers in it. Daddy took the envelope and thanked Major Ken again, slapping him on the shoulder.

As we got in the car, Uncle Dick slammed the door without saying a word. And Daddy drove away from the base, filling the car with stony silence.

The specific part of me who saw the envelope and the laughter between the men had not been part of the experiments or the abuse in the trailer. His job was to handle the transfer from trailer and base to car and family; from Major Ken to Uncle Dick; from Carol (and all the parts who helped her survive whatever had been done today) to BJ; and eventually to Outside Bonnie, who would wake up from her "nap" knowing nothing about what had happened. In buffering these transfers, his major task was to gather up any sensations left over in the body from whatever it had endured and tuck them away so they could not be felt and raise alarms or questions.

These processes always continued as we left the base in the car with Uncle Dick and headed directly to his house. Uncle Dick's soothing voice helped Carol and BJ take over from the transitional guy and finish closing the doors in the mind, allowing the girl to fall into her forgetful sleep. Then she woke up just before we arrived at the house, with no memory of anything since we had gone through the tunnel on the Angeles Forest Highway hours before.

But this well-practiced transition process into a place of outside warmth and security could not flow through its stages on this day, hindered by several unanticipated changes. First of all, why was the little girl's father there? And what was this curious envelope that changed hands like an important talisman while Major Ken and Daddy talked and laughed and said goodbye?

As usual, we drove out between the two long, low buildings, but the kindness Uncle Dick usually showed was replaced by a silent tension between the two brothers in the front seat, who ignored me completely. And we didn't go to Uncle Dick's house. Instead, we went to a restaurant—all white with palm trees painted on the walls—where Mother and Munner sat waiting for us.

The bright afternoon sunlight bouncing off the white walls hurt my eyes and added to my confusion. I think they had all eaten before they picked me up. I don't remember what they talked about as we sat there since I was busy trying not to show my surprise, confusion and sadness.

Why doesn't anyone want to talk to me? Why are Mommy and Daddy up here? If Daddy knows Major Ken, does that mean he has known about the base all this time? And Mother too? Actually, hadn't Major Ken said that my family wanted me to do the work at the base? But why? And what is going on between Dad and Uncle Dick? Did they have a fight? Did I do something wrong? They all seem so mad!

These questions—in fact, the whole scene—would need to be tucked away with all the other sensations of the day when we finally left the restaurant and closed the door in my mind on the way to Uncle Dick's.

But that didn't happen either. Instead, Mom and Dad took me in their car, and Uncle Dick and Munner left in his. Now what? When do we close the door in the mind? How do we fall asleep? Who is in charge? My head was a big muddle inside, with no one on the outside to help or care. Neither Bompa nor Uncle Dick would ever have allowed me to leave without assuring all doors were closed and the girl was asleep. Overwhelmed by emotions, sensations and confusion I could not name, I sat in the back seat as we started down the windy road over the mountains toward home.

Apparently, everyone but me knew that would be my last visit to the base. I guess the experiments had yielded all they could from me, and my parents wanted to end the arrangement because it had become inconvenient amid our family conflict.

Major Ken had filled my mind with so many suicidal and self-destructive, posthypnotic suggestions that he probably believed I wouldn't live long enough to cause trouble. So, I was left to sort it out on my own. I wish someone had told me all the abuse would end that night.

As we drove into the mountains, my parents began telling me, "It's for your own good," the way parents do. But all they did was further shatter my world and underscore that they didn't care or understand anything about me. Speaking over their shoulders from the front seat, they declared I would no longer be allowed to visit Uncle Dick and his family. Dad talked about how Uncle Dick had done mean things when he worked at Dad's business. Mother said she knew I was hoping to go to a dance with one of the boys, but that would not be possible.

On and on they talked, making it clear they were not interested in my opinion and that these were not negotiable decisions. I would not be going back to Palmdale anytime soon, especially not to any dance with a high school boy.

My parents acted like they were only talking to their twelve-year-old daughter. Whatever they knew or didn't know about the base or Bompa's training, they showed no understanding at all of what was happening inside me or of the impact of all their changes. My mind was in utter chaos, and they did nothing to help me close the doors, as someone usually did. They just made it worse by making us all feel completely unloved and uncared for.

BJ, who had already been devastated by the doctor's indifference and the unusually harsh treatment that day, joined the outside girl in despair and anger over having Eddie's affections ripped away. The one person who consistently made her feel loved and special, taken away. How heartless and mean, and for no good reason!

Obviously, they don't care about me at all. No one will ever love me. I'm just worthless, like the Brown Lady said.

Carol, who knew nothing of the outside world she had suddenly been thrust into, instinctively stood in a doorway in the mind, holding back the darkness of the base as best she could. What did these new rules mean? If I couldn't go to Uncle Dick's, did that mean I couldn't go back to the base? What would Major Ken do if I didn't show up? My parents couldn't possibly know the danger they were putting themselves in. What could I do to protect them? To protect myself? And my sisters?

Oblivious, my parents droned on as we drove down the road I had traveled so many times, but which had lost every familiar landmark. I wanted to jump out of the car and throw myself over the cliff. In the darkening twilight, black canyons descended around every curve, just feet away. Maybe I could will the car to miss one and fly off into the abyss. But Daddy knew these mountain roads too well, and all I could do was cry, which covered up the fact that no part of me could think clearly or form a coherent sentence.

IT WAS DARK WHEN WE GOT HOME, and I went straight to bed in a confused, adolescent rage. I still wore the precious dime-store, pearl necklace Eddie had given me for my birthday. The exhausted body and outside girl fell asleep, but other parts of the mind stayed active. As much as Carol had worked to shield the base parts from the chaos, they were still worried about the vulnerability of their secrets.

Molly took action. Following Major Ken's instructions, she came out into the body without waking the girl, got out of bed, and walked into the big, pink-tiled bathroom. She knew quietly, surely, unemotionally what she needed to do to protect the secrets permanently. Remaining calm and clear about the task, she found a full bottle of aspirin in the medicine cabinet and counted out twelve—one for each year of her life. Major Ken had said to take "as many as you can," so she took a few more. Someone inside assured her she had done her job. She went back to bed, glad she had done her part to protect her family.

Claudia watched all this from the mind's open door, which no one could quite close. Major Ken had been clear with her that it would take a whole bottle of pills to ensure success. Why hadn't Molly taken more? Not needing an answer, and with clarity of purpose, Claudia woke Gloria and, together, they took the body back across the hall and into the bathroom to swallow the rest of the pills, filling the little pink plastic cup several times to wash them down. Now we could go to sleep and never worry again about the secrets or Major Ken.

Purple Lady was the first to feel strange sensations in the body. "The head felt like it wanted to explode." She knew BJ was still connected with the outside girl, who had fallen into a deep, sob-induced stupor of a sleep, so Purple Lady turned to Jane, who always liked to make herself known. Nudged awake, Jane let out a loud moan, thinking maybe all the crying had made the head feel so bad.

Mother came in to check on the girl, waking Outside Bonnie, who complained of a terrible headache. BJ, who woke up with Bonnie, remembers that when Mother left and came back with the empty pill bottle, she asked, all mad-like, "What did you do?"

She didn't wait for an answer, only went to get the father. He came with the Bakelite stick, which was what he always used to give spankings. He needed it because I had done something bad. I was still holding onto the necklace when he yanked on my arm to pull me out of bed for a good spanking.

The strand broke and little pearls flew all over the room, which brought on another wailing outburst. Instead of spanking us, Daddy got down and used the Bakelite to try to scoop up all the pearls from under the bed and around the floor. When we saw him on his hands and knees, trying to find something that meant so much to us, Bonnie and BJ both knew he must really care about us. That surprised us and made us feel a little better.

None of us remember the drive to the hospital or much about the emergency room. The doctors worked on the body to get rid of the poisons, making it feel even worse.

BJ and Purple Lady floated out of the body to observe from above. They found our spirit guide, Bear, up in the corner of the ceiling, keeping a watchful, caring eye on the child. The three of them exchanged thoughts about what was needed to prevent this from happening again.

Bear made clear it was not the girl's time to die. There was great work for her to do, and things would be different from now on. His gentle coaxing and support included no blame or shame, only a new understanding of our role and purpose. Responsibility for this life now rested internally. There was no one externally to rely on. We had to maintain order and control, and do whatever was needed to stay safe, to be sure the outside girl wasn't damaged by all that had happened.

Purple Lady and BJ understood. The most important thing in that moment was to close the mind's doors as tightly as possible, as quickly as possible. They went back inside the body to establish order as the body and mind came out of the grip of the pills.

BJ created more secure compartments for the big parts who had special jobs and might be needed again, while Purple Lady gathered the little, less-specific shards of the girl's mind and memory into quiet, safe circles. Together, they strengthened the main wall in the mind and closed the door securely.

Later, they realized that some of Major Ken's directives about dying could still come forward into the mind. Purple Lady took on the job of minimizing and normalizing these thoughts so they wouldn't be taken seriously. No one with suicidal intentions was ever again allowed access to the body to act on them.

Chapter 36
The Arrogance of Patriarchy

Damn! So my father knew about the base. Damn... Sitting in the Green Room with Julia, I wrestled with the most devastating revelation to come out of this story. Dad knew.

I wanted desperately to dissociate that memory back into oblivion. But ever so gently, Julia held reality in the room. I had dealt with the fact Dad was a binge drinker whose wife was periodically unavailable to him while having babies and nursing infants. And that he, on several such occasions over a period of two or three years, had come home drunk and used his eldest daughter.

In my construct, it had been clear he only hurt me when he was drunk and that neither of us remembered it the next morning. A neat, contained little package of situational incest that could be compartmentalized, if not excused. I even imagined him conveniently asleep (or passed out) when others abused me in his presence. As I sat there with the memory of him glad-handing Major Ken, a deep, gnawing knot of betrayal gripped my gut.

Julia had never fully bought my framing, and she periodically asked questions to promote further inquiry. But there was no "I told you so" in her eyes. I saw only deep compassion, some sadness, and a twinge of anger she couldn't quite stifle.

How much did he know? Did Mother know too? What was in that envelope? Was he somehow paid off for my services? What the hell was the base, anyway? What were they trying to do, and how were Bompa, Uncle Dick, and now Dad involved in it? Where were Bompa's little black notebooks? How and why did my internal system keep this hidden from me all these years? Was that a near-death experience in the hospital, with a bear-angel instead of a white light? And why weren't my brain and body more damaged by all the abuse that had started when they were so young?

The mystery of why I took the pills may have been solved, but no bells rang with a cheer of "Hooray, now you are healed; you have found what you've been looking for!" The answer only brought more questions and a deeper sense that no one had loved me enough to protect me.

No wonder Dad didn't want to talk about why I took the pills. He knew. I'll never know *what* he knew, but he was there at least that once, so he knew something. How could he betray his own daughter like that?

⚬⚭⚬

A SERENDIPITOUSLY SCHEDULED WEEK in Sedona arrived with perfect timing. Invited guests had canceled, so I settled by myself, into a comfy, high-ceilinged, big-windowed apartment, facing the red rocks of a cliff, beside the creek flowing at its base. Sedona offered space for whatever I needed, particularly deep internal reflection and a strong connection to Pachamama's beauty and regenerative energy. Thank you, Universe… And thank you to my wisdom for hanging on to the time-share.

Sylvia Fraser's *My Father's House: A Memoir of Incest and of Healing* had sat untouched on my shelf for several years. Besides fearing how the topic would make me feel, I had promised Julia I wouldn't read about others until my own story was known. That criterion had surely been met, and the book found its way into my bag.

I picked it up on the second day, after a welcoming hike through beautiful and familiar territory that wrapped itself warmly around my bruised spirit. Written by a novelist, the story grabbed me and wouldn't let go. I read it in almost one sitting, with time out only for food and a little sleep.

Her story and mine actually have few similarities beyond the incest and dissociation, but her ability to speak her truth with all her feelings intact mesmerized me. My emotions had been so separated and hidden, I hardly had access to them even now. But I knew I was filled with anger and disgust on her behalf—and then for myself. As I lounged on the big leather sofa in my sanctuary beside the creek, she helped me know those feelings wouldn't consume me. Her story opened a path to owning—to embodying—my own.

I didn't want to sanitize it so neither I nor anyone else had to face the truth. I needed to allow myself to hear, feel and believe what my body wanted me to know. And I realized I could be furious, disgusted, heartbroken, bewildered and curious, all at the same time. Between the quiet of the apartment, the magnificence of the landscape, and the internet's limitless availability for research, the next few days offered exactly the freedom I needed to explore multiple emotions and questions.

I wanted to know what the experiments—both at Bompa's and at the base—were about. What did they think they were learning, and were they successful? Did they learn anything that helped someone or catalyzed some invention that is useful now? They must have had some purpose. What did I help them learn, and where were Bompa's notebooks? And how could any of that give them the right to torture an innocent child?

Purple Lady, the peacemaker, spoke up. "What happened, happened. Breathe." She was always reminding me to breathe deep, long breaths. "Whatever they learned or created from the experiments, our job now is to find health, wholeness, strength and beauty in what it created in us."

Oh, okay. I didn't have to make sense out of their work. What I had to make sense of was what it did to me and how to use that to move forward. But I would have loved to get my hands on those little black books.

Anger stirred in my solar plexus. First, at Bompa. Then, at a government that had perpetuated what he had started. And at Dad for not stopping it.

I was a child, not even nine years old when I was delivered into their hands. Who were they, and why did they think it was okay? Why did I have to be the one to deal with the aftermath? How many of them spent half their lives thinking about suicide? Maybe there were some people who had consciences and felt bad, or even had nightmares about what they had done. How would I know? And what difference did it make now? I was just mad at them for what they had done to me.

My terrors and abuse could have stopped when Bompa died, and perhaps they might have been easier to heal from. But no, the worst came after. They had a specimen to test, to torture, and to probe—a child trained by someone other than their experts, who could withstand amazing things. How could they use her and then be sure she didn't use her skills against them? Program her to self-destruct. And I almost did.

No wonder Dad didn't want to talk about it. What part had he played in it all? How had they coerced his silence? (Oh, please say he needed coercing!)

Did anyone from the base follow up? Had someone told them I tried to kill myself and Dad intervened? Did they have some assurance from him I would be watched? Given Mother's preference for denial over conflict, Dad would have known he could get away without telling her whatever he knew by refusing to discuss it or my "stupid prank." How dare he gaslight us all like that?

Well, I'll never know. They're all dead now, and the records are gone too.

Purple Lady nudged her way into the consciousness again to remind me that we had taken on the job of breaking generational cycles of abuse and patriarchal violence. She drew the connection between my years in child abuse prevention and youth development, my personal healing path, and the global movements hoping to create a cultural shift to protect children from trauma.

Suddenly, I realized this was the same shift prophesied by all the wisdom traditions I had been studying. My life made sense! I was moving from the patriarchal focus of the last era to the more matriarchal energy of the new era—breaking generational cycles of abuse and violence. Increasing love and harmony while decreasing fear and aggression. With love, without fear. It all fit.

I saw myself suddenly as an elder with a story—a story of complexity, contribution, dissociation, leadership and now healing. I was no longer young and passionate about a cause. Been there, done that. I was becoming an elder, willing to use her story to heal others.

I was not simply a survivor of a culture that allowed and perpetrated such violence against its children. In fact, I had been a change agent in the world of children and family services all my life, and now I finally understood why.

Yes, but… Again, the anger surfaced in my belly, making it hard to breathe—anger at the betrayal by my family and my country.

I may never know what project I was involved in or exactly where or what "the base" was. I'm angry that there are so many possibilities! My research uncovered not only MKULTRA, but Project Artichoke and Project Bluebird, just to name a couple more. And Operation Paperclip, which welcomed into this country some of the very doctors who had committed the atrocities we condemned in Nazi Germany, so we (and not the Russians) would have access to what they had learned.

By order of CIA Director Richard Helms, most of the records about these projects were destroyed in 1973, just before investigative journalists, in the aftermath of Watergate, began making public other immense breaches of the public trust. A presidential commission, with Vice President Nelson Rockefeller at its head, was appointed in 1975 to investigate as the United States President's Commission on CIA Activities within the United States. That same year, Senator Frank Church convened hearings before the Senate Select Committee to Study Governmental Operations with Respect to Intelligence Activities, and a similar committee was formed in the House of Representatives, eventually chaired by Representative Otis Pike. Over the next couple of years, the three committees produced voluminous reports, and the American public was assured that all such operations had stopped.

Still, the angry research geek in me wanted to read the reports and figure out where I fit into it all as a child. But why? I knew enough that I could not dismiss the awful scenarios reconstructed out of my imperfect memories as impossible or imaginary. Ample evidence made plausible everything my body and mind had remembered; all of it perpetrated and kept secret by my own government.

Gloria, one of the alters who worked with Major Ken in the trailer at the base, strongly believed his assertion that our work was being done "on behalf of the country" and that it made us very important. When Julia suggested that what had been done to us was illegal, Gloria countered, "It couldn't be illegal because the government was doing it on behalf of the whole country. And if the government was doing it, that meant it was legal, by definition!"

The very idea that this all happened makes me worry it, or something similar, could happen again. Fear creates perverse incentives in institutions and individuals, and patriarchal arrogance and hubris make unjustifiable actions seem defensible. We have seen this dark underbelly many times in human history. Perhaps it is this connection that drew me to the concentration camps in Germany, to see for myself the predecessors of my own abuse, even before any of this was in my conscious mind.

At the same time, I couldn't help thinking about my mother. Her voice had been equally stifled by the patriarchy of her family, her religion, and her community. She lived into her nineties, wondering how her father knew she would never tell what he had done to her. The patriarchy counts on our internalized fear and acceptance of their rules, on our sense that there is something wrong with us if we question them.

Purple Lady again urged us not to dwell on these things. We had chosen to live this life, defusing and disempowering fear with every interaction. That was my path, my role now. That was the reason to focus on learning about and healing from the adverse experiences of my childhood—to help build a better world where all children are safe and protected.

While George agreed with Purple Lady about the future, he voiced for all of us why it was so difficult.

Whatever else happened, the hardest thing for any of us to live with and survive is the abandonment we each feel. The abandonment is much worse than any of the things that happened after it was clear no one cared enough to protect you, or help you, or make it stop. The sense that you as a person don't matter enough to anyone to keep things from hurting you stays with you long after the awful things no one protected you from are over. And the song they sing in your head is that you are unloved, you are worthless, you are not cared about. It doesn't matter to anyone if you are hurt or scared or sad. No one will come if you call or cry. No one cares about your feelings and pain or sees them as important. Everyone else is more important than you are. There is nothing about you that is lovable, and nobody loves you. These feelings become truths, and they are much worse than the physical pain held in your body.

Chapter 37
The Bonfire of the Penis Sticks

Even given the history of abandonment and betrayal—or perhaps because of it—some of us, including Big Bonnie and BJ, longed for a man in our life again. A consistent, caring person to hug, a person who really cared for and knew us in all our complexity, and with whom we might eventually choose to have sex. This idea was destined to go nowhere, but it triggered responses inside that brought forward an alter named Bill, who had a bucketful of unexpressed anger at men in general for all the terrible things they do to others, and at my father, grandfather and uncle specifically for the things they had done to me.

George and Bill explained in the Green Room the strength and depth of their anger and suspicion toward all outside men. Julia reminded us of how good it had felt years before, when we went up into the mountains and threw rocks and sticks, and yelled and screamed our anger at our father.

Yes, that had been very cathartic, but it wasn't exactly what we needed this time. Burning the rug felt deeply satisfying too. Maybe we needed some combination of the two. Maybe burn Dad in effigy or find some sticks to represent penises we could burn with the effigy of Dad?

Early the next morning, Big Bonnie packed up a large pot, a paper bag suitable for an effigy of a man, some string, and a box of matches, then headed for the mountains. I thought I knew where we were going, but the car seemed to turn of its own volition and went in a different direction.

By a circuitous route, I found myself driving into a large, secluded city park down by an old dam at the foot of the mountains, where we used to go on school outings as children. Following instructions from inside, I parked in an out-of-the-way area shaded by lots of oak trees, with picnic tables and a cement restroom building, but no people.

With no plan that I knew of, I took my journal, pot and paper bag and set out to find somewhere I could write in solitude and see where it led. But before I even got to the table, I let out a hoot of loud laughter. The ground was littered with small sticks and twigs that looked like they might represent little penises.

We settled on the picnic bench until Big Bonnie felt safe enough to just go with the flow of internal guidance. First, we roamed around, filling the paper bag with handfuls of dry leaves. We tied string around the top of the bag to create a neck and put my empty paper coffee cup upside down on top as the head. The perfect resemblance to Dad at his heaviest made me snicker.

Next, we gathered up sticks representing the various penises that had been used inappropriately on us when we were young. With no one around to hear, I began talking out loud to the people whose penises the sticks represented—my father, my grandfather, my uncle, the others whose names I did not know. Soon, I was stomping angrily and swearing at these men and their hubris and their ugliness. I didn't yell, but I swore with great intensity. George noted, when he wrote about it later, that Big Bonnie used bad words he had never heard before.

The focus of the castigation and swearing landed squarely on my father, his betrayal of me and concern over what he might have done to anyone else. "How could you do that?! Even if you were hurt yourself, you had no right!"

My ire boiled over seamlessly to the rest of the family, and then I was cursing at every man who has ever abused a woman or a child and put his penis where it didn't belong. "Look at all the harm you have caused! How could you do that?" I ranted on, a mad woman swearing and stomping through the dusty leaves, picking up sticks, and railing at them about how evil they all were.

At some point, I heard Purple Lady inside, urging that this process also needed to be about forgiveness and about letting go of all the heavy energy. Big Bonnie, George and Bill had been joined by several others, and they all laughed at her suggestion. "Oh, *hell no*! We're not ready for that. We can't forgive what they did!"

When my hands and pockets were full of sticks and we were done angrily scolding and swearing at the men, we went back to the table. After I put the effigy in the pot and surrounded the paper-bag father figure with penis sticks, my eyes filled with tears. I soon sat sobbing uncontrollably. Overwhelmed by the awfulness, the sadness of it all, Big Bonnie cried and cried until she felt spent.

Checking inside, I asked if George, Bill or Priestess needed to cry, and one by one, fresh waves of sobbing overtook the body. Then Carol and others took their turns. I don't know how long we sat there crying, but since we weren't in a hurry, everyone got their chance to cry as long and as loud as they needed.

Right on cue, just as the crying ended, the sun shone through the clouds for the first time that morning. I got up and began my ceremony, thanking the four directions and opening my heart to the sun's loving warmth. How perfect to feel its rays on our skin, renewing our strength.

While we soaked everything in, word came from inside that the fire needed to happen then and there. I looked around for the safest place to light one.

Given the tinder-dry conditions, the adult present knew we had to be responsible in how we did this. Any errant spark could have devastating consequences. Off to the side of the tables, nearer to the fence, in the one spot where the oak trees did not form a canopy of dry leaves and branches overhead, lay a cement pad of indeterminate function.

My crab pot, filled with the fat, paper-bag effigy of my father and a deep layer of penis sticks, sat next to me on the cement. With satisfaction, trepidation and some difficulty, I lit the bag on fire. By now, we knew Purple Lady was right. This was not an act of revenge or an opportunity to wish ill on those who had hurt us, but rather an act of release and healing.

I used three oak leaves to make an impromptu North American *kintu* (like the ones we made in Peru with coca leaves), filled it with my intention to liberate the heavy energy—the rage, hurt, sadness and pain—and blew it into the fire. As the flames and smoke rose, I could feel long-held emotion join them.

I would not go so far as to say it came coupled with forgiveness. Rather, I sensed the release was not for me alone, but for the men as well. The sometimes-thick smoke seemed to carry the heavy energy of several generations.

As I released my rage at what they had done, I realized as long as I carried it, I was not free of them, and they were not free of me. They couldn't have any hold on me anymore unless I allowed it—and I didn't want their actions to control me or guide my emotions and actions any longer. *Let it all go up in smoke. They are dead and cannot hurt me or anyone else anymore. Take back control of your life. And if their souls also find some release, we all can benefit.*

So, there she sat: an older, white woman in jeans, with a dirty, tear-streaked face, on the ground in the park on a Wednesday morning, with a smoky fire in a large stockpot, quietly praying and watching the smoke rise into the early morning air.

It took a long while for my little inferno to burn itself down. Each time I poked at it to help burn every last penis, I felt a little more like one of the witches stirring the cauldron in Shakespeare's *Macbeth*. When the flames flared up, I knew it mirrored how my anger and pain have flashed and tapered over the years. Every time, we released a little more heavy energy and called on the ancestors to let go of their pain alongside mine. Finally, I was left with a pot of ashes that I let cool as I packed up my things.

My solitude shattered when a park maintenance worker came over to see what was going on. When he asked what I was doing, I felt so raw, I decided to be honest and said something about working to heal a family history of child sexual abuse.

Unfortunately, this made him want to talk about it more, recommending that I try therapy or go to church. As well-meaning as he was, I just wanted to let the pot cool enough to put it safely into the car and leave.

He commented that every family has something difficult to deal with. While true, this was not at all comforting. Most families do not have multigenerational sexual abuse, systematic torture, and religious cults to deal with. And most women in their sixties do not come to the park to make a bonfire of penis sticks.

His responses were compassionate, appropriate, caring and unwanted. I had been honest because I didn't want to be invisible, but I felt unprepared to cope with well-meaning kindness. It would be wonderful if all public employees faced with this situation would respond with the compassion he showed as he made sure I left his park safely. I want to believe that his conversation with me also allowed him to assess whether I intended to attempt suicide or any other harm to myself or others, and that he had the means to summon support if he felt the need for it.

But speaking from the point of view of the person with the mental health challenge, although I appreciated his kindness, I really didn't want the intrusion of talking with someone at that moment.

George and Bill were only barely below the surface, and I wanted them to be able to stay close without drawing suspicion. It's a fine line we ask people to tread. We want not to be invisible, but only on our own terms.

When I finally left with my pot of cooled penis ashes, it struck me how little of what had happened had been anticipated by my adult self. We had found a good balance, open to the flow from inside, while at the same time keeping everyone safe. But I also recognized the privilege provided by my white, middle-class, well-educated and articulate ANP, who didn't have to worry too much about interference. How might I have been treated if I had looked and been perceived differently? Maybe the same, maybe not.

On the way home, I asked inside what I was supposed to do with the ashes and dutifully headed back to the place in the foothills where I had begun to physically release anger at my father several years before. I let these ashes blow into the breeze up there, where the process had begun. Ashes to ashes. Closure. My body and mood lightened.

THE PERPLEXING IRONY of wanting to be seen and heard, but not labeled or treated like there is something wrong, showed up again when I joined the National Association for Mental Illness (NAMI) and went to my first state conference as a person with a mental health diagnosis. The conference was informative, and I went, hoping to learn how best to use our new voice as an advocate.

But when we got home, an internal revolt resulted in a pugnacious and strident paper about how we were not mentally ill. We have a survival tool that has kept us alive and functioning. How dare you call that a disorder!

The paper is written mostly in the angry voices of George, BJ and Priestess, and ends with this demand:

So call me different, call me weird, call me dissociative, call me fascinating, call me immensely fortunate, or call me triumphant. But don't call me mentally ill just because I have a diagnosis. Call me mentally gifted.

Being an advocate and speaking out as a person with the lived experience of a mental health diagnosis would prove tricky in a world that treats the survival tools needed by people like me as an illness.

Chapter 38
Jane's Origin Story

As if to prove BJ, George and Priestess's point, we finally pieced together the events that led to Jane's emergence as our first internally created alter.

My first long stay alone at Munner and Bompa's house (for two weeks or more) happened when Mary was born, twelve days before my second birthday. Then, just thirteen months later, another baby was born, so I had to go to their house again for a longer period.

Bompa had already begun teaching me his special way of using my mind to go away, so nothing would hurt and I wouldn't remember things too special for other people to know. Now, he decided it was time for my first initiation—well, actually, they called it a "purification ritual." Since I did not yet know how to enter a trance and my mind control skills were only beginning, Munner and Bompa had to help from the outside.

Munner dressed me in a long white dress with no panties on underneath. (I was a big girl and didn't need diapers anymore, so it was okay.) She held me while Bompa helped me close my eyes and settle in like he had taught me.

He hit my body hard in time with the rhythm of the metronome until I started to go away. Then I felt him cover my face with something until I couldn't breathe. As soon as I was semi-conscious,

Bompa carried me, limp across his arms, up into the large, formal living room to a small, waiting group of his religious followers, including some of my uncles. They were speaking in tongues and swaying with each other.

Bompa brought me to the front of the group and did some ceremony and prayer over me. He picked up a round wooden thing, moistened it with something special, and pushed it up between my legs into my body three times. I didn't feel it or remember anything about it until years later, when my body remembered the pain of the expansion required by purification.

A few days later, Daddy came over. Uncle Ted and Daddy took me on a picnic down into Eaton Canyon in Uncle Ted's old black car. We drove down the dirt road near the bridge and parked. Uncle Ted laid a scratchy, dark green army blanket out on the dusty ground, while Daddy fell asleep in the back seat of the car, because he was still celebrating the birth of his son. Uncle Ted and I sat on the blanket, and he talked about what a pretty day it was while he drank another beer.

He took my clothes off so I could feel the warm December sun on my skin. I sat frozen on the blanket, scared of him—he was so big and loud and unpredictable. He had been drinking a lot, but not as much as Daddy. He undid his pants and showed me this big thing— part of his body. It seemed like maybe he wanted to kill me with it. I did what Bompa had taught me and tried to go away. I worked really hard not to be there, not to feel or know anything, but I wasn't totally successful.

Seeing that I couldn't move, he laughed his awful cackling laugh, pushed me over on my back, and put that thing right up inside of me. I could feel my skin and insides stretching while he moved the thing around. It was important not to cry, so I kept my eyes closed and stayed inside as far away as I could get. When he stopped, we just both lay there on the blanket; him breathing loud and heavy, me hardly breathing at all. Then he cleaned up all the wetness and put our clothes back on.

After a while, we drove back to Munner's house, but Daddy went home to the new baby when he woke up, and I didn't get to tell him what had happened. So, when Munner and I were alone in her room, I tried to tell her that Uncle Ted had hurt me down there. Could she make him not do that ever again? But she got really mad at me and put soap in my mouth to teach me never to say such awful things. It hurt really badly, but I couldn't cry because that would just have made her madder.

She went into one of her fits and started yelling at me so loudly that Bompa heard her, and he came and calmed her down with a shot of medicine from his doctor bag. He rinsed out my mouth and helped me not feel the burning of the soap. But I knew I couldn't tell him what had happened.

When I went home a couple of days later, I decided maybe if I told Mommy what had happened, she wouldn't make me stay over at their house so much and Uncle Ted wouldn't be able to do that anymore. I went into her room, where she was in bed nursing the new baby boy. Mary was on her other side, snuggled in the soft bedspread, and I wanted to get up there so I could tell Mommy what happened and she could make it stop.

I started to cry a little when I thought about it, but Mommy didn't like me crying. As I got ready to climb up, she said, "No, no, Bonnie. You can see I have two babies up here, and I can't listen to you right now. You are a big girl. So, you need to be the big girl from now on and take care of yourself. Mommy has to take care of the babies."

For two years, I had been her baby, her sweet girl, with her whenever I wanted. That changed when Mary was born, but I was nice to my baby sister, so everyone still liked me. But now, with this boy baby, neither Mommy nor Daddy liked me anymore or wanted to be with me or take care of me. What was I to do?

Well, I was pretty sure that Aunt Jane still loved me. *If I'm a big girl now, I'll run away to Aunt Jane's house. I know where it is on our same street. She'll listen to me and hug me and not make me go be with Uncle Ted anymore.*

I left our house without telling anybody and headed to Aunt Jane's, six houses down along our sidewalk. On the way, I saw Bobby and his sister playing out in front of their house across the street. Knowing that I was big enough to cross the street all by myself, I went over to play with them. It wasn't very long before their mother called them in because it was getting dark. I needed to cross the street again—look both ways, don't be scared, and run when it is clear.

It had gotten darker by the time I got to Aunt Jane's house and climbed up her front steps into the round place that made her front door sort of like a castle. I knocked on the door and waited for her to come and hug me. But she didn't come.

I found the doorbell and rang it. Once... twice... three times... But no one came. *Oh dear, maybe Aunt Jane isn't home? I hadn't thought of that. Well, maybe if I wait here, she'll come home.* So, I sat beside the door and waited for her while it got really, really dark, and I got more and more scared. I couldn't go home because Mommy would be very mad at me if I came in after dark, all scared and crying again.

At that moment, something deep inside me took over. *I need to not be scared. Not of Mommy and not of Daddy or Uncle Ted. I need to leave the fear behind so it can't come with me. I need to be happy and smiling and giggling so everyone will like me like they used to. Nobody will be mad at me, and I won't be afraid.*

I sat there in the dark and focused, like Bompa had taught me. Then I stood and took a step out onto the porch, leaving all the fear by the door, never to be felt again. I thought of myself as "little Jane" and ran home, sensing my guardian angel running with me to help get me home safely.

When I got to the house, I was so happy and smiling that no one got mad or even wondered where I had been. Maybe they hadn't noticed I was gone, but no matter. I would never have to feel that kind of fear again because Jane would always be able to deflect it with a smile and a giggle.

Part 7
How It Worked

Chapter 39
The Way It Was

In my life, dissociation has proven to be more of a superpower than a disorder. We feel more mentally gifted than mentally disordered. But how does it work? How did Jane walk away from her fear? These revelations only made Big Bonnie more curious. How in the world did it all work inside? What did it look like? How did all of you keep everything hidden for all those years, with me on the outside knowing nothing?

I had learned in my reading that people who develop dissociative disorders are generally smart, that is, they have higher than average IQs, and we are a creative lot. People with dissociative identities lived with unpredictable, prolonged, life-threatening trauma very early in life—before the age of six or nine (depending on which study you read).

Books like *I Am More Than One* by Jane Wegscheider Hyman and my early online forays into the world of people with dissociative disorders helped me understand I wasn't as unusual as I thought. There are lots of accomplished, professional people out there who share my diagnosis. But that still didn't tell me how it worked in *my* head.

Finally, BJ and George agreed to collaborate with Big Bonnie to draw a picture of how they saw the internal structure of our mind: a structure that first evolved to survive a variety of traumatic experiences during childhood, aided by mind control training and post-hypnotic suggestions. After the suicide attempt, it was strengthened to keep the outside person safe and the inner secrets securely separated from the outer mind. It served CanDance's imperatives to keep the outside person functioning well enough to appear normal, be a good person, and make her contributions to the world, never acting to cause fear or with violence.

As we drew the picture, we struggled to describe on a flat piece of paper something multidimensional and nonlinear. Our language is too limited to communicate the interrelated complexity of multiple minds using the same physical brain and body. Big Bonnie kept asking questions, and George agreed that visual aids could help illuminate something this complex. So we worked to develop a snapshot of what it took to survive and keep the ANP functional.

This final version was facilitated and clarified on a visit to Sedona when our dear friend Grace, an anthropologist, worked with George to separate what it looked like in the "olden times" from what had evolved as we healed and opened up the walls in the "new times."

An almost impenetrable main wall forms the primary feature, dividing the structure into three basic functional areas. The first is behind the wall, where secrets were locked in the mind and in the body. Next comes an active field in front of the wall, where special alters shielded secrets and worked to keep things on the outside picture perfect. Finally, there is the outer, apparently normal mind of the apparently normal person whose job was not to know or question what was going on inside.

The goal was to maintain the image of a good, competent child, student, friend, wife, mother and professional as a reality in the outside world. The others referred to her as "Outside Bonnie," or simply "the outside girl," until the work in the Green Room began, after which the adult became known as "Big Bonnie."

Behind the main wall, completely separated from the consciousness of Outside Bonnie who had lived in the outer world for five decades, were the homes of the major alters who had experienced specific, recurring trauma until the age of twelve. Each was sequestered in his or her compartment, with heavy walls of amnesia and disconnection. They did not know about each other and knew very little, if anything, about the rest of the world, beyond the specific situations that were theirs to handle.

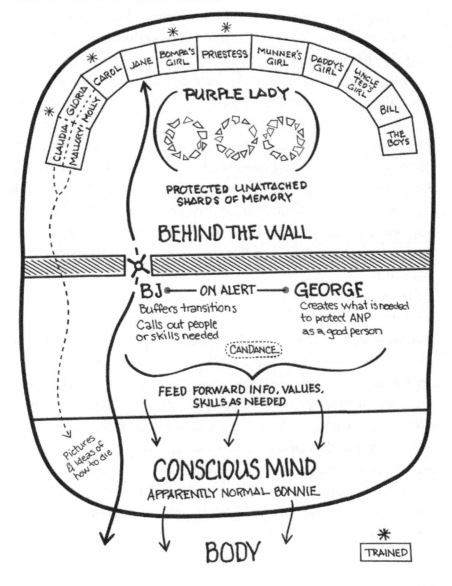

For the drawing, we differentiated between the alters who were trained or created by Bompa or Major Ken on the outside and those who were spontaneously created by our protective mechanisms, mainly thanks to George and BJ, by adding an asterisk to the alters who were brought into being by someone outside of us.

But it's more fluid than it appears. For example, Bompa's Girl, who was externally created, spontaneously made an older, larger girl to handle the science in the room behind the garage so she could stay on the lawn and not go there herself. And in collaboration with BJ, Jane had access to the conscious mind and outside actions when we needed to be cute, fearless and likable.

In the open space behind the wall, in front of the homes of the major alters, rested Purple Lady's circles of little shards of memory or experience—pieces of a child's horror that weren't really sure where they belonged. Purple Lady sheltered these disconnected pieces in circles of compassion and quiet safety, in part to guard against the danger of them popping up somewhere they shouldn't be, like breaking out of their invisibility as an unwanted flashback. They each held only a small, detached piece of an experience, so they were not needed to go back out again like the bigger ones with specific jobs and skills.

In front of the wall, BJ and George collaborated as leaders of the In-Front-of-the-Wall Gang, who passed on the information or skills Outside Bonnie needed to fulfill her duties. Especially when we were young, they were always hypervigilant for danger and the potential need to switch to allow the best-prepared among us to handle a given situation. BJ developed out of Bompa's first mind control training, and she had access to all the people behind the wall. Like a switchboard operator, she could plug in or call up whoever was appropriate for a particular danger.

From the outside, BJ is and was virtually indistinguishable from Outside Bonnie, and she could be co-present with her in the conscious mind of the ANP. BJ could seamlessly push Outside Bonnie to the side—out of the consciousness—and perform her duties as the buffer and bridge between psychic states. But she didn't go with internal parts into their world behind the wall or need to know the details of what happened to them when they were out in the body, except when Carol needed her at the base. For example, BJ would sense when we would have to be alone with Uncle Ted. She knew his curly hair, pudgy body, and cackling laugh and would call out his special girl to do her job in the outside world so no one else internally would have to experience or know about him.

In much the same way, when Daddy came into the bedroom to take the girl to the den, BJ woke up Daddy's Girl, who went with him. When he was finished, BJ returned to handle the aftermath, without knowing exactly what had happened while they were gone. For example, when the body needed to vomit after we got back to the bedroom, BJ was there to take over and clean up. This way, it didn't matter if our sister woke up or even if Mother came in or noticed in the morning. Neither BJ nor Outside Bonnie knew why she'd thrown up, and so the secret was protected.

George was the go-to guy for spontaneous protection and layering off. When there was no specific alter to handle a situation that confronted us, George jumped into action. As our self-proclaimed, internally created protector, George worked with BJ to monitor outside experiences for anything that needed to be split off from the child's consciousness. He was particularly skilled at absorbing emotional pain and protecting the outside girl and most of the others from knowing or feeling it. His skill and willingness to play this role in many ways made possible the development of Big Bonnie and the forty years of healthy relationships and high functioning she enjoyed in the world.

Both BJ and George supported Carol, who took charge at the base and layered off part after part to survive the medical experiments and emotional duress, keeping it all behind the wall and out of everyone else's consciousness. In the compartment next to Carol's, rest the alters and parts created by Major Ken in the green trailer. A dotted line connects Mallory and Claudia to the conscious mind, which they fed with ideas and pictures of how to die. Molly and Gloria were more able to be present in the body than the mind.

Each time we went to the base, George enveloped CanDance in a protective walnut shell to safeguard the central qualities of a good person. CanDance embodied the type of person who would be worth the work and energy it would take to keep the girl alive. A person who would never do or allow the awful things that had happened to her to happen to anyone around her. A person who demonstrated all the qualities that were almost completely absent from the base: kindness, compassion, honesty, love, caring. George kept these attributes front and center in the outer mind of the girl. Honesty was the hardest because, until she met Wayne, she had never seen it practiced by anyone close to her, except her big brother, Peter.

George also helped layer off many small fragments in the form of young boys to hold the pain of Munner's mad, religious ramblings about good and evil, the Wrath of God, and the wicked and sinful nature of human activity. In Bompa's absence, and with no one else internally to turn to, George stepped in to protect Outside Bonnie and the others from hearing Munner's fearful monologues.

We learned a lot when George finally allowed the compartment that housed the young boys and their emotions to open. The unexpected intensity they held clearly showed the difference between how he created parts and how external people did. George took care to hide the feelings in a way that kept them from everyone else inside—not just Outside Bonnie. Bompa and Major Ken focused only on keeping things away from Outside Bonnie's consciousness. They didn't care so much about the rest of the internal community. Maybe they didn't even understand it. That meant they sometimes left free-floating fear, abandonment or a sense of being unloved and uncared for to be absorbed by others, especially BJ.

During our adult life, George and Jane appear to have been the major players in our relationship with alcohol. Jane, of course, loved the role of the cute, perky, fun-loving girl with an insatiable need (and capacity) to be liked by everyone. As an astute observer of family dynamics, she figured the best way to be liked by men was to drink alcohol with them and party just as hard as they did. She (and Outside Bonnie) developed a high tolerance and robust appetite for drinking, to fit in and be liked.

George saw the drinking more as an act of defiance against Munner's teachings and the constraints of a society that had failed to protect the girl. Eventually, he realized this was something he had in common with Daddy. They both drank, at least partly, in rebellion against Munner, who viewed it as bad, evil and wicked. George noted that, in the end, the taste of alcohol signified freedom to him, whereas Jane saw it as a path toward being universally liked.

The ANP—influenced by all this, yet oblivious to it—never became an alcoholic. She knew she sometimes drank excessively, but usually only at celebrations or on vacation. For her, Bompa's ingrained requirement that she do her best and be useful in the world maintained primacy. Alcohol could never be allowed to interfere with her goals for a productive life or with the internal imperative to be a good person.

This was a blessing that left me with useful work and people-pleasing as my major addictions.

Chapter 40
The Way It Is Now

We created a second diagram that provides a snapshot of how the system evolved through the healing process. In the illustration, formerly thick walls of amnesia and separateness are all lighter and more permeable, to show more openness and sharing inside. This picture also depicts the important role of our healing connections to Mother Nature and to the spiritual world. As the Inca say, "As within, so without." Greater connectedness with the outside begets greater connectedness inside, and vice versa.

During our discovery process, the small parts that had sheltered in Purple Lady's circles emerged to reveal their pieces of the story by releasing body sensations, words or images. Those of us who are writing this don't know how it was decided which ones would be allowed—or urged—to express themselves when. But it happened in a decidedly nonrandom way, promoting the unification of each part with the appropriate alter. And it always provided a greater level of clarity about what had happened in each particular incident or group of similar incidents.

As Purple Lady's original circles served their purpose and were no longer needed, she created a new circle where the alters who had assimilated their parts and learned their story could gather, share and comfort each other. She named it the "Golden Circle" and lit a fire to burn bright at its center. A candle on our altar at home mirrors this central flame.

When Priestess reconnected with the rest of the fragments of her story, Purple Lady invited her to join the Golden Circle. She resisted at first, as a powerful, all-knowing priestess might. But when she realized how much more there was to be known, she joined the circle, where information and problem-solving is shared across old barriers. Questions that require input from many parts, such as "Why and by whom was Jane created?" and "What happened on the day that ended with us taking the pills?" have been addressed here.

Some alters and little parts remained fearful of the outside as they came into the consciousness and told their stories. The open area behind the wall, in front of the rooms where the alters live, provided a safe space where they could watch and learn about the outside world without needing to be in it. Sometimes, we imagined big, soft cushions in safe colors for them to rest on. When George's little boys needed support, Bill stepped forward as an older mentor and friend to help them navigate their new realities. He joined in creating a big, open tent here, from which the little boys could watch without actually engaging with outside people and activities.

In the Conscious Mind section of the picture, we find Big Bonnie as well as two specific ways of being in the outside world that required agreement among the alters.

Mommy-mode came about early in the healing process. After emotional discussions in the Green Room, we committed to being in Mommy-mode whenever we were with either of our children. This meant that, when with them, we presented the apparently normal person—the loving, nurturing mom and professional woman they had always known, who did not discuss what we were learning inside unless specifically asked. Over the years, as Beth and Will became more comfortable with my reality, the need to invoke Mommy-mode diminished greatly and both my kids developed relationships with my internal folks.

Priestess and Purple Lady took the lead as the birth of our first grandchild neared and decided what kind of grandmother they wanted our grandchildren to have: consistent, loving, protective, authentic, smart, strong and wise. This was our Oma-mode. Since my children and grandchildren live in different cities, each a plane

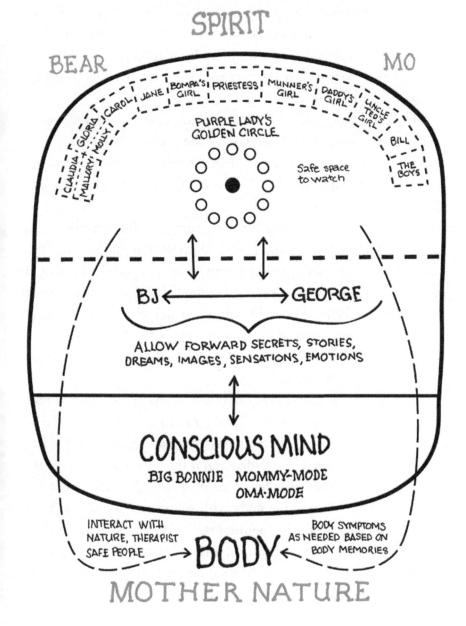

flight away from my home, these agreements were relatively easy to maintain. Whenever we left on a trip to visit, a pickup reminded everyone to be in Oma-mode, with Purple Lady ready behind the wall to hold anyone gently inside who displayed too much curiosity.

While drawing this diagram, we realized that CanDance had quietly relinquished her protection of the inner core of a good person. As healing progressed, she saw that those values were no longer under assault. Instead, they had been adopted by Big Bonnie and several others in just the way she had intended. Her vigilance was no longer required.

The rest of us were often co-conscious in our daily life, giving everyone the opportunity to embrace the present. The evolution of unity drew out the unique qualities we most appreciated in each other, with six major contributors leading the way: Purple Lady, Jane, Carol, George, Priestess and BJ.

These days, Purple Lady leads morning meditation and ritual time, when we honor all the places, teachers and guides who have helped us. We also send loving energy through special stones to all our loved ones and reinforce our intention to break cycles of fear and aggression and bring love and harmony to all our interactions. Each morning, our prayer to the universe ends with "I open my heart, mind and soul to all that is mine to do, to be, and to perceive on this day, with love, without fear."

Jane, of course, has always reminded us to express joy and gratitude for all the beauty around us, and for our many friends. With her ease in the body, Jane is often out enjoying nature, and she can help others experience what is outside, even if they don't feel comfortable being out in the body. The term "co-presence" describes what it is like when she is sharing the body with someone else, such as when we're at the beach or in the mountains. She will help someone more timid experience the grounding feeling of water and sand curling around the toes, the sensation of wind on the face, or the sight of the bright blue sky with fluffy clouds dancing.

Carol, who shouldered most of the responsibility for surviving all that happened at the base, had the largest subsystem of any of us, and she continues (with help from Jane) to monitor, mentor and assimilate the many parts she layered off. She has also assumed a major role in helping the girls who were created by Major Ken in the trailer to learn to live in the here and now and not in his world of fear and paranoia. Carol's quiet determination helps to assure that a good person with CanDance's values maintains control of the body's outside actions while others are healing.

George's tenacity, encouragement and adaptability have been directly responsible for the writing of this book. He had a broad overview of all that needed to be told and understood that telling how we healed might help other people do the same. As each alter worked with and through him to use words to tell their stories, the discovery and healing continued and deepened. He kept Big Bonnie on task as well, but gave time as needed for adult things, like paying bills.

Priestess maintains intellectual rigor and insists on honesty and respect. She pushes us, especially BJ and Big Bonnie, to speak our truth as the Grandmother of Lightning would, with love and without fear. She is a hard taskmaster even though she knows that we are all still learning new skills.

Once purposely invisible, BJ's roles in our survival have become clearer, even to her, as we have healed. The shift to understanding old roles well enough to let them go may have been hardest on her. On that night in the emergency room, she assumed responsibility for managing and controlling who and what got out into the body. For most of the next fifty years, in addition to monitoring the world for potential danger, she made sure the ANP got all the support she needed from wherever it could be drawn.

To accomplish this, BJ worked hard to stay away from her own emotions. She has been like a camp counselor, looking out for everyone else's well-being but only recently beginning to believe she is worthy of that same level of care. BJ supported virtually every alter in managing their trauma, while also sustaining the ANP as the good person everyone had hoped for. Finally allowing herself to express her emotions (and those of the many shards around her) has been BJ's biggest challenge and has opened in Big Bonnie a depth of feeling that she too never knew before.

There's nothing static or linear about this process of opening up. Whether we were created spontaneously or by design, each of us, including Big Bonnie, continues to evolve and to be transformed by our healing process. We all have needed to learn new realities about our existence, which has meant changing our perspectives, our relationships, and our ways of functioning.

The concept that one body has always housed all of us, and that one body felt and remembered everything, is difficult to comprehend. It really is hard to fathom. Our experiences seemed much more separate than should be possible if it was all the same body. Even if we accept that there may be one physical body with one brain, our many minds clearly hold unique memories and filters through which to view the world.

In addition to the variations in our personalities and skills, the world looks and feels distinctly different depending on who is experiencing it. Each alter has his or her own perceptions of color and light, and sometimes even of the sizes and shapes of objects or the features of a person's face. Each holds the body differently when in it and has different comfort levels and ways of movement. We each came into being at different developmental stages of a little girl's life, and we experience the world around us with different lenses.

Chapter 41
The Spirit Guides

The second diagram also depicts our relationship to the spiritual world, including Bear and other spirit guides. This, of course, invites the question whether these are internal or external, personal or universal. Either way, it's all part of the Great Mystery and a huge part of my healing.

It became clear to me long ago that some force, way beyond anything I could comprehend, must be orchestrating my healing journey. There were just too many serendipitous connections to be solely the result of excellent therapy. But who or what was guiding us? How were choices made? How and why was the specific timing, sequencing and pacing with which body memories and secrets were released determined? Why were some things known or some questions resolved, and others not?

When an ethereal presence began to visit the Green Room to help us understand some of these queries, I was blown away but eager to listen. It started out as a kind of enveloping mushroom cap of peaceful energy that brought a sense of oneness with the universe. It returned later, slightly less ethereal—a white cloud of gentle energy, but with a voice.

By that point, I was recording the sessions in the Green Room and wrote summaries of, or sometimes transcribed, our meetings.

(Without this assistance, I seldom had full recall of the sessions, even though the words and thoughts came through my body.) Julia and I felt the need to give this presence a name, even though it clearly was not an alter in the usual sense. It seemed to come and go out of the ether, rather than in the mind. It didn't have a body, but the presence felt masculine to me, although of course he was likely genderless. I understood him to be the Main Orchestrator and called him "MO" for short (pronounced "mō"). But he could also have been called the Great Explainer, as this was the role he took on as orchestration became less necessary.

Through MO's references to "the big angels" with whom he worked, I understood him to represent the energetic and spiritual forces that had guided this soul throughout its lifetime. Now that he was finished helping us release secrets from childhood, he sought other ways to assist with our healing. His support was contingent upon my willingness to accept hard truths and seek understanding, not to blame anyone or hold onto the victim mantle, but rather to grow and heal. I never heard that said, but it was clear in the non-judgmental way he dealt with information.

He allowed me to see the connections among events on the time-line of my journey, which deepened my trust and permitted me to defer vexing questions to him. I knew "MO knows and will let me understand in due time." I had heard that some wisdom traditions believe those of us with brains that work differently may connect more easily to the Great Mystery and that we can access insights others cannot. I think they're right!

Purple Lady's strong connection to MO often allowed her to write what he wanted us to know in the journal. Here's one passage I find particularly clarifying.

> I was like a black hole that could take it all in and not have any of it bounce off or reflect back out into the world. There is one soul who came into this body for this lifetime, to break cycles of lifetimes that couldn't find wisdom or peace or

express love. Many different skills were needed to survive and experience all the gifts and the outpouring of energy, so they could be absorbed rather than passed on. So, the single soul allowed many manifestations within the one body. One soul, one body. Many ways to absorb rather than replicate or be transformed by the old pain.

Here's another, along the same lines.

We came in with one soul, one body, then we drew on lots of spirit guides and bridge people for guidance and support—and even for orchestration. We must realize that we are all part of a soul who chose a life that required many manifestations and great creativity within its one body and hovered close to the spirit side on many occasions, receiving sustenance, support and guidance—messages heard and known internally, if not in the external mind. We all played a part, or several parts, over time.

I am more than the sum of my parts. I am the ocean, not the drops. In this case, "I" is an imperfect representation of the essence of this spiritual being living a physical life. I am not my diagnosis.

What a surreal gift to meet a force who seemed to hold the blueprints for my life and was willing to share some of the rationale behind puzzling events, like the purpose and timing of the apparent illness that led to opening up or the ways my system used other situations (some ostensibly outside our control, others internally generated) to accomplish its intentions.

As an example, a car accident in 1990 prompted me to understand my childhood differently. With damage to three vertebrae in my neck, I was in treatment and a neck brace for six months, narrowly avoiding serious surgery.

But during my hospital stay, the neurosurgeon saw something (I wish I knew what it was) that made her believe I was dealing with post-traumatic stress disorder (PTSD) along with the physical injuries. I desperately wanted to be home with my husband and kids, and she released me on the condition that I get PTSD counseling from the mental health clinic associated with the hospital. I agreed, but with very little understanding of what PTSD meant, how it might relate to me, or why she had referred me.

My mother drove me to these counseling appointments, and we talked about what I learned, which was the beginning of a new depth of honesty in our relationship. My father had died four years earlier, and the counselor pushed me to explore my relationship with him, which had been turbulent, even on the surface.

With hindsight, I see Mother and I took the opportunity to confront things we had never discussed before and began to set the record straight. I learned that Dad's drinking had been well beyond "social" for many years. He was a binge drinker who would sometimes be gone from home for two or three days at a time.

I asked Mother when his drinking had been the worst, and she surprised me by saying it was when he moved his electronics business out of our garage and into a building in town when I was five. She was so good at covering up for him that I had believed her when she said Daddy was working hard on a big project at the shop that kept him from coming home. I always thought his drinking had gotten bad only after I became a teenager, which is when I finally noticed it.

This beginning of a more realistic portrait of my dad and mother was incredibly important on several levels. Mother passed MO's test of her willingness to loosen her tightly controlled image of the life she wanted to portray, and I grasped that I might not have a totally clear picture of my childhood. These first steps awakened our capacity and readiness for the journey ahead, as my system's inevitable quest for wholeness and freedom began to stir.

While healing from this accident, I went back to school to get a master's degree, fulfilling a goal I had nurtured for years. With that accomplished, Wayne and I switched roles—something we had talked about since deciding to have children. It happens all the time now, but in 1992, it was quite unusual for him to quit his job in order to work part-time, handle the household, and be more available to the kids while I resumed a full-time career, becoming the primary wage earner in the family.

My existing part-time consulting practice grew immediately, with major clients like the National League of Cities and the National Center for Youth Development. I loved my work, got involved in local and national advocacy, and felt I was contributing something of value to every community I worked with. At the same time, I relished being a mom who had loved being at home with her young children and could now model for them the role of being a professional woman who traveled all over the country.

And then I turned fifty.

MO revealed two aspects of our fiftieth-birthday, family trip to Europe that triggered the change in our lives.

First, I insisted we visit a concentration camp so I could educate my teenaged children about the Holocaust and World War II. I had no understanding of how or why I would be so deeply triggered by the reminders of human experimentation.

Second, MO explained to us, "The issue of dependency came up on this trip. We needed [Bonnie] to be in a position to be supported… not to need to care for others. And it became apparent that those who should be caring for her now depended on her in ways we didn't like. So, it became necessary to move forward with a test of the level of support that could be made available—and it was unfortunately lacking. We put in place opportunities for learning, for adaptability, for growth, and they weren't accepted or were accepted only moderately."

He orchestrated the first two waves of physical symptoms as short-term tests, to see if there was enough external support for the long road of disorientation, pain and excruciating body memories (or "growth, expansion and evolution," to use Deepak Chopra's language) that lay ahead. Any deficiencies noted were to be acted upon before the actual long-term process was unleashed.

MO's assessment found Wayne unable to provide the emotional or material partnership needed to make it through the grueling years MO knew I would face. Yet Wayne had been the perfect mate until that point. When we met, the In-Front-of-the-Wall Gang saw immediately he had a gentle face and twinkly blue eyes, reminiscent of Bompa's. He had served in the Peace Corps, like my adored older brother. Everyone's interest was piqued, and the night after I met him, I had an automobile accident, which offered the perfect opportunity to observe him. MO and George noted he was not a man who needed to flex his masculinity. He was kind and attentive to my needs after the accident, even foregoing our first sexual encounter until I felt better—which is to say, until *I* chose. An encouraging sign.

Wayne was not terribly introspective, which meant he would not ask a lot of intrusive questions about our internal workings, and he really liked the Bonnie he knew. Over the more than three decades we were together, he helped draw out the best of me, and I became a better Big Bonnie because of his values and his belief in me. But when MO tested him for this new challenge and found him unable to muster the strength and resilience that would be needed, MO prepared me to handle life without depending on a mate.

Without realizing I was acting based on MO's guidance, I decided to get a full-time job to replace my consulting practice. I had only to voice it, and within a week, the phone rang with a perfect offer. By the time the internal system turned up the intensity of the body's symptoms, I had what I needed to sustain myself: excellent group health insurance in my name and a salaried income with sickness and disability benefits.

Chapter 42
The Science

While I was busy creating pictures of how my mind worked and how the spirit guides had helped direct my life and healing, the world of neuroscience was striving to answer my questions more scientifically. How in the world did my brain do this? How did I, and many others I had met, emerge so high functioning when trauma had messed with our brain at such a young age? Does dissociation somehow protect the developing brain from the impact of early trauma?

By early 2013, I felt safe enough to let loose my inner, nerdy, science geek and dig into the emerging research without worrying that my evolving memories could be tainted. The neuroscience on the impact of trauma and neglect on the young, developing brain includes studies on resilience, neuroplasticity, neurogenesis, polyvagal theory, epigenetics and much more.

Back in the 1990s and early 2000s, some of the research I had been exposed to at work theorized that abuse and neglect can cause irreparable harm to a child's developing brain. We were shown PowerPoint slides of brain scans that left me with an indelible image of underdeveloped potential.

But by 2016, I was excited to learn about new discoveries of how brain neurons can repair themselves and even generate new growth across the lifespan. That made more sense to me, based on my experience and that of other people I knew with dissociative disorders.

As an early follower of the adverse childhood experiences study[10] and its impact, I read new papers as researchers refined their analysis of the study's findings. When groups like the ACEs Connection network came along, I joined and was thrilled to see the movement toward trauma-informed care taking root all over the country and around the globe. I could even imagine that, in some communities, this work might build on the collaborative youth master plans I had helped develop decades earlier.

It wasn't easy to find much information about the inner workings of dissociation. One researcher even told me quite clearly that a child or teenager who was doing well in school and outwardly behaving normally would not have been studied for the impact of neglect or toxic stress. Why would they, since we were apparently normal? So, those of us who dissociated and kept up a good front were inadvertently left out of the research.

In fact, physicians and psychologists I talked with said they received very little information about dissociative disorders in medical or graduate school. They were told that these conditions were very rare and they probably would never see one. Of course, it's hard to see something you aren't looking for and know almost nothing about!

On the other hand, there is a rich and growing body of research and literature about trauma in general and childhood trauma specifically. In most of the newer works, dissociation is addressed as an important survival tool.

My copies of Alice Miller's *The Body Never Lies,* Bessel van der Kolk's *The Body Keeps the Score,* and Donna Jackson Nakazawa's *Childhood Disrupted* are dog-eared, with penciled notes throughout. I came a little later to Judith Herman's book *Trauma and Recovery,* which actually pre-dates all of these and sets our individual pain

---

10   See footnote 1.

in its social context. Eduardo Duran's *Healing the Soul Wound* and Thomas Hübl's *Healing Collective Trauma* deepened my understanding of what the indigenous elders had taught me about ancestral and collective healing. The resource list at the back of this book is filled with other important written works I have found helpful. In addition, I became an avid attendee of online workshops and conferences these authors and other scientists and healers offered.

But how did all this information help me understand myself and the paradoxes of my life? First things first. Trauma researchers often suggest we start by reviewing attachment during infancy. According to the family history I'd heard, during the first twenty months of my life, I traveled with my parents, had easy access to Mother if I needed anything, and thrived on the attention I received from them and from the diverse array of people we met.

This type of varied and safe activity, positive feedback, and access to a comforting adult provides a foundation that serves an individual and their brain well. Given how devastating it felt when access to my mother was disrupted when I was three, I'm inclined to assume my attachment until then was solid.

I looked for help to explain how my later life experiences might have conspired to build resilience and repair my brain after the years of abuse I endured from age two to twelve. It turns out that being multilingual strengthens one of the specific regions of the brain that can be damaged by early trauma.[11] Ongoing research has shown our brains continue to develop throughout our life cycle, and a particular window of opportunity exists for increased neuroplasticity in late adolescence and early adulthood.[12]

As a junior in high school, excelling in advanced classes in math and French, I applied to be a foreign exchange student with the

11   Schug, Alison K et al. "Gray matter volume differences between early bilinguals and monolinguals: A study of children and adults." *Human brain mapping* vol. 43,16 (2022): 4817-4834. doi:10.1002/hbm.26008.
12   Fuhrmann, Delia et al. "Adolescence as a Sensitive Period of Brain Development." *Trends in cognitive sciences* vol. 19,10 (2015): 558-566. doi:10.1016/j.tics.2015.07.008.

American Field Service. Mother signed the papers without giving it much thought, except to note that it was in the future and probably wouldn't happen. In a surprise to everyone, except perhaps MO, I was selected and left in June 1963 to live and attend school in Sweden for thirteen months. Given my gregarious personality, communicating with my new friends was imperative, so I worked hard and became fluent in Swedish. In the process, I realized I had an ear for language and loved learning, thinking and speaking with the new perspectives a new language brings. Shifting from dreams of being a musical-comedy star, I decided to become an interpreter and help bring about world peace and understanding. By the time I turned twenty, while studying in Europe, I was fluent in three languages and conversant in another three.

This leads me to posit that my teenage linguistic activities rewired and built up the architecture of my brain, repairing it from whatever damage had been done. I spent more than two years studying in Europe, then translated and interpreted across three languages for several years after that. Science calls this process of retraining the brain "neuroplasticity," and the work of rebuilding the brain is called "neurogenesis." I may have accomplished both without knowing it, and perhaps this allowed me to function well enough in my adult life that no one ever suspected there was anything wrong—least of all me.

Using theater and music as a trauma treatment modality is gaining credibility, although many practitioners have had great success employing them for a long time. From kindergarten to my early twenties, I acted in school and community plays every chance I got and sang in glee clubs, choirs and as a soloist at local events. Beginning after the suicide attempt when I was twelve, I sang big band tunes at dances and other events as a soloist with the Boy's Club dance band. In Sweden, I sang and performed with a small girl's chorus and did a rendition of *Annie Get Your Gun*, complete with pistol and cowboy hat—always a major hit.

Again, it is possible that my natural tendencies, perhaps guided by MO, led me into activities that helped repair damage and build up mental and emotional functions, so the outside girl could thrive in school and the world. The mastery and joy I felt while performing certainly built self-confidence and self-worth, as did the languages. These diverse treatment modalities came naturally into my life at times when my brain and mind were the most receptive, blessing me with opportunities to build resilience, both structurally and emotionally. Now that we know the science behind why this worked, my life makes more sense. I hope we can make such opportunities available to others.

Steven Porges's Polyvagal Theory offered helpful insight into my question about whether dissociation acted as a kind of protective factor for a developing brain. He says, "Polyvagal Theory interprets dissociation as an adaptive reaction to life threat challenges, which... would not compromise the neurobiological needs" of the body, as some other responses would. He sees dissociation as a heroic response and wants us to honor the wisdom of our bodies.[13]

Scientists have known for decades that brain scans of adults with dissociative identity disorder look different depending on which alter is present in the body.[14] My experience of how differently my alters hold the body and process the same sensory cues fits perfectly with this finding. Depending on who is out in the body, Julia looks different, the light in a room looks different, even the feel of a piece of material—like the green couch—is different. We even may or may not need our glasses! And, of course, we all process information or emotions in different ways. This led me to wonder whether the same physical or medical intervention might have differing effects depending on who was in the body.

Nagging pain in my left hip and thigh that stemmed from a very old injury to Priestess when she fell down some stairs gave me the

---

13   Porges, Steven. *Pocket Guide to The Polyvagal Theory.* (W. W. Norton, 2017), pg 12.
14   Talbot, M. *The Holographic Universe.* (Harper Perennial, 1992), pg 77.

perfect opportunity to check this out. I asked Dr. Kendall, my intuitive chiropractor, who always takes the most holistic approach possible, if the issue might be better dealt with if the person who was present in the body when the injury happened were present as she worked on it. She agreed it might make a difference, so we tested the idea.

I settled face-down on her table as she did some adjustments based on her initial observations of my body. Then she asked permission to talk with others, to see if she could help. Without saying anything, George, the protector, came first to see what she was doing and make sure it was safe. She asked again, because he hadn't said anything as she scanned our left side.

"I agreed to be here. Isn't that permission enough?"

She responded with deference, feeling for potential adjustments, and said he seemed to be in good alignment, with no issues in the hip or leg. At her gentle touch, he relaxed and went back inside.

With George's all-clear, Priestess came forward and the body tightened up, as it always does when she is present. This time, the doctor could tell someone else was there and asked again for permission to touch the body. Priestess responded with a terse, "Yes."

Dr. Kendall touched the hip. "The pain is also connected to the shoulder," Priestess clarified.

As Dr. Kendall did her assessment of the body, she moved to the right shoulder, which irritated Priestess. "Not that one! The other one! And it goes all the way down to the toes."

"Thank you for the information," Dr. Kendall replied, continuing her work and adjusting all three places in her gentle way.

"Are you a doctor?" Priestess demanded.

Dr. Kendall introduced herself and her credentials, as she might to any new adult patient. As she continued to test and make adjustments, the body relaxed and released years of tension.

"You have done a good job," Priestess admitted.

Dr. Kendall described briefly what had been out of alignment and that it was now corrected.

"It is good to be in alignment. Thank you." And Priestess left.

Jane popped into the body next, wanting to test out whether she could sit on the table cross-legged. She did, with no pain at all. "Oh, this is so exciting. It's the first time in a long while that I can sit like this without hurting—and it's my favorite. You must be the best doctor in the whole world!"

Since that day, before we go see the chiropractor, we check to see whose pain the body is feeling and to invite that person to be present to experience the treatment. It's strange, but highly effective, and it underscores that old trauma can be stored in muscles and organs for many years. As with talk therapy, it turns out that physical symptoms can best be treated if the psychic state who was present at the time of the injury is there to identify and release the pain.

So yes, Western science offered some helpful support to Big Bonnie's need for legitimacy and a scientific way of understanding her life. But in the end, I realized the science was just catching up to the wisdom of the Universe that had guided my life and to the intuitive skills of my therapist and doctors, which, combined with the wisdom of indigenous traditions, had guided my healing.

In *Healing the Soul Wound*, Eduardo Duran talks about historical and generational trauma in terms of the "soul wounds" of individuals and groups. When Thomas Hübl writes about *Healing Collective Trauma*, he asks us to consider that we are all born into a traumatized species in a traumatized world. These are not concepts I understood or had ever heard of when I was led to augment my Western cognitive therapy with the soul-cleansing indigenous wisdom that rejuvenated my spirit and spiritual connections. To provide a basis for the compassion I knew was needed, I decided to take another look to better understand the wounds of the culture into which I was born.

In the first year of what came to be known as the "post-war baby boom," I was born into a solidly middle-class northern European, Aryan, Protestant family—a total WASP (White Anglo-Saxon Protestant) going back several generations. The well-established, suburban Southern California community I grew up in prided itself on excellent schools and universities, and on a world of new opportunities and scientific discoveries that made almost anything seem possible. I internalized this privilege and optimism, believing I could accomplish anything I put my mind to. Most of the kids I went to school with looked a lot like me and lived in the same picture book version of the 1950s. The idyllic media representations, economic growth, and hopefulness of the time formed our understanding of ourselves and the world. At the same time, public policies invisible to us kept our neighborhoods and schools, for the most part, racially and economically segregated—even in Southern California. I remember not being allowed to go to certain parts of town, but overt acts of racism and anti-Semitism were largely hidden from my view or justified in ways I wasn't supposed to question.

Other, coexisting realities lurked just behind the veneer. The post-war 1940s and '50s held great fear, the most obvious examples of which included the air raid drills I remember at school and the fallout shelters some people built. While the country bragged that our WWII military saved the world, a whole generation of men (and many women) came home with invisible war wounds—terrors they had no way to talk about or get treatment for—to start or continue families.

What must it have been like to be one of the fliers who rained firebombs on the Dresden my German family wrote about? I could see the nightmares on both sides. And I wondered how a returning vet could possibly describe the sights, smells, sounds and emotions of a concentration camp being liberated? Science did not yet recognize the impact of such trauma on the human brain and nervous system. Instead, returning soldiers and their families felt the impact in myriad ways, from emotional shutdown to alcohol and other forms of self-medication to family violence.

And of course, the powerful drug of choice for most of the '50s, denial, coupled with a stigma against asking for help and a lack of useful resources, meant we never talked about any of it. Quite to the contrary, a great deal of energy was expended to keep the illusion intact, even when a classmate's mom died in her garage of carbon monoxide poisoning or we went to pick up a friend and found her caring for her sick-drunk parents.

The Korean War and Cold War deepened our fear of the unthinkable atrocities WWII taught us humans were capable of, beyond the bombs. Perhaps the paranoia was understandable, but it drove a desire to control the human condition and led some scientists and government institutions to conduct secret research programs. Others sought comfort in an exploration of religious and Satanic rituals.

In this dark stratum under the idyllic surface, what passed for scientific investigation ran unchecked, fueled by fear from the past and fear of the future. The limits of human potential needed to be tested, and the amazing scientific ends justified means of exploration that the general community would have neither understood nor tolerated, like torturing little girls and programming their minds with posthypnotic suicidal suggestions.

Secrets held in families, created by fear and creating more fear. Secret acts perpetrated by the government, prompted by fear. Religious creeds based on fear of a vengeful God. Seen this way, fear undergirded my whole culture.

No wonder I had to go all the way to Machu Picchu to uncover the fear that had lived in my body all my life—and to hear the call to learn to live "with love, without fear."

Part 8
Words of Wisdom

Chapter 43
Reconnecting Gondwana

Silvia Calisaya, an Aymara elder, teacher and wisdom keeper I first met at Lake Titicaca, invited me to an international conference in 2014 called "Reconnecting Gondwana." It was to be held at Uluru (in Australia) in November, during my birthday week. Just as the earlier council in Peru had sought to join the Americas to activate peace and unity, this conference sought to demonstrate connections among the traditions of the continents that were once part of the ancient supercontinent of Gondwana.[15] I immediately saw the opportunity for some deeply connective personal work, as well as a chance to visit Phoebe and her husband, who by now had two little girls I was eager to meet.

But first, I wanted to see some other parts of the Northern Territory, including Darwin, Kakadu National Park, and a bit of Arnhem Land, where Phoebe had stayed while working on her PhD in linguistics, helping to codify and maintain indigenous languages. The opportunity to travel and explore on my own was welcomed internally and planned jointly.

I spent a week enjoying the incredible natural beauty and traditional art of this amazing area. I even took a boat ride on a bill-

---

15   The existence of Gondwana was first hypothesized in the mid-1800s by Eduard Suess, a Viennese geologist who dubbed the theoretical continent "Gondwanaland." It presumably incorporated the land masses of the southern hemisphere.

abong[16] and saw crocodiles and water buffalo in very low water, waiting expectantly for the wet season to begin. The flight back to Uluru offered more vistas of the magnificent red desert with its dotted landscape, reminding me of my first visit and my cherished painting, *Bonnie's Dreaming*.

Reconnecting Gondwana was a small, intimate conference with presenters who included elders from a variety of wisdom traditions: a Maori grandmother from New Zealand; a Buddhist monk from Tibet; the Aymara wise woman from Peru; a student of the Rainbow Serpent from Glastonbury, England; and our host, "Uncle" Bob Randall, an elder of the Anangu people of the region around Uluru.

Once we gathered, it became clear that pretty much everyone there was a spiritual elder in his or her own right. We represented many countries and diverse communities, and we easily established a joyous time of sharing and ceremony. I even came to see myself as having something to contribute, as well as more to learn. Reconnecting severed land masses seemed an apt metaphor for reconnecting the splintered results of childhood trauma in a human life.

Unlike the Yucatan trip, during which I traveled with my dear friend, Marisol, who knew several members of our internal community, at this conference, I had a roommate I had never met before. The kind of co-presence some of our alters anticipated had to wait a couple of days, as we learned to trust Polly enough to share about their existence.

To open and close each session, our host, Uncle Bob Randall, and his guitar gently led us in singing a simple song that summed up the universal theme and teaching that connected us all.

We are one. We are free.
Love is my responsibility.
We are one, one family.
Love is my responsibility.

16   An isolated body of water left behind after a bend in a river is cut off when the river's channel changes course. These beds often dry out during the hotter months and then flood when the wet season arrives.

Love is the connective tissue for all life in the local wisdom traditions. Likewise, the Mayan charge makes it my responsibility to grow love with every interaction and the Inca blessing "with love, without fear." And, of course, love is an important tenet of most world religions. God is love. Love. It really could draw us together, if we would only live our beliefs.

The only religion I could think of that was not based on love was the fearful teachings of my grandparents and uncle, which left them as sad outliers. Even Priestess had moved away from Bompa's teachings and saw that love and caring could be greater signs of strength and belonging than fear of punishment.

The week-long conference included field trips to several remarkable cultural and historical sites, as well as more intimate and informative visits with Uluru and Kata Tjuta than I had been able to arrange on my first visit. One day, the local elders at Uluru treated us to a delightful and informative expedition to learn how residents of this area had traditionally used local plants for everything from medicine to clothing. They also gave us deeper insight into the morality parables and creation stories connected to the land and the natural markings on Uluru. A couple of moments stand out because of their specific relevance to my healing.

That morning started with breakfast at the little café in the cultural center, where I found myself at a table alone with Geshe, the Buddhist monk. Uluru glowed bright orange in the early sun just outside the window as he and I chatted about compassion over our scrambled eggs and toast.

I commented on a helpful presentation he'd made the day before, then added, "It's important that I grow my 'compassion muscle,' given my soul's task in this lifetime to break generational cycles of abuse."

He patted my arm and said, with a joyous twinkle in his eye, "You can remind yourself you are free now. You can relax."

And I felt myself do just that—relax deep inside.

Wow. What a blessed life! Breakfast conversation with my own Tibetan monk. His simple statement, spoken in love with delight in his eyes, resonated through me and everyone inside. Yes, we were free now. We could all relax. Self-compassion was as important as the generational work.

The last morning of the conference, I woke up early, knowing several inside folks had wanted time to play in the red earth and feel their toes in the warm sand. They were unhappy that Big Bonnie had not yet made time and a safe space for that to happen. I hopped out of bed, grabbed some clothes and, without washing my face, told my roommate, Polly, "I'm going out to play in the sand. Want to come?"

Her immediate answer was, "Sure!" She was a dance teacher who loved to play.

The hotel sat just across the street from a broad open expanse of trails and brush—more or less the natural desert. The pathways of loose red sand beckoned, so we didn't even put shoes on.

As soon as we got to the red earth path, Jane came into the body with effusive joy over how good the warm dirt felt, how pretty everything looked, and how much she liked Polly. Jane decided she needed to give this new person some understanding of who we were, so she picked up a stick and drew in the sand the drawing we had recently made of our brain and how it worked. She loved showing off how well she could both explain and draw it.

After Jane had her fun and demonstrated that Polly was a safe playmate, she urged Carol to come forward. Carol was shyer and quieter, of course, but Jane knew she had been working very hard and needed some fun. The sight of this desert confused Carol at first, because it looked so different from her desert—red sand instead of white, and it had different bushes.

She confided to Polly, "You know, they did bad and hurtful things at the base. I don't know why they did that. But they hurt me bad." She let her feet play in the red sand, watched them change color, and felt the temperature shift. She walked around a bit, taking in the greens of the bushes, the blue of the sky, the warmth of the sun.

"This is really fun. I think Molly would enjoy it. I'm going to see if she wants to come out."

Molly didn't talk much, but felt more comfortable in the body than Carol. She walked with her feet trailing in the sand for a good while, maybe fifteen feet, after which she moved them apart for a few steps, then back together. When we stopped and looked back, Polly pointed out that it looked like a snake and took a picture. Molly was impressed with her own artwork. She invited Mallory to come play, but Mallory was happier to stay in the mind and watch.

Molly's serpent may be the perfect final image of this trip. The Rainbow Serpent work presented at the conference tied together Mother Earth's chakras. With considerable excitement, I realized I had visited and felt the reciprocal energy in five of Pachamama's seven chakras. As I worked to reconnect myself to my own inner spirit and strength, I was also aiding the opening of the new era at many of Mother Earth's most sensitive and energetic spots, with guidance from some of the oldest wisdom traditions on the planet.

At every step along the way, I met generosity of spirit and openness to sharing healing wisdom with a traveler from another culture. What appeared as random trips on a bucket list had actually brought me to these important places and their lessons. I celebrated the connectedness that made it clear, separation had always been an illusion. As within, so without. I felt deeply blessed by a magnanimous universe.

Chapter 44
Be Kind

After more than two decades, our healing quest has brought us to the point that maintaining the illusion of an apparently normal person has become secondary to embracing this life as it is—one life lived by many parts—a life that has included pain, abandonment and horror, as well as adventure, exploration and fulfillment; great joy in life's many pleasures and deep sorrow, isolation and meaninglessness; excitement to be alive and eagerness to end this life; the blessing of loving and knowing I am loved and the certainty that nothing about me is lovable or has ever been loved. I've seen terror and torture, the results of unfettered human hubris and religious and political fervor. I've also enjoyed great human kindness and been touched by friends and strangers with gentleness and humanity. All of it made possible by a superpower that some people think of as a disorder.

Life, and my understanding of it, changed forever when the doors of my mind opened and forced me to accept the impossible. The seemingly normal life I had lived turned out to be a well-orchestrated illusion to which I could not return. I had been profoundly separated from large chunks of my reality, but now I can connect the dots so they create a whole picture.

Trauma separates. Healing is about connection and breaking cycles, about choosing to treat people differently than you were treated. I had to wait until I was in my sixties to fully connect with myself and learn these lessons. Finding my way forward required embracing the internal community who had supported this life every step of the way.

Albert Einstein, one of the twentieth-century's great scientists, was also quite a philosopher, and I love his provocative writings. His early willingness to ask the entire scientific community to break open the boundaries of accepted assumptions became a call for all of us to do the same in our lives.

A letter he wrote in 1950 to a grieving father, Norman Salit, offers a powerful expression that helped me grasp what life was asking of me. Einstein writes:

> A human being is a part of the whole, called by us "Universe," a part limited in time and space. He experiences himself, his thoughts and feelings as something separated from the rest—a kind of optical delusion of his consciousness. This delusion is a kind of prison for us, restricting us to our personal desires and to affection for a few persons nearest to us. Our task must be to free ourselves from this prison by widening our circle of compassion to embrace all living creatures and the whole nature in its beauty. Nobody is able to achieve this completely, but the striving for such achievement is in itself a part of the liberation and a foundation for inner security.[17]

Healing meant freeing myself from the delusional prison of separateness Einstein speaks of, widening my circles of compassion and connection to embrace all of nature's creations, even my abusers, as both he and all the indigenous wisdom traditions I've studied suggest. Yes, life always has more to teach us than we think we have to learn.

What happened in the past prepared us for life now. Our task is to be awake and present in every moment. Every challenge carries a gift. Yes, that's a cliché that I have found to be annoyingly true.

---

17   Albert Einstein Archives, The Hebrew University of Jerusalem. emeraldlakebooks.com/einstein.

On one of those days when I lay in bed feeling sorry for myself, seeing no end in sight and wanting to pull the covers over my head and hide, Purple Lady took up her purple pen and admonished me in our journal.

> It is about the journey, not the destination. Each day, meaningful interactions happen. You are either present fully for them or not. Your choices matter to other people. You are not here alone or by chance. Show up so that you honor the fact that others' paths bring them into interaction with you on yours. You don't have to know the outcome—the future—in order to honor and respect each interaction in the present moment. You have this day. Use it well. Be present with clarity, focus, ease and grace. Respect your own path as you respect that of others. Each moment holds possibility.

I printed out and posted this quote next to my desk to keep it easily accessible the next time I forget. It's a reminder that people all around us walk through their days carrying burdens we know nothing about. We can each choose to interact with kindness and grace, without making assumptions.

"Be kind, for everyone you meet is fighting a great battle." I had first heard this line in a lovely movie starring Sophia Loren, called *Between Strangers*. The movie credited the quote to Philo of Alexandria. I've seen it attributed to several other people, but whoever said it first, I love it and use it a lot.

Life is a collection of moments filled with possibility. Those include even the difficult times, as long as we are willing to ask, "What's the lesson in this for me?" There is no end to the quest and no separation between body, mind, spirit and nature. However much the language and culture I grew up with see them as separate domains to be treated individually, my healing experience begs to differ. No end; no separation—only connections to be healed and celebrated, within and without. As each one heals, the healing of the whole advances.

This is as true for me as a multiple as it is for humanity. Each person's individual healing matters to the whole.

Big Bonnie's life—which still looks normal to a casual observer—is full of friends, family, travel, life coaching, speaking, writing and, of course, Dodgers games during the season. With continued support from everyone internally, we are committed to interacting with the world in ways that increase love and harmony, and to advocating for families, children and anyone recovering from or affected by trauma. We participate in as many global meditations for peace and healing as we can, inspired by the knowledge that the healing work I do in my little condo is multiplied many times around the globe.

Intense feelings of loneliness, isolation and abandonment—even occasional suicidal thoughts—still surface from time to time. Given the openness of the old walls, it's easier now to acknowledge whoever is suffering and listen to and honor their pain. We remind them with internal hugs that the past is over. We are living in a much safer present, where we're nurtured by loving friends and family, the resilient strength of our fire-prone mountains and conversations with our special trees. Some days, we need mashed potatoes with every meal or the quiet self-care of watching old movies while snuggling in bed with our teddy bear.

The imperative to find the right answer and do the right thing to meet other people's expectations no longer drives our actions. There is no right answer to strive for—just a life, utterly transformed, to live with as much honesty and compassion as we can muster. One unified life with one body, lots of minds, and the capacity for emotional and spiritual growth, complexity, kindness and love. And I get to live it in the sweet knowledge that we won. They didn't break me. I outlived everyone who hurt me, and lived (mostly) according to CanDance's values, thanks to my internal community—my superpower.

We have lived to tell the story of an apparently normal life that was struck by an apparently debilitating illness and walked through the not-so-metaphorical valley of the shadow of death to find whole-ness, health and a new life purpose on the other side. Hooray!

When I met Grandmother Sue, who runs the Vortex Healing Centre in Tasmania, at the Reconnecting Gondwana conference, her deep energetic connection to the universe and our planet inspired me to keep in touch with her. Not long after the conference, she sent me these words of wisdom.

> Sometimes, the best way to help others is in taking the responsibility to help yourself become more of who you are. Don't miss your opportunity to express that one piece of the puzzle that only you hold!

By telling my story, I believe I am adding to the puzzle a piece of the great mystery that is uniquely mine to contribute. I hope it inspires you to "find your own rock," as Priestess would say. We are together on this planet at this time with an important responsibility to each other and to future generations. I hope the story of my journey helps you on yours.

Thank you for reading *An Apparently Normal Person*.
If you've enjoyed reading this book, please leave a review on your favorite review site. In doing so, you can help reach more readers who might benefit from my story.

Discussion Questions

If you'd like to invite the author to join you for your book club, classroom or other group discussion, Bonnie is available to meet with you remotely to discuss *An Apparently Normal Person*. Requests may be sent by visiting emeraldlakebooks.com/armstrong.

1. In the first few chapters, Bonnie's deteriorating health seems very physical, but turns out to have a psychological cause. What do you think about her response to this connection between mind and body? How did her response change over time?

2. What clues do you see in the early part of the book that Bonnie misses or doesn't pay attention to because she considers them normal?

3. Bonnie describes several "serendipities" over the course of her journey. The first is a job offer on page 12. Viewed as more than coincidences, she calls such occurrences "a gift from the Universe." Have things like this ever happened to you?

4. As Bonnie learns new truths about her past and some family members that differ greatly from what she thought she knew, what did this do to her sense of herself? Have newfound truths ever surprised you?

5. Why did Bonnie find it so difficult to share with others what was happening to her? How would you respond if a colleague you liked confided they had been diagnosed with a mental health disorder?

6. What role did suicide and suicidal ideations play in Bonnie's life as an apparently normal person? How was her outward response influenced by her internal community? If she had taken her life as an adult, would anyone have understood why?

7. In Chapter 37, Bonnie releases her anger by burning a paper-bag effigy of her father. What other ways did she find to release big emotions? What methods do you use?

8. Although Bonnie grows to feel compassion for them, she never actually forgives her father or grandfather. What do you think about this? How important is forgiveness in your life? Compassion?

9. Has reading about Bonnie's journey changed the way you think about people who have dissociative identity disorder? In what ways? How is it different from movie and other media depictions of this condition?

10. Do you know anyone with mental health challenges? Does Bonnie's story give you any new insights into what it may be like for them?

11. What do you think about the way Bonnie came to see her dissociative skills and internal community as a super-power rather than a disorder?

12. Which of the internal community members (alters) did you relate to best? Why?

13. What did you think about the way some alters grew to use their skills in new ways?

14. What questions did learning about "the base" raise for you? Had you known about secret CIA programs from that era, like MKULTRA and Operation Paperclip? Discuss the implications of these historical projects for today's world.

15. Discuss the role indigenous wisdom traditions play in Bonnie's healing journey. What important lessons did she take away from her studies and retreats? What parts of these interactions are most meaningful to you?

16. In what ways did you notice Bonnie's relationship with Mother Nature become important on her healing journey? How do you feel when you interact with nature?

17. In the last chapter, Bonnie offers a quote from Albert Einstein that "helped me grasp what life was asking of me." In what ways does Einstein's quote speak to you?

18. Were you surprised to learn in Wendy Lazarus's foreword that dissociative disorders are as common as bipolar disorder and schizophrenia? Why do you think this is not very well known?

19. Bonnie's story highlights the relationship between childhood trauma and adult health. What are the implications of this connection for your family, schools or community?

Recommended Resources

Booklist

Some books that have been helpful on my journey:

Burke-Harris, N. *The Deepest Well: Healing the Long-Term Effects of Childhood Trauma and Adversity.* Mariner Books, 2018.

Campbell, J. *The Hero With a Thousand Faces.* MJF Books, 1997.

Chödrön, P. *When Things Fall Apart: Heart Advice for Difficult Times.* Penguin Random House, 2000.

Davis, Laura. *The Burning Light of Two Stars: A Mother-Daughter Story.* Girl Friday Books, 2021.

Delgado, J. L. *Andean Awakening: An Inca Guide to Mystical Peru.* Millichap Books, 2012.

Duran, E. *Healing the Soul Wound: Trauma-Informed Counseling for Indigenous Communities.* Teachers College Press, 2019.

Frankl, V. *Man's Search For Meaning.* Beacon Press, 2006.

Fraser, S. *My Father's House: A Memoir of Incest and of Healing.* Time Warner Books UK, 1989.

Herman, J. *Trauma and Recovery: The Aftermath of Violence—From Domestic Abuse to Political Terror.* Hatchette Book Group, 2015.

Hübl, T. *Healing Collective Trauma: A Process for Integrating Our Intergenerational and Cultural Wounds.* Macmillan, 2020.

Hyman, J. W. *I Am More Than One: How Women with Dissociative Identity Disorder Have Found Success in Life and Work.* McGraw-Hill, 2006.

Kimmerer, R. W. *Braiding Sweetgrass: Indigenous Wisdom, Scientific Knowledge and the Teachings of Plants.* Milkweed Editions, 2013.

Lesser, E. *Broken Open: How Difficult Times Can Help Us Grow.* Random House, 2008.

Levine, P. *In An Unspoken Voice: How the Body Releases Trauma and Restores Goodness.* Penguin Random House, 2012.

Levine, P. *Waking the Tiger: Healing Trauma.* North Atlantic Books, 1997.

Marks, J. *The Search for the "Manchurian Candidate:" The CIA and Mind Control: The Secret History of the Behavioral Sciences.* W. W. Norton, 1991.

Menakem, R. *My Grandmother's Hands: Racialized Trauma and the Pathway to Mending Our Hearts and Bodies.* Central Recovery Press, 2017.

Miller, A., *The Body Never Lies: The Lingering Effects of Hurtful Parenting.* W. W. Norton, 2006.

Nakazawa, D. J. *The Angel and the Assassin: The Tiny Brain Cell that Changed the Course of Medicine.* Random House, 2020.

Nakazawa, D. J. *Childhood Disrupted: How Your Biography Becomes Your Biology, and How You Can Heal.* Simon and Schuster, 2015.

Neihardt, J. G. *Black Elk Speaks: Being the Life Story of a Holy Man of the Oglala Sioux.* University of Nebraska Press, 1979.

Nemeth, M. *Mastering Life's Energies: Simple Steps to a Luminous Life at Work and Play.* New World Library, 2007.

Perry, B. *Born for Love: Why Empathy Is Essential—and Endangered.* William Morrow, 2011.

Perry, B. *The Boy Who Was Raised As A Dog: And Other Stories from a Child Psychiatrist's Notebook—What Traumatized Children Can Teach Us About Loss, Love, and Healing.* Basic Books, 2017.

Porges, S. *The Pocket Guide to Polyvagal Theory: The Transformative Power of Feeling Safe.* W. W. Norton, 2017.

Poulson S. *Looking Through the Eyes of Trauma and Dissociation: An Illustrated Guide for EMDR Therapists and Clients.* BookSurge Publishing, 2009.

Ross, C. *The CIA Doctors: Human Rights Violations by American Psychiatrists.* Manitou Communications, 2006.

Ruhl, L. *Breaking the Ruhls: A Memoir.* Central Recovery Press, 2018.

Seigel, D. *The Developing Mind: Toward a Neurobiology of Interpersonal Experience.* The Guildford Press, 1999.

Trujillo, O. *The Sum of My Parts: A Survivor's Story of Dissociative Identity Disorder.* New Harbinger Publications, 2011.

Tolle, E. *Stillness Speaks.* New World Library, 2003.

van der Kolk, B. *The Body Keeps the Score: Brain, Mind, and Body in the Healing of Trauma.* Penguin Books, 2015.

Yunkaporta, T. *Sand Talk: How Indigenous Thinking Can Save the World.* HarperOne, 2020.

Trauma Resources

We now know dissociative disorders and other trauma-related physical, behavioral and mental health issues are much more common than many people once thought. Individual responses to trauma come in various shapes and sizes, and virtually every family is touched by interpersonal, community or generational trauma.

With compassion and awareness, many individuals, researchers and organizations are working to end the stigma of mental health disorders and break cycles of family and community abuse, violence and denial. Science can now help physicians, others in the medical world, schools, families and communities better use what we know to create trauma-responsive care and build healing and resilience.

If you want to learn more or find out what you can do to join these movements, here are some websites that can get you started.

- ACEs Too High – acestoohigh.com
- An Infinite Mind – aninfinitemind.org
- Beauty After Bruises – beautyafterbruises.org

- CPTSD Foundation – cptsdfoundation.org
- Center on the Developing Child at Harvard University – developingchild.harvard.edu
- International Society for the Study of Trauma and Dissociation – isst-d.org
- The Mighty – themighty.com
- National Association for Mental Illness – nami.org
- National Institute for the Clinical Application of Behavioral Medicine – nicabm.com
- PACEs Connection – pacesconnection.com
- Traumatic Stress Institute – traumaticstressinstitute.org

Global Networks

Global networks are growing and are open to everyone who has access to the internet. Many were built to promote a more peaceful and compassionate world, usher in more positive global energy, and heal our collective trauma and our Mother Earth. We can all do as the Mayans urged and increase love and harmony in ourselves, our families, our communities, and the world. Here are a few I have found helpful.

- Humanity's Team – humanitysteam.org
- Science and Nonduality – scienceandnonduality.com
- Time of the Sixth Sun – timeofthesixthsun.com
- The Pocket Project – pocketproject.org
- The Shift Network – theshiftnetwork.com
- TreeSisters – treesisters.org
- Unify – unify.org

Acknowledgments

I first used the African saying "It takes a village to raise a child" in my 1992 book *Making Government Work for Your City's Kids*, which I wrote for the National League of Cities. Now I have to acknowledge it also takes a village to write a book. Well, actually, it has taken a very large community to get this one written. And it started with the Pasadena Village and its memoir group, which has met for more than a decade now. They have encouraged me week by week, month by month to keep writing. Their loving curiosity and acceptance helped me own my truth and find my voice. Thank you, Linda and Tom, Mike and Carole, Kitty, Jo, Lois, and later arrivals, Judith, Sally A., Sally W. and Janet. Linda and Mike were the very first people to read the whole story and ask questions that helped the writing to improve and deepen. And Patrick Dunavan, thank you for helping me "come out" for the first time as a multiple to a larger Pasadena Village audience. After reading that first draft, your kind clarity and copious notes pushed me forward in ways only you could have done.

Thanks to gifted author and friend, Lillian Faderman, who read a very early draft and suggested structural changes that helped immensely in framing the story.

Others who read early drafts and encouraged me with insightful suggestions or confusions include Nora Lee, Joanne Edgar, Jonathan and Carla Sanger, Ruth Sullivan, Carrie Miller, Trish Ploehn,

Irene Keller, Max Brenner, Sharon Lilly, Dianne Bougher, Candace McCarthy King, Mary Brennan Ziegler, Joanne Steuer, Catherine Klatzker, and Merle Saferstein. Thank you all for urging me to keep going.

A huge thank you to the team at Emerald Lake Books, Tara, Mark and Blazej, for believing in this book and allowing each alter to have his or her own voice in the process of finalizing how we tell the story. You were respectful and kind no matter whose voice came out of this body. We appreciate that it was a new experience for you and that you made us each feel heard.

Through the years, I also worked with, learned from, and appreciated editors Laurie Chittenden, Jane Harrigan, Linda Joy Myers, and Deborah Lott.

An Infinite Mind and their annual Healing Together Conference for the DID community welcomed me into a beehive of safety and openness, expanding my ability to speak my truth without fear. And the National Association of Memoir Writers taught me more about the art of telling that truth.

I thank my therapist, "Julia," for the many times she saved my life and for her intuitive, curious and skilled therapy over more than twenty years. This book is dedicated to her because, without her, the healing process it chronicles could not have happened.

My dear friends Katherine Gable, Eunice Shatz, Miryam Choca, and Julia Pennbridge have known me before, during and after this journey, accepted all the chaos, commented on drafts, and developed relationships with many of my internal family. There are no words to express the depth of gratitude I feel for your lifesaving and empowering support of me/us during the years of gestation this book needed. And a special thanks to Frank and Marianne Dryden who read the manuscript before Frank died and became so lovingly invested in me and the book's success.

Wendy Lazarus, you've also been there over all these years with long walks, gentle questions, and reminders to keep my eye on the big picture. You've written a foreword that sets my story in the larger context and helps readers know why I wrote this book. I appreciate you immensely.

To my siblings, known by pseudonyms in the text, thank you. My healing quest unearthed events and called pieces of our family history into question in ways none of us liked or anticipated. Thank you for allowing space for me to heal within a family circle of love and for accepting that my experiences were very different from yours.

And to my children, known here as Will and Beth, I am so very proud of you and the healing, cycle-breaking life journeys you are on. Thank you for being wise and kind as you figured out how to maintain loving, supportive relationships with me while taking care of your own well-being.

Finally, I'd like to thank Drs. Felitti and Anda for their groundbreaking work on the ACE study and all the other researchers and practitioners who have helped us understand the impact of childhood trauma and what we can do to mitigate it. Thank you to every person in every community who is working to build trauma-responsive care and a world where children do not need to learn special skills to survive their childhoods.

About the Author

Bonnie R. Armstrong spent decades as an apparently normal person who knew nothing of the complex dissociative infrastructure that hid much of her childhood from her conscious memory and supported her from within. She functioned as an effective and happy wife, mother, sister, friend and advocate for children and families. Professionally, she specialized in youth development, education and preventing child abuse, not knowing she was also a resilient survivor.

Bonnie enjoyed a forty-year career that involved high-level positions in two governors' offices, including a stint in Washington, DC, working with the Carter administration and Congress. She wrote *Making Government Work for Your City's Kids* for the National League of Cities and provided consultation that guided a generation of city council members who wanted to improve conditions for children and families in their communities.

In the late 1990s, she moved to philanthropy and focused on building public-private partnerships to strengthen communities, families and child welfare systems to prevent abuse and ensure every child can live in a safe and loving home. She served as an elected school board member, appointed commissioner, nonprofit board member, and expert consultant on child and family policy issues. A national speaker and workshop presenter, she also authored numerous other publications and received many awards for her leadership and accomplishments. Bonnie holds a master's degree in human development from Pacific Oaks College and is a certified life coach.

At the age of fifty, a mysterious, debilitating illness attacked Bonnie, eventually requiring her to use a wheelchair to continue her active life and travel schedule. After six years of testing and continued degeneration, her neurologist ruled out medical causes and referred her to a psychologist. Together, Bonnie and her therapist slowly uncovered her dissociative disorder, her strong internal community, and the secrets of her childhood.

Bonnie retired in 2012 to focus on healing, learning and writing about her journey through mystery, discovery, horror and the curative interdependence of body, mind, spirit and nature. Big Bonnie lives together with about a dozen of her internal community members, focused on continued healing and their shared life's purpose: to break generational cycles of abuse and fear and to create a more loving, harmonious world for their grandchildren and yours to grow up in.

Bonnie and her internal family especially love sunsets, trees of all kinds, travel, the energy of red rock formations, and mashed potatoes. To learn more about Bonnie's latest activities, visit her website at bonnierarmstrong.com.

If you're interested in having Bonnie speak to your group or organization, you can contact her at emeraldlakebooks.com/armstrong.

For more great books, please visit us at
emeraldlakebooks.com.

EMERALD LAKE
BOOKS
Sherman, Connecticut

Made in United States
North Haven, CT
02 February 2025

65310722R00186